WHY IS *SHE* STILL HERE?

WHY IS *SHE* STILL HERE?

My Ungraceful Journey from the Playground to the Boardroom

PATTY AZZARELLO

NEWTON PARK

Why Is SHE Still Here?
My Ungraceful Journey from the Playground to the Boardroom
Patty Azzarello

Publisher: Newton Park Press
Chicago, Illinois

First U.S. Edition, 2025

Hardcover ISBN: 979-8-9998280-0-2
Paperback ISBN: 979-8-9998280-1-9
Ebook ISBN: 979-8-9998280-2-6
Library of Congress Control Number: 2025917771

Produced by Spoonbridge Press

Printed in the U.S.A.

To Mom and Dad and Kerry

Contents

Suit Up

6:00AM

I stood there, scanning the row of black suits and grey suits and navy suits in my closet. I wrapped my hands around my favorite coffee cup, the one with the grey spots—I was trying to extract some extra life force from the heat.

The right cup or glass is important. It has to be beautiful to look at. And it has to have the right shape, weight, and balance in your hand. It also has to have the right color, texture, thickness, and rim profile, depending on the drink, and be of a material that enhances the taste. Otherwise, you might as well be drinking a martini out of a Styrofoam cup.

As I sipped my coffee, I pondered my situation. *I was an executive. And I was a woman.*

Each day I needed to really hold on to the belief that being female would not be an absolute obstacle blocking my way forward. Having boobs just created a different set of low expectations I had to overcome to build and maintain my credibility. I took a deep breath and reminded myself:

Be prepared to assert your existence. Don't give them any reason to bounce you out of the room. Suit up. Hair up. Glasses on. Check.

7:30AM

I arrived at the office. When I scanned my badge at the front desk, the beep, like Pavlov's bell, started up the background program reminding me not to do anything to wreck my career today:

Pay close attention to how you look.

Serious suit—and simple accessories only. Nothing too showy or artsy.

Take note of posture and energy.

Mind your conversations—always practical. Manage content and tone.

Don't tell stories that make you seem female.

Don't be too creative. Your creativity annoys your boss.

Don't smile too much.

Really try not to react to the flirting with nervous laughter.

Never miss a step in your work, your communications, and your seriousness about the business.

Don't reveal that you are a fun person outside of work or that you like your family or your weekends (or your coffee cup) too much.

I walked to my desk and sat down to gear up for the big meeting. The background program continued . . .

One little thing out of place—one wrong move, one tiny mistake—and you give them the reason they have actively been looking for to bounce you out of the room. Don't do anything to make them take you less seriously, even for a second. Don't give them any excuse to push you out.

I swear sometimes it felt like the wrong earrings could doom me to exile at any moment.

8:53AM

I walked into the planning meeting a few minutes before it was scheduled to begin. I was never late. I was excited to share my proposal that I had worked so hard on during the past two weeks. There were about twelve men in the room.

There were always good men who respected me and helped me throughout my career, but they were not in every room—and they were not in this one.

In this particular room, as I entered, most of the men just ignored me, while others—their eyes made boob contact or did a full body scan. As I got near the table, one of the friendly ones stroked his hand from my shoulder down my back as he greeted me. I picked up my pace to avoid his hand going further down. A couple of them, already sitting in the back of the room, shot each other a "what is she doing here?" look.

I reminded myself, *Women's careers are not considered important here. They think that you are not the primary earner so your income doesn't really matter. Or they think you are going to disappear to have babies. To them, the value of your career falls somewhere between quaint and annoying.*

As I started to approach the conference table to take my seat and focus on the excellent points I was going to make, one of the men looked at me and said, "Hey, hon. We're about to start—how about you get us some coffee?" Then his colleague came up and said, "Want to join us for drinks tonight? We could use some company that's easy on the eyes."

OK, here we go. Hang in there. Force field up. Stay focused on what you need to do here.

"Sam's secretary sits right outside. I'm sure she will bring us all coffee if you go ask her."

That special-combo disrespect of being hit on and discounted at the same time always felt like a downgrade of my humanity. They might as well have just said out loud, "Why can't you just be pretty and interested in giving me a hand job instead of wanting to compete with me for my job?"

Ignore them. Get a seat at the table. And make sure not to be too small. Elbows wide. Take up some space like they do. Prepare to interrupt—remember, no one will ever invite you to speak.

1:45PM

I sat at my desk eating a dry turkey sandwich from the cafeteria.

Well, I got my proposal heard. But I haven't won them over yet. But on the positive side, I also didn't get fired or demoted today, at least not that I know of. Or . . . did I? Did I do something in that meeting that damaged my credibility? I'm never sure . . .

I replayed the tape in my mind again. And again.

7:45PM

I cautiously walked to my car in the dark parking lot in my heels lugging my very heavy soft-sided briefcase, which in those days contained a 16-pound laptop and 47 pounds of paper. I carried my work around with me all day. I carried it home every night, and I carried it back every morning. *Always be prepared.*

Sitting in my car, I tried not to damage the back of my new suede pumps as I hit the brake pedal a million times stuck in traffic that night. I thought about the day, and my career and my soul, and what cocktail I will have in what glass when I get home. I thought about how this constant worry of being on the razor's edge of being pushed out of the room never leaves me. I felt that I could never just relax and feel free to be a normal human if anyone from work was looking.

"Never compare your inside to someone else's outside."

—Anne Lamott

Part 1

I Want What They're Having

—

"Lord, grant that I may always desire more than I can accomplish."

—Michelangelo

Afraid of the dark

1.1

I'm snuggled up on my sofa, in fuzzy pants, with a glass of wine and a comforter—not an afghan mind you, not an elegant throw, not a $7 fleece blanket from Costco—but a proper comforter like you would put on a bed.

It's really dark outside—and really late in the evening, maybe even 9:15—when suddenly . . .

Someone is knocking on my door.

SOMEONE IS KNOCKING ON MY DOOR.

IN THE DARK.

I panic.

In the daytime, an unaccounted house noise or an unexpected knock on the door—it's jarring, but not dangerous. But in the *dark* . . .

It must be a serial killer or an advancing army of marauders. I mean what sort of sociopath knocks on someone's door AFTER DARK? The house is buttoned up and closed for any further input today—the force field is UP. No one should be arriving at this point.

So, I did what any normal introvert does at a crisis moment like this. I kept perfectly still and pretended that I wasn't home.

But the damn knocking persisted, more and more urgently. So, heart in my throat, I army-crawled my way to the door. My house is very secluded, so it's creepy enough at night already, even without a murderous intruder at my door. But it is also mostly made of glass, including the front door—so it lacks any line of defense to hide behind. There was no way for me to see what horror awaited me outside that door without it seeing me too.

As I peeked around the corner, in a failed attempt to stay invisible, I saw that it was not a looming figure in a hockey mask with a machete.

It was my neighbor. My irrigation system had sprung a leak, and it was geysering all over his property.

OK, so pretty much, I'm afraid of the dark.

I was thinking about this home invasion and my paralytic fear response when one of my most senior executive clients asked me, "Patty, are you ever afraid?"

She was going for a big promotion and was worried she wasn't ready.

"Of course," I responded. "I'm afraid all the time."

"But how can that be? You seem so confident. It seems like you are not afraid of anything."

"I'm afraid of all kinds of stuff."

"Really? Like what?"

I knew it was important to answer this question honestly, because I wanted to let her know it's OK for her to be afraid and still go for this big job. But I thought I probably shouldn't mention *all* the goofy things I am afraid of. Like the dark. Or throwing up. Or stumbling to my demise and paralyzing myself, even on flat ground.

I probably should also skip that I'm afraid of getting lost. And I have a profoundly terrible sense of direction. One time when I went to interview for a CEO job, I could not find the front door of the building. I wish I was kidding.

She continued, "But you are such a high-level executive. You have been so successful, so I just assume you must not be afraid of anything at work."

Ah, now I know how to answer her question.

"Are you kidding? Work is the scariest place! I'm always worried about proving my credibility or not being good enough or that I am a fraud."

"Wow, you feel those things too? I wouldn't have guessed that."

I have had this same conversation over and over again with ambitious, nervous people. As far as I can tell, everyone is walking around afraid of stuff all the time. Quite frankly, it helps me to know that I am not alone in this regard.

I can tell you that with every big, worthwhile thing I've ever done, I've needed to figure out how to do it before I felt ready—while feeling uncomfortable and sometimes downright terrified. Whatever you might take from my life's accomplishments, I can tell you that they are not a result of my not being afraid.

And thus we arrive at the essence of my story:

1. This awkward little girl, in a spectacularly unlikely chain of events—and at a young age—became a high-level corporate executive of a global billion-dollar software business, then a Silicon Valley CEO, and later the CEO of her own thriving company with clients across the globe.

2. Most importantly, that CEO is still this little girl.

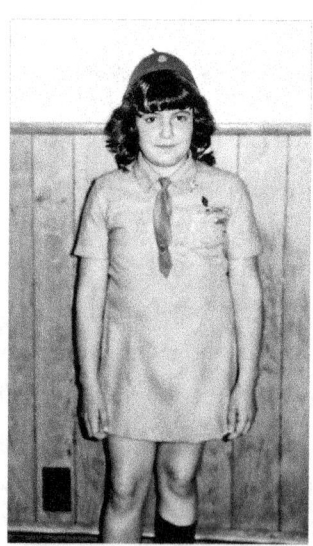

Not this again

1.2

So what happened to that little girl?

Let's start the story decades later, on a cold winter's day in Italy. My Italian friends had taken me on a long bike ride in the hills around Florence. When we finally took a break and walked into a café, I ordered a coffee and a sandwich (because I was cold and hungry). But, to my surprise, my order immediately caused everyone in the place to seize up in horror.

As it turns out, Italians have very strict rules that dictate everything about their food: how to cultivate it, certify it, transport it, label it, sell it, store it, cook it, present it, serve it, and, perhaps most importantly, how to eat it in nonnegotiable combinations and in an exacting, specific order.

So my ordering a coffee and a sandwich at the same time was a transgression so grave, that showed such a blatant disregard of the food combination/order rules, that it broke my friends' hearts and disgusted them in equal parts. And it wasn't just my friends on that day. Every other Italian friend I have ever mentioned this to in search of some support uttered some form of "Coffee and a sandwich together? Your friends were right—I would vomit."

While I often get the rules wrong, I have to admit that all this unwavering commitment to food protocol makes Italian food both delicious to eat and gorgeous in its presentation. Thus, eating Italian food in Italy has become my drug of choice.

One day in Italy, I entered a sprawling fresh food market, where grandmothers and chefs alike were buying ingredients for their dinners. I made my way to another part of the market, which was set up for eating, where I was practically assaulted by a staggering array of food stalls displaying cheeses, fresh pastas, crusty breads, artful piles of sizzling meats, seductive pizzas, endless panoramas of bruschetta and veggies, mounds of cookies and pretty desserts—and wine bars tucked in the gaps between all the beautiful displays of food.

After making my selections, I looked down at my tray and the glass of wine in my hand. I was breaking no rules as far as I could tell. And I smiled that whole-body smile of anticipation I always get when I come face-to-plate with virtually any food item in Italy.

I then turned toward the common eating area and looked at the rows of tables, all of them teeming with lively, smiling people.

And suddenly, the happy-food feeling started to drain out of me . . .

If I walk over and try to sit down, time will stop, and the people will look up at me and say to me with their forks and their faces, if not their actual words, "What do you think you are doing? You don't belong here with us. We don't want you to sit with us. Ew. You're being weird standing there. Go away."

And then there it was . . .

I was 10 years old, standing in the school cafeteria, holding my tray. Rejected and alone.

OK. Hang on a minute.

I have run a global, billion-dollar organization, leading thousands of people internationally. I have been a CEO in the tech sector. I've been flown across the world many times to take the stage in front of thousands of people. I've been granted rare access to exclusive groups and events. Famous people have sought my counsel. I've accomplished more than I'd ever dreamed. I have amazing friends all over the world.

But here I am after all of that, standing with my tray and no place to sit, and the jury has ruled once again: "You are undeserving of a seat at the table. There is no place for you here."

How can it be that I still walk through the world feeling shy and insecure and fearing rejection—like an unwelcome intruder who no one wants to be with or talk to—and yet I managed to become a highly successful corporate executive and CEO? Really, how is that possible?

Everyone hates Patty

1.3

On my first day of kindergarten, I bounded up the steps of the school bus in my patent leather (OK, shiny plastic) Mary Janes, with my Sesame Street lunch box and my unbridled enthusiasm. I had waited my whole, long, four-year life to finally start school. My impressionable little brain and my wide-open heart could not have been more enthusiastic for what was about to come.

Yvonne and I started kindergarten together. Her mother worked, which was unusual in our neighborhood at the time. My mother, thinking she was doing a kind and good thing (which she was), offered to watch Yvonne after school. She also thought it would be good for me to have a friend to be with at school. Sounds good—on paper.

The only flaw in this otherwise perfect plan was that Yvonne was my bully. And now she was coming home with me every day.

So my social anxiety started pretty much the very first moment I dared to be social—at age four. I sometimes wonder, is it really accurate to call it social "anxiety" when people are actively saying to you, "I hate you, Patty"—really, those exact words—on a daily basis?

It continued beyond kindergarten. By second grade, it was a pretty steady chorus: "Ew. Go away. Don't get so close to me. You're gross. You can't sit here. How dare you even think about coming near us? I HATE YOU. Don't you know that everybody hates you?"

Wait, what? Everybody hates me? Was I supposed to know that? Why does everybody hate me?

I never understood *why* people hated me, but man did they fall in line—because my bully Yvonne told them to. Yvonne was a cute, skinny, blond pixie with a confident smile and a twinkle in her eye. Yvonne had all the social power. I had no social power.

And she used her power to spread shame directed at me, not so much for being fat, or smart, or nerdy (of which I was all three). Yvonne made it clear that I needed to be hated just for being Patty.

One day, as I was sitting by myself on the lawn at recess making a braid out of some tall pieces of grass, a girl in my class came over and said, "Hi."

Wait . . . she doesn't sound mean. Is this really happening? Is she going to talk to me? Is she going to be my friend?

Then she looked nervously over her shoulder to make sure she was not being watched, and she whispered, "You know, I really don't hate you, but I have to pretend I do because of Yvonne. You understand, right? I do like you, it just can't be out in the open."

All I could muster to say was, "Yeah, OK."

She walked away, and I cried. My little brain could not take this in. All I could think was, *Why can't you just be nice to me if you like me? I have never been mean to anyone. Why is this happening to me? This just isn't fair.*

And what on earth do you do with "I do like you, it just can't be out in the open" when you're seven?

Does that mean that when you jumped off the seesaw so I crashed down and hurt myself . . . or when you went along with it when Yvonne said that I tried to drown her in the lake and you called me a murderer for a year . . . I am supposed to just be OK with all that because I know you secretly don't hate me?

(I'd like to go on record—I did not try to drown Yvonne.)

These secret confessions happened many times over the years, and they were way worse than the active bullying. It would always start with my naive hope of kindness or friendship and end with "I really do like you, but it can't be out in the open."

School would have been unsurvivable if not for one thing: Wendy. Wendy was my friend—boldly and out in the open—from the very beginning. She was somehow impervious to Yvonne's control.

Wendy was really smart. And we laughed. And out of nothing but our imaginations, we invented endless, stupid games. Laughing with Wendy was the one joyful thing I experienced outside of my home, in a world that otherwise offered me indignities and shame. Wendy showed me that being joyful out in the world was even a thing. Ever since we were four, we supported and respected each other. In school, any moment I was with Wendy, I was OK. But Wendy could not be my protector at every moment, especially on the playground.

The bullying started when I was four and lasted till I was about twelve. And I just had no frame of reference to put it into a context outside of myself. I was me and nobody liked me. That was the only context.

This formed a deep groove of programming I've never been able to fully shake: *Patty is not welcome in the world.*

Little patty really wanted to have more friends. She was so hopeful. She always tried to be nice, but she endured so much rejection. But she kept on trying, longing for someone to like her back.

Semi-lethal playgrounds of hot metal

1.4

At this point, you might be asking, "Where the fuck were all the adults? Why didn't your mom do something? Why didn't the teachers do something?"

Well, all I can say is that in the 1970s, it just wasn't a thing for adults to get involved in the playtime and social lives of children. It wasn't that the adults were bad or stupid or didn't care. My mom and teachers were just doing what all moms and teachers were doing at that time: their respective jobs. They were focused on other things.

So, as a kid, you were basically on your own to work things out socially and not die on the playground.

And back then, it was almost as if the playgrounds themselves had been engineered specifically to hurt children.

There was a metal carousel that a group of 20 could get rotating so fast that kids would get shot off and torpedoed onto the pavement. "Oh, Billy is face down and bleeding . . . let's go again!"

I avoided this nightmare at all costs. I didn't want to fall off and paralyze myself. I typically observed the scene sitting by myself from a more bully-resistant distance.

Also on the playground, there were metal slides so tall you actually could die if you fell from the top. And if you didn't keep your legs perfectly centered on the way down, the hot metal sides would rip the skin off your ankles. No child escaped this particular injury.

In those days we had lawn darts. *Lawn darts.* Imagine a regular dart, pointy and dangerous, but make it twelve inches long and about three pounds. You could actually murder someone with a lawn dart.

Every moment of recess on the playground reminded me that I am weird because I don't think any of this is fun. I only liked the learning part of school that happened indoors. Lunch, gym class, and recess—those were just pointless agony.

But what I didn't know at the time was that my ferocious inner drive to learn about everything would be met with some more obstacles.

The middle of nowhere

1.5

T hey say that an acorn does not need any extra help to become a great oak. It has everything it needs within it. That's great. Poetic even. You are good enough. You have everything you need already inside yourself to reach your full potential—in a Wizard-of-Oz-y sort of way.

OK. But what if the acorn lands on the pavement?

As a child, I could feel myself bursting with potential and the desire for more. But whatever and wherever that fertile soil for my own potential was, it seemed unknowable and very far away from where I was sitting in this small, isolated place in the countryside where I grew up and Nothing. Ever. Happened.

We Didn't Have iPads

I can pretty accurately describe my hometown as the middle of nowhere. And the middle of nowhere was different before the internet. In 1970, it wasn't possible to see "somewhere" for contrast—I had no idea what the opposite of "nowhere" would look like. There were no world travel adventurers posting photos and stories on social media. You didn't see other places unless you went there.

And we didn't go anywhere.

Small and Brown

I was longing for something exotic and beautiful. In my small world, we had trees. But not interesting trees. No magnolias, or aspens, or jacarandas or palm trees. Just maple and pine trees. Maple and pine. That's it. I was pretty sure that palm trees were not actually a real thing. I thought they were just fake props on the TV show *Hawaii Five-O*—and that Hawaii probably wasn't a real place either.

The unexoticness of the nature in my hometown did not waver. There were no large or colorful birds. The birds were all small and brown. We didn't have marvelous, large, green bullfrogs that sat on lily pads. We only had small, mostly dirt-based brown toads. In our small lake, we only had small, brown fish. We didn't have colorful butterflies. We had tan moths. The universe, for all intents and purposes, was small, brown, and unvarying. And my main source for imagining what beautiful, colorful, exotic flora and fauna might look like was the encyclopedia in the school library—which was printed in black and white.

To reinforce the small, brown vibe, then there was our house. Our house was tiny. And for a while it was brown. Inside and out. My mom had a thing for wood paneling.

But a wonderful, mind-exploding thing happened when I was about 10 years old, when I saw the movie *The Sound of Music*. It was during the storm scene where all the kids come into Julie Andrews's bedroom and get in bed with her and sing "My Favorite Things." When she lifted up her bedcover and folded it over, my heart stopped.

Oh. My. GOD. What is THAT? Is that a blanket? That thing must be 10 inches thick! I've never seen anything like that on a bed. It's so big and fluffy and wonderful!

As I stared in awe, my fingers grasped the scratchy, crocheted afghan on the sofa and worked their way through the square holes where cold air would shoot in. *Why would you purposefully build holes into a blanket?* I also thought of the thin, stiff, troublingly slick polyester "bedspread" on my own bed that might as well have been one of those gross outdoor tablecloths, with the shiny red-and-white checked plastic on one side and creepy fuzz on the other, compared to this miracle I was seeing on the screen.

After learning this magical, puffy creature was a called a "comforter," I was obsessed. And *The Sound of Music* was no longer a movie about the kids or the love story or the music or the Nazis or the war or the escape. It was the movie with "the comforter scene." And thus began my lifelong obsession with comforters, which I will tell you decades later has not dwindled in the slightest from that moment—and was to play a much bigger role in my life.

Note: Yes, I know it's called a "duvet," but I like to call the whole yummy combination of the duvet nestled inside its cover a "comforter" because it seems less pretentious and more, well, comforting that way.

Anyway . . . my mom did not share my enthusiasm for fluffy things. She had a very practical view of decor. She optimized for durability, cleanability, and low allergic reaction, so everything in our home had to be as flat and smooth as possible. The carpets, for instance—think Astroturf in the bedrooms and you're getting close. Like the carpet in conference room B, but of an indoor–outdoor synthetic material that could also withstand a monsoon. The idea of a comforter on my bed was an idea shot down on arrival in our smooth, flat, hypoallergenic universe.

But within little patty stirred a quiet rebellion that sparked a lifelong quest to have beautiful (and fluffy) things in her world.

The girl who would be CEO

1.6

People often ask me, "If you could go back in time, what advice would you give your younger self?" I struggle with that question, because my first thought is: *I am often the one who looks to little patty for answers.*

Many people, as adults, seem to lose track of their little person. Or if they think about them at all, it's in a therapy session. And sure, while little patty is still afraid that no one will like her back, the more important thing for me to consider about her is this: What was she like *the day before* the world hurt her?

Because that version of little patty was powerful.

And when it came to the things she wanted in life, she was brave and curious and joyful about pursuing them—*and she wanted big things*. It has served me well not to forget that.

Many also seem to lose track of their little person's dreams—because those big ideas turned out to be *too big*, or too impractical, or just too much work. But little patty is unrelenting when it comes to her goals.

If little patty had wanted to be astronaut—I would be an astronaut.

Honoring little patty in my adult life is like having a built-in teammate who is kind of a badass.

Here's what I mean.

Fast-forward and I am in a room of 15 men and 1 woman. I am the woman. I am 31. The guys all look 20 years older than me. Little patty and I are both in awe of this room and my new responsibility. We watch their vigorous hand-shakes as they bunch into groups. We note their big smiles, comfortable banter, and silvering, executive hair—they all look very impressive. I had just been promoted, and these were my new colleagues.

My focus was split between two things:

1. I deserve to be in this room. I'm smart. I won this promotion fair and square.
2. It is undeniable that I am actually very young for this job—and I'm the only female.

The thought reverberating through my entire being was *I am not like them at all.* Here I was, adult Patty, in my classy black suit and high heels, feeling way too young and very small—like I might as well be wearing my mother's lipstick.

But little patty, as ever, would not let me back down, telling me, "Hang in there even if they are being mean to you. You need to stay here to learn important stuff."

So, I told myself, Just hang on. Just take a breath. Just stay in the room.

Just stay in the room.

Just stay in the room.

Just stay in the room.

Like a mantra.

Watching all these men in their relaxed conversation circles made me think back to the very first job I had in my career. I was 17 and in my second year of college. I was a student engineering intern working for the US government. I had big hair and big boobs.

All the full-time engineers were men and all the other interns were male, and, by contrast, they all had neat hair and tidy, flat chests.

I walked into the shared office and found them all talking. Their eyes met my boobs upon entry, but they did not invite me into the conversations. As I stood on the sidelines, it struck me like a bolt of lightning . . .

These conversations are where everything happens. Everything. Everything at this job, everything at every job, and everything in the world. And—I am not in these conversations.

I saw my whole career flash before my eyes. Endless groups of people over the course of my lifetime talking about and doing all the important stuff—without me.

And I thought, *This internal story about being unwelcome and unlikable, is not serving you. And you will never be invited in. If you want a career, you need to get yourself into those conversations no matter how shy you feel and awkward it feels. You need to break in.*

I knew I needed to put myself into that conversation circle of men, even though the thought of doing so in that moment made me feel panicked. But I took a deep breath and went in. It felt like that moment when you jump off the high dive. I was in motion but didn't know what would happen when I hit the water.

Everyone looked surprised, like, "What is she doing here? She's not part of this group? She's never been in these conversations before."

Then, they basically ignored me. I felt weird that I didn't have anything to say. But I stayed in it and just listened. I listened while they talked about the new car dealership on 71. I listened when they talked about the baseball game last night, and the new secretary's sweet ass in her tight skirt. But then, the conversation got to a new computer system being delivered tomorrow that we had an opportunity to get trained on if we wanted to. I leaped to the front of the line. None of the male interns leaped; they didn't even volunteer at all. I was the only one.

A couple of weeks later, someone needed to demonstrate the new system to all the visiting generals. And it was me.

I realized something super important when I got that opportunity: As uncomfortable as it is to break into a conversation circle where I am not invited, and as much as it sometimes feels like I am going to die when I do, if I can shove my way in there and just listen, just listening can create opportunities.

So now, here I am in the present, after my big career promotion in my first big room of big corporate executives.

I thought about the interns and the generals, and how I had forced my way into the conversation (and didn't die), and how there had been a benefit. So once again, I willed myself to walk into this intimidating conversation circle. And once again, they all ignored me. But I stayed there. I lurked. And I listened. And that was enough for the moment. I did not back away.

Just stay in the room . . .

In life's game of musical chairs, I have a choice to make. I can choose to be the one left standing on the outside and skulk away as the loser, or I can go find myself an extra chair and unceremoniously shove it into the circle. That will cause the music to come to a screeching stop, and then everyone will look at me like "Why did you do that? That's not how this game works. What are you doing here? You've never been in this game before, and now you just ruined our game. We were having fun until you showed up. You don't belong here."

I realized that developing the ability to enter a conversation circle without dying was an important habit I was going to need to master. I can choose to stay comfortable on the outside, or dare to be uncomfortable and go in.

Little patty reminds me, "Feeling weird is not fatal—I should know. You have to go in."

"You're too nice"

1.7

"**W**ho are your enemies?"

I was 22 the first time I was asked in a job interview to name my enemies.

I sat across the desk from the grizzled executive interviewing me, thinking I was doing well mesmerizing him with my competence and enthusiasm for this job. But then, when I failed to produce an impressive enemy list, he looked at me with disdain, like, "How can you claim to be competent if you haven't made powerful enemies? Why are you even wasting my time?"

Despite my natural shyness and social nervousness, I was always pretty good at job interviews—they were like taking a test. That I could do.

But this question really threw me. I thought, *Do I have enemies? Am I supposed to have enemies? Can I be successful without enemies?* It was so weird.

Little patty was like, "Are you kidding me? Are you seriously considering making enemies *on purpose*? This can't be the right job for you if this guy is telling you that you need enemies."

As I left the interview, I thought, *I have a very important choice to make. This enemy thing is my invitation to turn into a bully to advance my career. I don't want to be like the bullies who hurt little patty. I choose instead, even at work, to be the kind of safe person she needed back then. If that is not good for my career, so be it. That is my choice.*

Little patty would have been so disappointed to have survived all of that torment only for me to become a bully later on.

I was asked this interview question throughout my entire career. And I came up blank. Every time. No enemies.

But I finally came to understand that this enemy thing was rooted in the male idea of power. Generally speaking, men tend to see winning and power like this: For me to win, you need to lose. You haven't won hard enough, apparently, if you didn't create enemies in the process. Therefore, having no enemies means you are weak and irrelevant.

But I kept thinking, "If I can win *and* you can win, how does that hurt me? Why is that not better?"

But even after I was actually in big, executive jobs (despite my lack of a mortal enemy list) for years, I was still told, "You are too nice. You are not aggressive enough. Corporations are nasty and competitive places. You need to be that way too if you want to get ahead."

Was I really limiting my career by being too nice?

I was on one executive team where all of my peers and the CEO were men. These men were angry a lot. The staff meetings felt like a WWE fight. Seven of us would sit around the conference table and they would all shout at each other. "You're an idiot—you are too worried about margins. We need to take more risk." "Your risk will kill us. Can you possibly be that stupid?"

I just couldn't imagine myself jumping into those fights. They weren't even productive. Everyone just got angry, we accomplished nothing, and then we left the room.

One of my peers revealed to me, "Patty, the CEO is concerned about your ability to be effective here, because he says you are not enough of a fighter. I think you might need to start fighting."

Joining the fight did not seem to be a solution to anything. And I couldn't have done it even if I wanted to. I had none of those moves. So here's what I did instead . . .

In the next meeting, when the fight spun up, I remained silent for about

45 minutes. Then I interrupted the yelling and said calmly, "In listening to this argument, it seems that you all agree that increasing market exposure on our second-largest product is our desired outcome, and so do I. Is that correct? Might we focus the rest of the meeting on choosing which of these two options will be the most effective way to get that outcome?"

This dynamic happened for months—but over time when the fight would rage on in the meeting, after about 40 minutes, one of them would stop shouting and say, "Patty, I think we need you to do that thing you do that gets us to stop fighting so we can make progress."

Ha! I was actually able to stay true to myself and not lose my job.

I decided that coming to a good solution together was always going to be better than a fight to the death with no point other than getting to feel like a powerful winner with enemies.

I still often wondered, though: Would being "too nice" eventually put a limit on my success? But I decided that no matter what, I was going to honor little patty. She would never be mean to people. And she had another even more important life lesson to teach me.

The birth of amazement

1.8

As a kid, I wanted more out of life but had no idea what that would look like exactly. It was just a nagging feeling: Life should not look like brown industrial carpeting.

My big sister Kerry, on the other hand, was way more insightful and action-oriented. Also frustrated with our small, drab environment, she was smart enough to realize that the antidote for a dull place was to go somewhere else! Kerry was rebellious and talented, and she lived with the idea that the world was already big, she just needed to escape our tiny universe

Me and my brilliant big sister, Kerry.

as soon as possible to go there—which she ultimately did, becoming a world adventurer with her first trip to Europe at age 17.

I would regularly walk into Kerry's room to find her doing something that delighted and inspired me. I'd find her drawing, singing, dancing, sewing, doing math, or being masterful at Spirograph. Her room was like a portal to new possibilities. *What is Kerry doing now? How is she doing that? I want to do that!*

I would always be desperate to copy and match her abilities, but my results were often a disaster. My Spirograph skills at age five were appalling! No matter how hard I focused, my little plastic wheel would always jump the track and I'd drag a harsh, unwelcome line across my budding work of art. I'd need to start again—like a million times.

There was a Christmas garland incident, stringing popcorn with a needle and thread where Kerry had made yards and yards of the stuff. After hours of work, at six years old, what I had to show for my efforts was a strand of about 12 broken kernels soaked in blood.

I so wanted to be capable of doing everything Kerry did, even though she was more than five years older than me. It was not in my worldview that a five-year head start on developing motor skills, brain power, and perspective would create a difference between her functional capabilities and mine. It was so frustrating.

Once, when I entered her room, I was met with a vision that made me feel like I had been transported into another universe.

She was making a poster for a school contest featuring the Peanuts character Lucy. I had left the room after seeing the blank poster board, magic markers, and small cartoon of Lucy she had cut out of the newspaper.

I had my own crude sense of what could be done with a blank poster board and markers. But when I returned, what I saw on that same poster board was a large, vibrant, exquisitely colored Lucy. It was staggering. It looked like it had been printed professionally by a machine, but since I didn't know what "printed professionally by a machine" even meant, to me at age six, it was just pure wizardry.

My brain was reeling. *HOW IS THIS POSSIBLE? And the WORDS! The words are so big and puffy. What am I even looking at?*

I'd never seen words written like that. She told me they were bubble letters.

BUBBLE LETTERS! OMG. How could she have done this using only markers and blank poster board? I need to know! I need to make bubble letters on poster board with markers right now!!!

I remember this moment with such physical clarity. I can relive that exhilarating feeling of amazement every time I think about it. I think this moment was so potent for me not because of the poster itself (which I still hold was a masterpiece) but because it was the first time in my life that I experienced amazement.

Little patty had discovered something wonderful that, before that moment, she had no idea existed in the whole world. This was BIG!

At that moment, I felt an overwhelming wave of shock, energy, excitement, possibility, and hope. I'm not sure I had a label for this feeling at the time, but I was instantly hooked on whatever it was. *This is what a more fantastic life is supposed to feel like.* Being amazed for the first time was my first real clue to that unknown thing that my little life was lacking.

I wanted to be brilliant and artistic, just like Kerry. Kerry continued to inspire me with her mind-blowing talents and her willingness to throw herself out into the world to find adventure. My big sister was such a strong and steady example of what it looked like to seek amazement in life.

Little patty had discovered the value of amazement—and that was *enthusiasm.*

She knew it then, and she keeps reminding me now: **You get extra life force from enthusiasm.** And—although little patty didn't know it at the time—she was gonna need it, and I would too—forever after.

I want what they're having

1.9

It was a sunny, fall day right after I had started third grade. We were at one of our epic, extended-Italian-family picnics. I was sitting in the grass coloring. I was trying to draw a picture of Galileo for the cover of a science report I was working on, and I was annoyed that there was no flesh-toned crayon. I mean come on . . . am I the only one who's ever wanted to draw a person with a crayon?

There were so many aunts, uncles, cousins, and random strangers at this picnic. I didn't know most of these people, and as the youngest, they were all way more interested in me than I liked, which meant everyone squealing "Look how big you got!" and pinching my cheeks—which I hated because it hurt.

I paused my work and watched the adults unload all the cars. They carried a grill, tables, chairs, coolers of food, and a *stove* so they could cook pasta outdoors. My adult brain still can't take this in. I have the utmost respect for Italians and their obsession with perfectly prepared pasta—but at a picnic? As much as I love pasta, I would never be moved to carry a stove to a picnic.

I continued with my drawing when some random adult (I could never keep them all straight) walked up to me. "What are you doing?"

"Working on my science report."

"You should stop doing that and have some fun."

I am having fun, I thought. I never understood other people's version of fun. So I kept to my work—which was fun for me.

I begrudgingly colored Galileo's face with the yellow crayon but immediately loathed my choice. *I'm going to have to start this all over again as a black-and-white sketch because coloring people with yellow is just hideous.*

I looked up from my work and watched the women prepping, cooking, serving, and cleaning. They did this on repeat all day. I watched the men playing ball and taking breaks to lie down in the sun and drink.

When I looked at the women around me in my life, I saw moms, nurses, teachers, bus drivers, waitresses, and secretaries. And I noticed other jobs on TV that were just for pretty, skinny women: models, flight attendants, hostesses, and Dallas Cowboys cheerleaders.

All the jobs that I found really interesting, only men did. The men were the bankers, police officers, athletes, advertising executives, scientists, astronauts, newscasters, politicians, builders, and doctors.

At that time, there were no females in my world doing those jobs. Most were at home taking care of their houses and their families and their men— so that the men could do all those things.

When I was growing up, the plotlines of the vast majority of movies, books, and shows could be entirely described as "men doing stuff."

At this picnic, I found my head darting from the women to the men, from the women to the men, from the women to the men, ultimately landing on the men. I thought, *That's what I want.* It was so very clear to me.

I wanted to create things in the world and work on important and interesting stuff—the things I saw men doing. And on the weekends, I wanted to be able to do fun things instead of cooking and cleaning all day.

When I look back to that time, I don't remember thinking that was an unreasonable or even unusual thought to have.

It never occurred to me that I was required to want the life of a woman as it was being shown to me. I thought, "Women are people, men are people; I am a person. I choose to do what the men are doing. There is no reason I can't choose that because I, too, am a person." I have always been fiercely invested in my personhood.

Recently, I was watching an old home movie of our family on Christmas Day. I got a baby doll and a toy carpet sweeper. My sister got an Easy-Bake Oven. And my mom got an ironing board—for real. I had unceremoniously thrown the doll aside face down like "What the hell am I supposed to do with that?" And the toy carpet sweeper sat untouched with the bow still on it in the background. Instead, I was elbow-deep in Lincoln Logs.

I guess even from the start, I had the sense that I'd rather build a house than clean one.

Memo to women: You are not supposed to want stuff

1.10

I was the keynote speaker at an international women's leadership event where I heard from professional women from all over the world about what they had to go through to have a career.

A woman from a country in Southeast Asia told me, "My father said I was evil for wanting a career—my family shunned me." A woman from the Middle East said to me, "Patty, I like your advice on how to advocate for myself, but I don't know how to apply it because if I am in a room with men, I am forbidden to speak." Another told me she was not permitted to make eye contact with a man under any circumstances. A woman from a country in Africa told me that her husband beat her and she was afraid he would kill her—and her family, instead of providing protection, sided with her husband as was the social norm. Literally her only way to stay alive, let alone have a career, was to flee her home and country alone.

I know that as a white person from a Western culture, the problems I faced as a woman in life and work were, on a global basis, at most quaint by comparison.

But there is one question that women of all backgrounds still ask me all the time: "Patty, how am I supposed to be confident and advocate for my career when I have been told my whole life that it's wrong to stand out?"

My response to every woman who has ever expressed this concern to me is always the same: "I know I don't understand all the aspects of your culture. But this advice that we are not supposed to want things for ourselves or have power over our own lives is *not* told to us girls to serve *our* best interests; it's told to us to keep us quiet and subordinate and out of the way. It's to keep us in the role of prioritizing and taking care of everyone except ourselves."

Part of the story we women are all told from birth that soaks into our DNA is that we are supposed to sacrifice our own lives for our families, and that this sacrifice is the most important and valuable thing we can do—along with *all* the housework. "Look how she gave up everything for her family. What a wonderful woman!"

Some little girls want to grow up to be moms and homemakers, and some want to be scientists or artists or athletes or businesspeople. And some want to be both. All are good choices—as long as you get to make your own choice.

As I grew up, the voices telling me "NO, you shouldn't want that, that's a man's career" were always present.

By the time I got to high school, I would hear things like "Patty should take home economics, not mechanical drawing" and "*She* shouldn't be allowed to take this engineering potential test. It's ridiculous—this is a waste of time and money." (I ended up getting the highest score in the group.)

Mom herself had been caught in the ancient programming. She was brilliant and always wanted to be a marine biologist. But as a female, she was forbidden to go to college. So, with her daughters, she was determined to break that cycle and put aside those old-world expectations.

While my mom could be kind of a bummer with her anti-fluffy policies, she was extraordinary in her intention for our lives. "You can be anything you want," she told us over and over again. "You will go to college. You will get a good education and a good job. Never expect a man to support you. That's your job."

Making the decision to go against thousands of years of expectations of what women should want and what they can be is a massive hurdle for many women to overcome. I was in awe of these brave women at the conference who were told by their cultures, religions, and families that to want a self-directed life and a career as a woman is fundamentally wrong, selfish, and even immoral.

I didn't need to overcome any of that disqualifying messaging because my mom put the idea in my little brain early on that I could direct my own life. I had an enormous head start and unwavering support. I just needed to take Mom's encouragement and run with it.

It was aways clear to me that my path was not to become a mom myself. Not once in my life did that thought even occur to me. And Mom gave me the space to make my own choice about that too.

But it would quickly become clear to me that the rest of the world didn't believe that I could be anything I want as much as Mom did. I would come to learn that as a woman, pursuing an executive career in tech was never going to be an easy path. It was going to require a lot of swimming upstream with a steady countercurrent of people telling me, "You shouldn't be here" or "You shouldn't do that."

But from the beginning, little patty was an ambitious dreamer who wanted her life to be bigger. She was determined to embark on a journey to learn about absolutely everything and to find beautiful things in the world that amazed her. And she was always determined to be kind to people along the way—and kept hoping that some of them would like her back.

Part 2

At Least They Drilled Air Holes

—

"We do not have to become heroes overnight. Just a step at a time, meeting each thing that comes up, seeing it is not as dreadful as it appeared, discovering we have the strength to stare it down."

—Eleanor Roosevelt

Stupid rat

2.1

A box of normal rats arrived in the lab. They were randomly split into two groups and placed into two boxes labeled "smart rats" and "stupid rats." There was no actual difference between these rats. Same rats.

The goal was to see if the "smart" rats would be faster in the maze than the "stupid" rats.

This was part of a study done in 1963 by Robert Rosenthal to test if the performance of a subject can be modified by the expectations of the observer.

As I read about this study I thought, *These are the same rats. How would the rats even know if they are in the smart or the stupid group? They can't read the labels. How could there be any performance difference? What are they even testing?*

What do you think happened when the rats ran the maze?

Well, the results were not even close! The smart rats outperformed the stupid rats by a wide margin.

What on earth was going on here?

OK, so here's Josh, a studious chap in a white coat with a clipboard and a stopwatch. He takes a rat out of the box, puts it down at the start of the maze, waits, watches, records the time, then takes the rat out and puts it back in the box. It's the exact same process whether the rat comes from the smart group or the stupid group. The rat itself has no idea which group it's in.

So how were the "smart" rats faster? The only conceivable difference is that Josh saw the label on the box, so *he believed* he was testing either a smart rat or a stupid rat.

Could what Josh was *thinking* have made the difference?

I guess maybe when Josh picked up a smart rat, he was thinking, "Hey, little guy, you're going to do great!" And because of that thought, he handled the rat gently and with some interest.

Then when he picked up a "stupid rat," maybe he was thinking something more like, "All right, let's get this over with, you useless rat." Then he just grabbed the rat and placed it in the maze with an apathetic thud.

Could it be that the expectations the students had in their minds about the smart and stupid rats were somehow transmitted to the rats themselves through only the subtle difference *in their handling of them*?

The students themselves were not even aware that they were doing something different, yet *the stupid rats' performance suffered from invisible cues* they got only from how they were handled. The expectations in the students' heads actually caused the difference.

The subtlety of this blew my mind. I had made it all the way through my executive career and into my 50s when I learned about the stupid rats. And one second later, my whole career flashed before my eyes . . .

Low expectations

2.2

Looking back, I came to realize that the low expectations of women—just like with the stupid rats—were mostly invisible. It was all in the subtle "handling." I had just learned to absorb and accept the underlying apathy and disregard from low expectations as the way the world worked.

Early in my tech career I was a sales engineer providing demos and technical support to the sales team for technology products. The low expectations were ever present. Like the time I stood in a client's office next to the sales rep who said, "I've brought our technology expert." Then everyone moved their heads back and forth looking around and right past me, thinking, *Is he in the bathroom? Is he coming later?*

When it became clear that I was in fact the technology expert, then came the side-eye, the sighs, people looking at their watches—their assumptions being that I could not possibly have anything of value to say. Their silent disengagement was palpable, so I couldn't just start. If I just started talking, the men didn't listen. (I have a colleague who calls this "woman deafness.")

I first needed to overcome their low expectations, their disregard. I'd have to say something so super clever, to ask such an incisive question, that their shock at something important coming from *the girl* would break them out of their low expectations.

Over and over again, I had to first earn my right to exist—not just when I was young, but at every level in my career where I met males of the species.

The low expectations and the unspoken, subtle "handling" that communicated them came in many forms. Once, my sales manager said to me, "This is an important client—I need you to wear a short skirt for the demo tomorrow." Subtext: *Your demo will not stand on its own, so let's give him a distraction he will enjoy.*

The demo went so well (based on my actual skill vs. my legs—I didn't wear a skirt) that the sales manager was utterly amazed. He said to me, "I just can't believe it. I can't wait to tell the guys that a 'skirt'"—that's what he called me—"did a demo even better than they could!"

Low expectations for women are so ingrained that some men have no idea how insulting it can be when they are so very impressed when a woman is competent.

Another form of low expectations was not even recognizing my identity. In one company, I was one of eight sales engineers. Two of us were women. I had long black hair, she had short red hair. She was much taller. Physically, we could not have looked more different. Yet none of the men in the company could tell us apart. Each of us was simply known as "the other one." I got called Barb as often as Patty, and the same thing happened to Barb.

Even as a top executive, when there was one other woman at my level, I was again known as "the other one" or called by her name. Alas, this dynamic persisted in part because there were never more than two of us. And to the men, it was just never worth learning to tell us apart.

I wish I could say that at some point, a switch flipped, and the expectations of those in power were generally high instead of low. But that never happened.

When I was the general manager and vice president of a billion-dollar software business, I was in a meeting room with the CEO of a partner company. I sat on one side of the table flanked by two men from my team, across from him and his two men.

The CEO would not look at me or address me in any way. I outranked everyone in the room, including him, as his was a much smaller company. I never got a direct question, answer, or look in the eye from him. He refused to acknowledge my existence. My guys kept saying, "You need to ask Patty that" and "Patty will respond to that," but he would only look at them, even when I was talking directly to the side of his face.

The reason it is so frustrating to deal with low expectations is that there is no explicit, concrete bad behavior you can point to. *It's in the handling*, like with the "stupid" rats. It's subtle. If you tried to raise an issue about how you are being treated, you would look like you were complaining about nothing. It's like a form of gaslighting, where you are being brilliant and contributing and everyone pretends you are not even there.

Constantly needing to prove your right to be in the room—when everyone seems to be asking "Why is SHE still here?"—comes at a slow drip cost to your energy, well-being, and confidence.

So even though I wasn't really conscious of these subtle cues along the way, just like with the stupid rats, my performance must have suffered.

Low-expectations "stupid rat" memo:

Welcome to your new job. You don't seem capable enough of doing anything really important. And because you have boobs, you are likely to be overly emotional, unpredictable, illogical, irrational, and prone to erratic behavior. But the boobs are nice.

But since you are here, go over there and work on this really hard, time-consuming, thankless stuff—while it needs to be done, you can't do any real harm if you screw it up. And do this peripheral work silently until you die. By the way, could you organize the office Christmas party?

High expectations are like rocket fuel for your success.

Low expectations are like a slow-acting poison that makes you weaker and weaker until you finally want to give up and go away.

Action Park

2.3

O K. Let's talk first jobs. Everyone had a first job, and in most cases, there was something uncomfortable or kooky about it. And for us women, we also had our first experience of being on the job as a female.

Mine was at Action Park.

Action Park in New Jersey was a theme park of sorts built in the 1980s on the mountainside of a ski resort and is still referred to as "the most dangerous amusement park in the world." People walked around there bleeding every day. People died there.

And I worked there for three summers.

Action Park was so lethal that a movie was made in 2020 called *Class Action Park*. The website for the film says, "Lying somewhere between *Lord of the Flies* and a *Saw* movie, Action Park is remembered as a place so insane and treacherous that, decades later, anybody who ever stepped foot in it is left wondering whether their memories could possibly be true."

I concur.

The main attraction in the early days was a ride called the Alpine Slide. This was, basically, a cement bobsled track that ran down a ski slope and killed people. You rode the chairlift up, and then you got onto a plastic sled with wheels and a wonky hand brake to zoom down the track.

The main feature of the Alpine Slide was that it ripped your skin off. I got my first lesson about not judging people based on the color of their skin at Action Park because as I watched people walking around bleeding, I thought, *Wow, look at that . . . no matter what color a person's skin is on the outside, getting the top several layers ripped off by the Alpine Slide reveals the exact same disturbing, glistening color of wet pink.*

This injury had a very particular look. It was about an inch and a half wide and ran the length of whatever limbs it was on. It didn't look like road rash; it was eerily smooth, more like something from a ham slicer.

One day, I got assigned to work at the top of the Alpine Slide, I took the chairlift up. As it ascended the mountain, I took in the big, beautiful view. It was glorious. Fifteen minutes of peace and delight and a *big* view.

But after my shift my manager said, "Get back down to the bottom and work the ticket booth next." I headed for the chair lift.

"No, that takes too long. Grab a sled. Get down there."

OMG, he is telling me I need to ride this death trap? I was terrified.

I placed my sled onto the track, sat down, and tentatively let go of the edges of the track. Clutching the (*dear lord please let this actually be a break*) plastic hand break, I attempted to make my way down the course slowly and safely. But then, *WHACK*. A speed maniac came up from behind and smashed into me. He began pushing me down the track at a high speed—out of control. I was terrified that he would launch my sled right off the track and the crash would paralyze me.

Every time I had to work at the top, I worried through my whole shift about surviving the ride back down. Thankfully, I never personally had a big accident, but the daily terror was quite draining.

At Action Park, there were also insane water slides where part of the fun was a ride in an ambulance. You would slide at high speed into a tunnel, then get shot out the side of a mountain 20 feet above a watering hole where others were swimming. Humans would just start falling out of the sky onto your head.

There was also a wave pool that was so big, deep, dangerous, and rough that a few times a day, they made everybody get out so they could scan the bottom for bodies. Really.

(The park had a fleet of ambulances on hand each day.)

Looking back on it, their premise—"YOU are responsible for the ac-tion!"—could have been a beautiful, super fun thing if they had:

1. Used *any* engineering and design oversight to eliminate or fix the rides they would later find human teeth stuck in.

2. Provided just 10 percent of actual management attention instead of relying on drunk teenagers to manage the attractions—the same teenagers who told the people riding the motorized mini-tanks they could set the tennis balls on fire before shooting them and who arranged the sex parties in the ski hut.

But then it got weird . . .

At least they drilled air holes

2.4

One Saturday, I was tasked with a special job of selling beer tickets for the Action Park Bluegrass Festival. Because I was 14, I was not allowed to actually sell beer, but apparently, it was legal for a 14-year-old to sell tickets that one could exchange for beer.

The festival started in the afternoon and went well into the night. I was put into a wooden booth the size and shape of an outhouse, about three feet square, made out of plywood, with a plexiglass front and air holes drilled in the sides and back. I managed a cash drawer that sat open on a shelf just behind the plexiglass.

So there I was, selling tickets, collecting cash, making change, and being polite to the guests. It was a little unnerving because I was locked inside the booth—I couldn't get out unless someone came with a key. And I had no means of communicating or calling for support.

This work didn't trouble me much at first, as things were going smoothly. It really wasn't so different from the regular ticket booth I often manned, except that I was locked in. But since my shift was to end at 5:00pm, I would be fine. But after a quick break at 5:00pm, the plan changed, and they locked me back in the box again until someone could come to relieve me.

But then it was 6:00pm. And then it was 7:00pm. And then it was 8:00pm. And then it started getting dark.

No one is coming to let me out. I guess I'm stuck here. I need to memorize the cash drawer so I can still make change in the dark.

Then it got *really* dark.

There was no light in the booth at all. A small shiver passed through me. *The guys outside are getting pretty drunk . . . it's getting kind of loud and chaotic out there . . . I'm stuck in here and I can't see anything. But I think I can still do this.*

"Hello there. Here are your tickets and your change, a ten and four ones."

It went on like that for a while. *So far, so good. This will be OK . . .*

Then a man's hand reached in under the front plexiglass. *Uh-oh . . . he's trying to grab the cash! Let me pull the drawer back a little. I think it will still balance. OK. Problem solved.*

"Hello. A ten, two tickets . . ."

Wait . . . someone is grabbing my left arm through the side. Oh, great—their hands can fit through the air holes. This isn't good. Uh-oh . . . I forget, was that a ten or a twenty? I yanked my arm away, then another hand grabbed my right boob. I swatted that hand away too.

"Here you go, one ticket, a five, and two ones."

It's pitch black. I can't see anything in here. Now, a hand is going for the cash drawer, AND someone has ahold of my left leg from the back. I slapped the front hand to protect the cash and wriggled out of the grip on my leg. "Wait, how many tickets did you want again?"

My simple job of selling tickets and making change had taken on a ninja/self-defense/memory-game combo that I was not expecting. They just kept grabbing my arms and boobs and legs while I was still trying to sell tickets and make change in the pitch black and protect the cash drawer from frontal attacks.

Then it got scary . . .

Uh-oh . . . Now what's happening? Oh no—they are trying to tip over the whole booth!

At some point near the start of the attempted booth tipping, some other employees finally saw what was happening, found someone with a key, and let me out.

On my way home that night, I chalked it up to just another difficult day at work. I always thought: *Work is not fun. That's why you get money for it.* But none of this seemed worth mentioning to my parents when I got home.

The next morning, I was called into the general manager's office. He sat me down, folded his arms across his chest, and said, "Do you have something you want to tell me?"

"Uh . . . what do you mean?"

"*Do you* have something you need to tell me?"

"No, I don't think so."

He said again, "*Are you quite sure* there's nothing you should tell me?"

I really hadn't the faintest idea what this conversation was about, but I was getting nervous because he seemed pretty upset.

"I'm sorry, I'll tell you whatever you want, but I don't know what you want to hear."

After several rounds of this, he finally said in an aggressive tone, "Your cash drawer was short fifty dollars. What do you have to say about that?"

Well, my response bubbled up and gushed out of me uncontrollably as I said, beaming, "Wow! Only fifty dollars! I did pretty good! I was locked in there for ten hours. And then it got pitch black. There was no light in the booth. I had to guess at making change. And then all the drunk guys were trying to reach into the booth to steal the money or grab my body. They tried to tip the booth over. I'm pretty impressed with myself that with all that, I was only down fifty dollars!"

My memory of this experience was not trauma about the groping, because by age 14, like most girls at that time, I had become accustomed to getting groped by men. This was just part of life. No one in the work world would have given it a second thought or believed something should have been done differently. You were on your own to protect yourself. We girls all have our stories.

For me, there was the orthodontist who always slid my shirt off my shoulders to look at my tan lines, the mailman who would grab my thigh from his mail truck while I was riding my bicycle, and all the creepy doctors who insisted that I take off my shirt and bra even if I was there for a cut on my leg.

By age 14, I had already dulled my nervous system to this type of "attention" and accepted it as a non-optional part of being a female out in the world. But this was the first time I was supposed to manage a tricky work task at the same time. I was really quite proud of myself for getting the job done and protecting the cash drawer.

The general manager looked stunned. He just told me to leave his office, and the cash drawer was never spoken of again.

Mom, the Slovenians, and WORK

2.5

I started my working life at Action Park at age 13 because in our house, once you reached the age of work, you worked. There was no other way of viewing the universe.

Like, one Christmas break from college, Kerry was home napping.

Mom came in, yanked off the covers, woke her up, and said, "I just got you a restaurant job. You start in two hours." And just like that, Kerry went from napping to working for the full four weeks of Christmas break.

Work was genetically required in our family, a state of being, infused into us by Mom's Slovenian parents.

Family legend has it that my grandfather stowed away on a ship to America from Yugoslavia.[1] We assume this is true because we found records of entry into the US for our other three grandparents, but not for him.

This was the story I pieced together over the years from what he was willing to talk about:

- A 17-year-old boy in the early 1900s is spreading manure on the fields and hears that "things are better over there."
- He thinks, *I don't have any money, but you know what I'll do? I'll leave behind my family and everything I know in the whole world and stow away on a ship to an unknown, faraway land—with no plan, and no sponsor waiting for me.*
- Now he's on a boat, hidden away. He'll spend approximately infinity days at sea, trying not to die from one thing or another.
- Finally, he arrives, weakened and sick, and he has to sneak off the boat so he doesn't get caught for stealing passage and sent back or arrested (or murdered).
- Then, even though he doesn't speak English and has no clue about anything, he thinks, *OK. Now I'll go look for a job.*

My own fear of being lost away from home forever makes me shiver just writing this (only two generations later) as I'm snuggled up on my ample sofa with a glass of wine and my living room–assigned comforter.

To find work in New York, my grandfather would show up for any job someone could point him to, whether he was qualified for it or not. I imagine

---

1 Note for sticklers in geo-political history: The country my grandparents left was not yet Yugoslavia, but they proudly considered Yugolsavia their homeland for their entire adult lives. It became a country in 1918 and remained such until 1992 when, in an ugly, complicated war, it became Slovenia.

My Slovenian grandparents, John and Angela (Levstik) Sterbenz

him standing there in his farmer's work shirt, dusty pants, and boots. His strategy was to just keep showing up, and nodding "yes" to get hired—then, when he failed, getting fired—until he finally landed a job that he could actually do.

My grandmother, who also came over as a teenager but with official passage and a sponsor, became a housemaid. She kept hearing the word *supper*, which in her language meant "upstairs." So for weeks she kept running upstairs instead of cooking dinner—so she got fired too.

After they married, they both took any work they could get just to survive. Nothing deterred them. They *worked*. No amount of risk to life and limb, embarrassment, or awkwardness was too great if it meant an opportunity to build a life in America.

My grandfather ultimately found his long-term career driving for Rheingold Brewery, and they built their dream life in New Jersey.

In reality, there was no way that Kerry and I were going to avoid some sort of work as soon as our opposable thumbs kicked in. And there was no way we were going to sleep through college break.

My grandparents also built their own house and farm and grew much of their own food. Growing up, Kerry and I did not totally escape farm labor, which was called "vacation at Grandma and Grandpa's house."

We sat at the big metal table in the screened-in porch for hours and hours, chopping green beans for canning or peeling apples for strudel.

Once we dragged the piles of apple peels to the compost heap, it was time to bake the apple strudel, which was a multi-hour endeavor in its own right. The dough for this strudel would be stretched out to the size of the kitchen table and was so thin you could read a newspaper through it. Then, with a bunch of various magic and butter, you'd roll up the apple mixture in a precise way to maximize the deliciousness of the layers. I've never tasted anything like this since, even in Germany, Austria, and Slovenia.

Then there was The Filling. This was my grandfather's recipe:

Take several loaves of bread including white, wheat, rye, and pumpernickel and cut into cubes. Set aside.

Fry a pound of bacon in a pan. Chop it up in the pan and leave it soaking in the fat. Set aside.

Mix 6 eggs and pour into the giant bowl of bread cubes.

Add the bacon and all the fat from the pan to the bread-and-egg mixture. Combine well, and then press, using power tools, this enormous mass of bread and grease into a single loaf pan to make a new type of bread with the density of a black hole. Bake till brown.

To serve, cut into slices, put the slices in the toaster to reactivate the bacon grease, and then spread with butter. Eat in the lobby of the hospital.

But as impressive as my Slovenian grandparents were, it was simply not in their worldview that educating girls beyond high school was a thing. Mom really wanted to go to college, but she was forbidden to even think about it. Having the agency to choose her own future taken away from her must have been heartbreaking, but it made her insistence that we must go to college more understandable.

So, what did my mom do instead of pursuing education?

Well, when it came to the only role she was allowed to have—homemaker—Mom unleashed all her intelligence, talents, energy, and inherited work ethic into the job of homemaker with the skill and intentionality of a four-star general. She always had plans for non-optional home activities and weekend family outings. She had schedules and processes for shopping and cooking and errands. No room or drawer was left unorganized.

Among many other useful things for my career that Mom modeled for me, one that had a huge impact, was organizational effectiveness.

Bullies and lying down

2.6

I came home one day from second grade and walked up the three chunky cement steps into our home, across the flat, blue, industrial carpeting in the living room, and into my parents' bedroom. The carpeting in there was also thin and flat, and brown, with a pattern that was supposed to look like wood planks.

I found Mom in bed. I fit my feet between the edges of the "wood" and shuffled in not breaking the lines as I considered my day.

I always felt excited about stuff I'd learned at school but weary from the bullying. I was happy to come home now—without Yvonne. Thankfully, Mom figured out that *that* was a disaster after the first year.

I crawled into bed with Mom and hugged a pillow.

"How was school today?" she asked.

I snuggled deeper into the bed and sighed.

Then Mom rubbed my back, and we had a long conversation about why people are mean.

My mom suffered from a back injury for about five years starting when I was eight. Suffered in the sense that, for the most part, she spent those years unable to get out of bed. Though she regained her mobility later, she was in pain for the rest of her life. But for her whole life, her pain did not define her.

While my mom could be tough and practical and we would not always agree on things, like plush carpets and fluffy comforters, she was the strongest, most nurturing, most positive person I've ever met. Mom would never even speak of her pain. She was never in a bad mood.

But since she couldn't channel her energy into the house and the family activities while she was bedridden, all that super-mom energy seemed to get channeled into our emotional well-being. As a kid, I would crawl into bed with Mom after school—it was the safest, most yummy place in my world.

I buried my head even deeper into the pillow and listened to her voice.

"First, I need you to really believe, deep down, that when people are mean, it is *never about you*. It is *always about them*. It's very, very important to not take it personally."

"But Mom, every day when people tell me, 'Patty, I hate you, everyone hates you,' it really feels like it is about me."

"I know that feels really awful, but you have to understand that some people need to hurt others because *they* are hurting. Yvonne needs to make you feel worse than she feels on the inside. People who are mean feel really bad on the inside."

Mom's message wasn't "it gets better" so much as "you need to understand this so you can deal with it." She gave me and Kerry tools and advice so we could work our way out of tough spots on our own. It was like she was telling us, "I'll never let you be a weak woman. You will know how to take care of yourself in the world."

Mom's guidance on bullies and resilience were big lessons that helped me make it through school (and turned out to be very good training for my Silicon Valley career as well).

But since it was clear that the bullying wasn't going to stop, I needed a bigger plan than just "it's not about you." I needed to create some sort of force field to protect myself and maintain some self-confidence.

So I made a decision.

I knew that I was smart, so I thought, *I'm going to be a super excellent student. That is going to be good for me, even if I am being bullied along the way.*

Having an actionable thought like this was a big moment for me.

It was the first time in my eight years on the planet that I realized I had the power to alter the course of my own life: **When something feels wrong or not fair, I can make my own decision to make my life better.**

I am going to be extra focused on learning. My bully can't touch this. Yes, she can be mean. She can get everyone else (except Wendy) to be mean. But when I am learning, I feel safe and happy. I don't feel scared or hurt when I am learning. My bully can't make me do bad at school. I control that.

And at that moment, the world felt entirely different. The moment before, I was confused and scared. The next moment, I felt clear and confident. It was like I had discovered a secret passageway. A way forward. Something no one else knew about. *Open sesame* . . . and suddenly the world is better.

So, from that moment on, super-student became my identity and learning became my whole reason for being. If I can overachieve in school, the world will hurt less, right?

Red flag? Masterful coping? Either way, I was on a mission.

I would go on to discover many more secret passageways, and every time, the new insight made me feel more confident and powerful, knowing specifically how to move forward.

And every time it is kind of thrilling.

Little patty loves it when I find secret passageways because they always feel as exciting as discovering bubble letters.

Fatty Patty

2.7

In the '70s, Sears sold a brand of polyester jeans called Toughskins. Mom became instantly hooked given her lifelong aspiration to avoid natural fibers. Why have comfortable, breathable, sturdy, cotton jeans when they could be stifling and stiff and have a weird sheen? And, adding indignity to injury, because of my weight, I had to get them in the "Husky" size. I would like to travel back in time and murder the marketing person who came up with that name. Some of you may want to join my support group on this.

As a child, clothes shopping was a grueling exercise in self-loathing, discouragement, and confirmation on a visceral level that I was not accepted by the standards of the world. The clothes were telling me quite literally, "You don't fit here."

There were no clothes for a heavy little girl back then. There were no leggings, jersey tunic dresses, or cute sweatshirts. Can you imagine, there was actually a time when there were no stretchy clothes? There were no sweatpants. No yoga pants. No tracksuits. Every day of your life, you had to button and zip things up that didn't budge. Everything was stiffly constructed with seams and zippers and buttons, distinctly not-stretchy, and not made in my size.

Mom: "Try this on."

Me: "I hate it."

Mom: "There are no other choices."

Me: (start crying)

I'd try on the skirt in the largest size and attempt to button it up as my fat squished out over the waistband. I would strain to get the two sides to connect—and they wouldn't. The sense of failure and shame was all consuming. We would go from one or two hideous choices to no choices at all.

There was nothing big enough for me in the whole world.

Man, did my mom and I struggle through this endeavor. Every article of clothing that we could both afford and get on my body was both a victory and a tragedy. I don't know which I hated worse—getting bullied on the playground or shopping for clothes.

I'm forever beyond grateful that my mother and my family never shamed me for being fat. I think they thought I would grow out of it. Although I have seen that happen to other kids, I don't know what wondrous sorcery you tap into to "grow out of" being fat. My fat was there to stick.

My body was my adversary for much of my life. As a kid, my physical self-image was overweight, slow, weak, sickly, and awkward. And I was a person whose name, in some twist of unplanned, universal tragedy, rhymed with "Fatty."

You're not allowed to be bored

2.8

"**M**om, I'm bored."

"Bored?" she said sharply as she wiped the spotted Formica counter in the kitchen in a hopeless attempt to make spotted Formica look better. "You're too smart to be bored. I don't want to ever hear you say that again." Then, with a decisive shuffle out the door, "Go outside and play."

Once you tripped over this particular land mine, you tended not to ever reveal that you were bored again. There was no scary anger, just a super clear intention that this rule was not to be disobeyed—ever.

But figuring out how to not be bored was entirely up to us. Mom made creativity obligatory. She probably saw it as a form of working. As far as she was concerned, as long as we were using either our bodies or our brains in some sort of creative play, we were acceptably honoring our Slovenian genetics.

And thank God, Mom was never upset if we made a mess, because I was (and still am) a tornado when being creative. Even today, I can make a cup of coffee in a perfectly clean kitchen, and judging by the aftermath, you'd think it was done by a raccoon on meth.

As a kid on a creative mission, I splashed paint, glue, and clay all over the house with reckless abandon and left an impressive trail of felt, yarn, beads, Styrofoam, colored pencils, bits of paper, and markers in my wake on a daily basis.

This was the cost my mom paid for instilling her "you're not allowed to be bored" rule with me. My creative answers (messes) to this challenge had no bounds. Like, one Christmas when I was 14, I decided to make a gingerbread house. It involved approximately 6,472 ingredients and destroyed the kitchen for a week.

"Why do you have to make so many different things? Isn't there an easier way? It's just a gingerbread house."

(*Just* a gingerbread house? An *easier way*? *Geesh* . . . Mom could never appreciate the sophistication of my creative visions.)

"But Mom, real houses don't have roofs and siding made from the same material. I want the walls to be actual gingerbread but I want the roof to be chocolate chip cookie bricks. I'm baking them now."

I made windowpanes out of a sugar solution that would dry into clear hard candy that would also dry onto the kitchen cabinets, the outside of the dish washer, and the knobs on the stove.

Mom later inquired, "How did you manage to get frosting in the bedrooms and on the meat in the freezer?"

The reason this endeavor made it into family lore, and why my mom reminded me of it over and over again for the next 40 years, was that within seconds of declaring victory, before I even got to behold my creation myself, I had a fever spike. My vision blurred and I couldn't stand up anymore. I fell into bed with a five-day flu. Which left Mom standing at ground zero to clean up the total devastation up . . . by herself. The "you're not allowed to be bored" rule does not protect the innocent.

Mom's "you're not allowed to be bored" rule turned out to be one of her greatest gifts to Kerry and me, because we became experts in relying on ourselves to make our own lives feel happy and interesting. We learned that we could generate our own enthusiasm from within—which has proven to be strong medicine for when adult life gets lonely or tedious.

What rules?
Dad, FOOD, and the Sicilians

2.9

T he Slovenians were hardworking, rule following, and orderly. They enjoyed life, but only after you finished your work. On my father's side of my family, the Sicilians were, shall we say, less rule-oriented.

You could see the difference, even in their houses.

My Slovenian grandfather built a very well-engineered, sturdy home with rectangular rooms that fit together coherently, designed with a detached garage that was neat and organized.

My Sicilian grandfather built something more like a mystery fun house with multiple sections, each built with different and totally random (sometimes stolen) materials, tacked together over the years at odd angles.

But his garage was one of the most exciting places to me as a kid in my otherwise dull world. It was always a little spooky to enter and be engulfed by a swirling mist of dust particles—like a magical, ancient spell had been cast upon the place and would render you unable to leave.

I poked my way past workbenches, feeling very small among the piles of mysterious objects that loomed over me. The shelves on the walls sagged to the brink of collapse from the weight of hundreds of jars and cans and boxes and car parts. The walls were covered with hanging wrenches, screwdrivers, and every kind of hammer that had ever existed. Stepping among the piles of salvaged wood and dismantled furniture was like navigating a maze.

But the most thrilling part was finding the secret door in the back. When I opened it, there was another room . . .

This one is full of crusty paint cans. Here are stacks of bricks and a jungle of electrical wires . . . oh, there are more steps that go around a corner . . . and now we're in a different room. Wow, look at that anvil—and there are three sewing machines and a bunch of iron feet sticking out of the wall. (My grandfather was a shoemaker for a time.) *Wow, this room has a door inside too. Oooh, now we are in another room with sagging shelves holding 8,000 glass bottles of tomato sauce!*

Giuseppe Azzarello making his washtub of fresh tomato sauce in the backyard.

This journey through his garage-maze felt like something straight out of a *Scooby Doo* episode but with a secret room just for storing tomato sauce.

I loved this journey because it got even more amazing before it was over. I started outside in the driveway, traversed this dark, mysterious labyrinth through all its crazy rooms; then, upon opening the very last door, I was suddenly *inside the house*—having been magically transported into the bright light of the kitchen to greeted by my grandmother holding a spatula.

I made this amazing journey over and over again.

As an adult, I know that I can be frustratingly structured sometimes, but when I'm being creative, I am the messiest person I know. I like to think that two halves of my brain are like my two grandfathers' garages.

This is one of my favorite photos of my Sicilian grandfather, making said tomato sauce in a washtub in the yard. He used to bottle the tomato sauce in glass Coke bottles and store it in the secret sauce room.

Vincenzia (Mazzola) Azzarello in her garden

My Sicilian grandmother brought food to the Olympic level. She could get a multi-course hot meal on the table with 10 minutes' notice at any moment of any day, without a microwave.

Sunday family dinners (which were required atten-dance) with my Sicilian grand-parents would start with a shot of sweet vermouth. At age six, I started getting half a shot.

I have always enjoyed the taste of liquor. In fact, my first fond memories of alcohol were of the whiskey-soaked Q-tips used to soothe my gums when my teeth fell out or grew in. To this day, I can remember thinking, *Ow, this hurts . . . but mmmm, that tastes nice.*

After the shot of vermouth, the first thing that would come to the table was The Bowl. My grandmother would bring an enormous bowl of pasta (with sauce from the washtub) to the table. To this day, I'm not sure I have ever seen a bowl that big.

Italians can make a simple pasta seem like the most delicious thing you have ever eaten in your life. Now that I have obtained my Italian citizenship, I can let you in on the secret. Whenever the sauce is so delicious you can't believe, it's because half of it is olive oil or butter.

After devouring a delicious mound of pasta, an inexperienced new-comer would be in a happy food coma—but what they didn't know was that the dinner was just starting. Once The Bowl was removed, a lot of open real estate was left on the table to be filled with sizzling steaks and sausages, a bubbling pot of meatballs, fried potatoes, garlic-soaked artichokes, more vegetables, and a massive pile of bread. Friends' eyes would just glaze over at this point in an equal mix of amazement and horror.

After school one day, when I was about 13, I got off the bus at the top of the hill to say hi to my grandparents before going home. There was always food on offer. And when I say "on offer," I mean "required." It didn't matter what time of day it was or if you had just eaten a moose.

As I walked into the kitchen, my grandmother beamed. She gave me a painful, overly squeezy hug, and even though I was a teenager, she still pinched my cheeks. And I still hated that. Because it still hurt.

I sat down at the table.

"Do you want some pasta?"

"No thanks, Grandma, I'm not hungry."

Her disappointment in me filled the room. That was clearly the wrong answer.

"No pasta? Then have some cake."

"No thank you. I've already eaten."

"You want to break your grandmother's heart? Then just some cookies."

The cookies appeared on the table. I didn't eat them.

"You need to eat some cookies. Don't you love me?"

This could go on for a long time.

Eating was not optional. You show up. You eat.

I've heard there is a myth that a Sicilian grandmother's life is shortened by a week every time someone turns down her food. That's certainly what it felt like.

Since I always struggled so much with my weight, I just could not eat every time she offered. So I had to be strong, but the guilt was heavy.

I believe that one of the reasons I later developed the necessary assertiveness to protect my boundaries and use my voice to defend my positions in the workplace was that I learned to turn down food at my Sicilian grandmother's table.

High school disorders

2.10

It started out innocently enough. High school was a fresh start—and completely away from Yvonne. I joined things. I got a leading role in the school play. I started dating a senior. And I had lost weight. I was feeling more OK socially and in my body than ever before. There was a real sense of *me* forming, and I liked it.

One morning before geometry, a junior-level class I had tested into as a freshman, I found the older girls in the class talking in the hallway on morning break. I approached the circle to join the conversation as I normally did. But this day, something felt weird. The circle didn't open to let me in. Instead, the girls made a show of tightening the gaps to lock me out, and then they totally ignored me. I just stood there dumbly on the outside of the circle. Rejected. *Why is this happening? They were nice to me yesterday. What's different today?*

So, I went into the classroom and sat by myself for the rest of the break, not quite realizing the impending sharp social decline that was to follow, or that I had just experienced the origin story for my lifelong fear of conversation circles.

For some reason, these older girls with the social power had decided once again that it was not OK to be Patty, and the new campaign against me began.

A week later, a photo of the four leads in the play was published in the local paper. The theater group got dozens of extra newspapers and posted the photos all over the school to promote the play. The next day, my face in every one of those photos had been vandalized in one way or another: scribbled out, torn out, gum stuck over it, drawings of penises on it.

For the rest of my first year, when I walked through the hallways or the lunchroom, I got called a slut, a teacher's pet, a bitch, a weirdo. And if they didn't use a slur outright, they would point at me and laugh in a mean way.

Once again, it felt like everyone hated Patty.

I did have a small group of musical theater and study group friends who stuck with me, which made parts of the day bearable . . . but the next fall, things took a bad turn.

I started gaining weight uncontrollably. The problem went undiagnosed for two years because doctors saw me as a teenage girl who got fat and was looking to blame it on something other than myself. I knew how to diet. I had just done it. Super-student Patty had figured that out and performed it with the same rigor she did everything else. But now, I was dieting and gaining weight for no explainable reason, and it was terrifying.

I was so miserable. Once again, I couldn't find clothes that fit on my body. Every day required a self-loathing effort just to find something to wear to school. I hated my body. The standards of the world at that time were telling me that any bit of extra flesh is repulsive and no one should ever be required to look at the fat of a fat person because it is disgusting. So, every day, I stepped into the world believing that I was disgusting and that I was supposed to hide.

And it wasn't just my embarrassment about my existence. I also felt sick all the time. I was having trouble concentrating. I had low energy. I would slide into periods of depression. I had hot flashes and joint aches, and I was losing hair in clumps. And to add more embarrassment to injury, my boobs were enormous—and painful.

Big boobs are no fun if you didn't choose them. There are no cute lacy bras to caress your breasts. Big bras back then were more like a hoisting device made from the kind of sturdy material you might find on a sailing ship.

I had permanent dents and often bleeding wounds on my shoulders from my bra straps. And my back always hurt. Living in my body was torment.

Near graduation, a group of guys put on a funny senior awards show. I was surprised when they called me up on stage for an award. They presented me with a varsity letter "F" for the name of my high school and announced, "This is the only F that Patty will ever get," referring to my perfect grades. It felt kind of nice to be included in the festivities.

But then, in keeping with the flow of the show, they went on to describe a fictional future state about each person who got called onto the stage. For me it was "... where she went to live in a developing country to feed *all* the small children." It took a couple of beats for the joke to land with people, including me ... and when everyone started laughing hysterically, there I was, just standing there on the stage with my big boobs, mortified, having to pretend that was funny.

I had no idea just how many stages my career would later put me on, but I can tell you that I have never again feared that I would feel worse on a stage than I did at that moment.

I had gained 50 pounds before a doctor finally stopped treating me like a stupid girl and started treating my thyroid problem. But the treatment didn't make the weight automatically fall off. I gained another almost 50 pounds because I had become so depressed, and I was bingeing and out of control with food. Which was yet another source of my shame.

But I gutted my way through my problems, just like I did in grammar school, by deciding to keep my focus on being a great student. I took extra classes at every chance so I could graduate early—I was so desperate to get the hell out of there as soon as possible. So, I went to college at age 16.

Getting into college

2.11

I walked tentatively through a huge entrance into the biggest and most ornate building I'd ever seen. We approached a grand staircase. My heart was pounding. I was 15. I was in awe of the towering marble columns, swirly, sculpted ceilings with artful inlays, and gold plating everywhere.

Mom had gotten me an interview for a full, four-year academic scholarship. (Kind of like getting Kerry a job while she was sleeping.) And right now, I was in this crazy, giant marble mansion to make it happen.

I wanted to go to college so very badly. Going to college was not optional in our family. But it would not have been an *actual* option without financial help.

This interview was the biggest thing to ever happen in my life, and I was terrified. I'd never been interviewed before. I just kept staring, dumbfounded, at all the marble.

I was led to a room that seemed even fancier than the rest of the building. Then there I was, suddenly face-to-face with a group of adults unlike any I had ever seen in my small, brown world—all formal and tweedy, with clipboards. They wanted me to talk about my life experiences.

Life experiences? I'm 15.

I grew up in the middle of nowhere.

Let's see . . . I could tell him about the brown birds and toads, and how the big event at school was that we tasted a pineapple one Thursday . . . uh-oh . . . I've got nothing to say. I am a blank.

OK, Patty, don't panic. Stay in this. You're smart. Say something smart. OK, nothing smart coming to mind? Then just say something—anything. If you can't say something smart, say something true.

So I focused on the only card I had to play. The truth, with a side of super-student.

"I'm very nervous to be here. I've never even been in a building like this. This building is amazing to me. I grew up in a tiny country town. But I want to go to college very badly—it's been my life's focus since I was five years old. I have worked really hard and studied really hard the whole time. I am at the top of my class even though I am two years younger than everyone. I promise I will work and study really hard here too. I can't afford to go to college without a scholarship, so that's why I am here today, and I hope that I'll be able to do well in this interview and be considered."

It was a bit one-dimensional for sure, but it was true, and it was all I had.

I had discovered another secret passageway, a technique that has helped me deal with uncomfortable conversations forever after: ***If you are uncomfortable, say so. Name the reality. Say, "I feel awkward about this conversation" and explain why. That will break the silence in a relatable way, and the honesty will create a positive path forward.***

Even though I was feeling defensive and scared, I got that burst of confidence from discovering a secret passageway, and I overcame my panicked silence with the truth. I didn't try to make up interesting stuff to sound smart. Instead, I set the interview on a good, authentic course—and I got the scholarship. Which allowed me to continue my pursuit of my whole reason for being—learning.

It amuses me to include this picture taken decades later, with the president and the chairman of the board of Monmouth University in New Jersey, on that very same marble staircase.

Me at a holiday ball on the grand staircase with the president and chairman.

When I arrived at college orientation, I was registered as a fine arts major. I had wanted to be an artist since I was four years old, but Mom did not approve. As I looked around at all of the students standing in various lines to register for their majors, I heard Mom's ongoing refrain in my head: "You need to get a good education and a good job. You need to make your own money and support yourself."

It's so funny—growing up, Mom made me and Kerry do creative stuff as if our lives depended on it, and we were constantly told we could be anything we wanted. But apparently my mom's real message was that we can be anything we want, as long as it's not an artist. Our choice of majors needed to be as practical as our industrial carpeting.

So, with my mom's voice in my head, and considering my excellent performance in math and science to date—and also, to be fair, fearing that I would grow to hate art by struggling to make a living at it—I scratched out "fine arts" and penciled in "electronic engineering" on my admission form, and stood in the electronic engineering line.

What I really learned in college

2.12

The only time I ever traded sexual favors for some sort of gain was to get help in my third-year engineering class on thermodynamics. Don't worry about me. It was fine. I was 18 (finally). He looked like a 30-year-old Mikhail Baryshnikov, with all the muscles and the wavy hair. He might still have helped me without the sex, and I might still have had the sex without the help, but that's how it was, and we were both OK with the deal.

And I was desperate to get the help because I was failing the class. It was killing me.

I said to him, "I look at these problems and I just don't understand how to start."

"That's the easy part," he replied. He then showed me a super practical way to look at the shape of the problem, and to pick the right equation to match that shape as the first step. That was the missing link. After that, it was just math again. He explained it so much better than the professor did. The class became almost easy after getting that one insight.

It is remarkable to me that so often, the difference between struggling and failing in lonely agony, and confidently gliding through to success, is simply getting someone to show you the secret passageway.

On campus, I was always carrying at least five of my textbooks at every waking moment of my life.

I would see the other students carrying no books. I'd think, *Where are you going with no textbooks and not a care in the world? How will you survive if you can't study at every spare moment? What else could you possibly be doing in college that you don't need all your books with you at all times?*

When I'd enter my dorm room after classes, I'd finally let all the books slide out of my arms. I'd fall down with them onto my bed and close my eyes for 10 minutes to chase away the chaos and insecurities that had built up through the day. Crawling into bed after school was already a lifelong habit from those wonderful afternoons with Mom. I was learning how to reset my nervous system when I am overwhelmed—and that I *had* a nervous system that needed to reset when I am overwhelmed.

Every day of engineering classes greeted me with totally new impenetrable problems that felt crushing, consisting of some new permutation of weird graphs and scientific nomenclature that I had never seen before.

One day, I walked into a midterm exam for Electromagnetics to find this on the test:

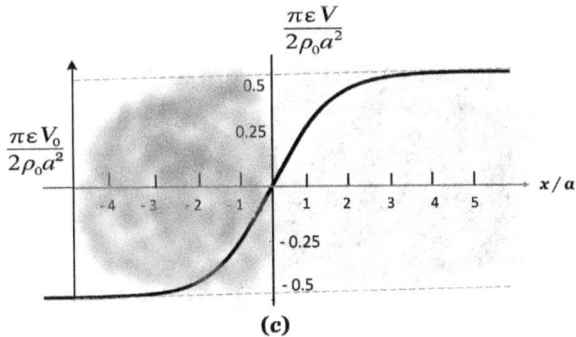

(c)

Let the charge distribution of Fig. 7.3a be represented by $\rho = \rho_0(x/a)e^{-x/a}$ for x > 0
and $\rho = \rho_0(x/a)e^{x/a}$ for x < 0.

(a) Show that $\rho_{max}=0.368\rho_0$ and that it occurs at x = a.

(b) Use a development parallel to show that $C = dQ/dV_0 = \varepsilon S/(8a)$.

OK, come on now . . . Show that $C = dQ/dV_0 = \varepsilon S/(8a)$? What does that even mean? Am I in the right room?

Seriously, I looked around the room. I was checking to make sure it was the right teacher—*OK, there he is*—but then I desperately thought, *Maybe this is a different class of his and I'm somehow here at the wrong time, because I have never seen a single thing on this test before.*

I scanned the room, hoping not to recognize the other students from my class, but one by one they came into view. *Oh God. I really am in the right room. THIS IS ACTUALLY THE TEST. I am going to sit here for an hour and not have a single thing to write down! I don't have any idea what any of these questions even mean!*

Every week of my first year became more soul crushing. What was happening to me? No more super-student. No more fastest learner in the class. No more straight A's. Now I was struggling sometimes for a C. It was like being slowly eaten alive by acid with a side of existential crisis. *If I'm not a straight A student, who am I?* For the first time in my life, I feared that I could actually get an F in a class. I had been officially smacked down.

The electronic engineering program was where my internal critic, who would become a companion for the rest of my life, first spun up in a big way. Here it goes . . .

YOU SHOULD NOT BE IN THIS ENGINEERING PROGRAM. IT'S WAY TOO HARD FOR YOU. YOU SHOULD HAVE LISTENED TO THOSE TEACHERS WHO SAID ENGINEERING WAS NOT SUITABLE FOR YOU. YOU ARE NOT LIKE THESE OTHER STUDENTS WHO DESERVE TO BE HERE. YOU ARE GOING TO FAIL THIS TEST, YOU ARE GOING TO FAIL THIS CLASS, AND YOU ARE GOING TO LOSE YOUR SCHOLARSHIP, AND YOU ARE GOING LIVE UNDER A BRIDGE AND DIE.

Losing my scholarship would have been the end of the world for me—a brutal end to my whole reason for being. It was terrifying.

OK. Patty, you need to stop panicking. Slow down. Look closer. You must know something—you studied this stuff for five thousand hours. Let's page through these 10 exam problems for the 47th time.

OK, wait . . . I see something. This equation reminds me of the middle part of a homework problem I studied last night. Let me write that down.

OK, now maybe I can find a hook to get to the first step. I can at least part-way solve this one . . .

By stopping the panic, I would usually find a way to get at least partial credit on a few of the problems. And that was typically enough to keep me from failing.

During the exam, I noticed other students calmly filling pages in their little blue test notebooks without a drop of sweat. I had to admit that they also seemed to generally know what was going on during the classes and dealing with it all without the agony and fear that I endured.

My internal critic reminded me:

YOU ONLY THOUGHT YOU WERE SMART, BUT YOU ARE NOTHING LIKE THESE REALLY SMART PEOPLE. I KEEP TELLING YOU, YOU ARE NOT SMART ENOUGH FOR ELECTRONIC ENGI-NEERING. ALL THESE REALLY SMART PEOPLE KNOW HOW STUPID YOU ARE.

I realized that I was immersed in a level of smartness all around me that I never conceived of in the little world that I came from. When I looked at these geniuses, I was in awe.

So what did I do?

I asked them for help.

All the time.

(It only involved sex the one time.)

Despite what my internal critic was telling me, I did not feel threatened or insecure around smarter people. For starters, I was too desperate not to lose my scholarship, *and* they inspired me. Their greatness didn't make me feel bad about myself or resentful of them. It just made me want to be like them. I learned that getting inspired by brilliant people was a good way to get my internal critic to shut up.

And the way to do that was to learn from them. Asking smarter people for help is what saved me in college, and it continued to save me for the rest of my career and life.

Mom used to ask me, "Why don't you just choose an easier major? Why did you choose the hardest one? You wouldn't have to be afraid of los-ing your scholarship if you switched to an easier major."

As much as Mom encouraged me that "You can be anything you want," she could never quite get her head around the scope of my various ambitions—just like with the gingerbread house. *An easier major. Geesh.* I always did extra. I always did more than necessary or required. I always built the gingerbread house.

But by being so mercilessly barraged by scary, unavoidable problems all the time, my panic eventually began to dull. And, as it turned out, I ultimately did really well in the program and got lots of As—because I got lots of help. I can tell you that I don't use the specifics of my engineering education at all—and I have huge, nagging guilt (and regular nightmares) about the fact that I can no longer do calculus—but two things I learned at college have been among the most valuable secret passageways I have ever learned in my life:

1. ***Don't panic when faced with an impossible, scary problem.***
2. ***Always ask for help.***

I use these lessons every week of my life, if not every day, so I am very grateful for the engineering program that almost killed me.

It really does get better

2.13

When I got to college, I assumed the social scene would be as brutal as ever. But in this bigger pond, I was invisible, so no one had any particular reason to torture me. That felt like a distinct upgrade.

One day in my first-year electronics lab, I met two older students when our hands touched, grabbing for the limited tech equipment needed to do the experiments. It was like a Hallmark movie.

Mike and Nabi liked me. And they sensed how in over my head I was in this lab. They took me under their wings, and over our four years in the engineering program together, we laughed, cried, ate pizza, and built a robot. I had actually made two lifelong friends with other students at school.

I realized that my timid, socially tortured, introvert self was beginning to figure out that I did not have to go to parties or even be outgoing to have a social life. I could make good friends, one at time, by working on things with someone and having deep, productive conversations—which was always my version of fun anyway.

Also, in my second year of college, I finally started feeling better physically and started losing weight. I lost about 80 pounds over two or three years by making small shifts in my behavior, one at a time. I kind of snuck up on the weight loss instead of making it a big ordeal. I gave up *over*eating without ever giving up *enjoying* eating. (But my weight was and is still the focus of far too much of my mental energy, and it remains a juicy topic for my internal critic.)

Also, in a wild plot twist, I even made friends with some girls in the dorm. (Still just one at a time—let's not get too crazy here.) Karen, Ann, Bonnie, Sue, and Christine made me feel truly loved among my peers for the first time in my life, and I never once went out to a party with any of them. They seemed to know better than to invite me.

You can't live here for free

2.14

Right before my last year of college, my stress exploded like an electrical fire. I called my mom in a full meltdown from the payphone at the end of the hallway in my dorm. I was standing there, tethered to the wall by the metal payphone cord. People casually walked by, not carrying any books, as my life was coming to an end. *How is no one ever carrying any books?*

I was inconsolable. "Mom, I just found out I can't get a single dorm room next year. The senior year of the engineering program is going to be the hardest ever, and there is so much work to do, and labs, and a big senior project. I need a private space to work. If I get a roommate who likes to party, I'm going to fail. I won't graduate. I don't know what to do! If I have to share a room, my life will be ruined!"

Mom was always a rock in a meltdown. "Patty, you will be OK. Your life will not be ruined over this. I understand what you need. We'll work this out."

Then Mom crafted a plan to help me live off campus, even though I couldn't afford it.

It included the use of a family car. My parents also subsidized rent for an apartment. My parents' offer to let me use the family car was not like, "Here, you can borrow this car," but instead, "Here is a lease agreement at a family rate that you will accrue debt on throughout the year and owe us after you graduate." The apartment subsidy was on a similar debt accrual program. Mom then added to this a year of future rent that I would owe when I moved back home after college. All in all, the debt totaled $6,000.

This level of support propelled me through my studies to graduate with honors, without the chaos of drunk roommates getting home late from parties with strange men while I was trying to learn digital signal processing.

On graduation day, my parents took me out to dinner to celebrate.

We were sitting at a local restaurant, which—like most of my world to date—had an entirely brown interior.

My mom said, "We're so proud of you for graduating from such a difficult engineering program!"

Then, after all the warm congratulations and bottomless fried shrimp, Mom reminded me of our earlier agreement. As the cheesecake arrived, she continued, "You know the $6,000 we agreed upon that you will owe us when you started your senior year off campus? Well, for your graduation present . . . we decided that you don't owe us $6,000."

My brain jolted. *OMG—are they going to waive this debt as my graduation present?*

"Wow, that's amazing!" I responded. My imagination was taking flight with possibilities.

Before I could properly say thank you, Mom continued.

"As your present . . . we are reducing your debt to $5,200."

When I think about how I achieved various successes in my life, my first thought is always how much my mom's encouragement and support helped me. She pushed me to be independent and told me I could be anything I want, in a "you deserve anything you want, now figure out how to go get it yourself" kind of way.

But when I try to pin down what practical career things I learned from Mom, specifically, I come up kind of blank. But there was one place where I can absolutely draw a direct line between Mom's input and my career success:

"You can't live here for free."

. . . I'm 8 and I want to color. "Do your chores first."

. . . I'm 13 and I want stuff. "Get a job."

. . . I'm in college full-time. "You need to work during all your breaks and summers if you want to stay at the house."

. . . I'm out of college. "You are a college graduate now. If you live at home, you need to pay rent."

People today are horrified by Mom's rent policy. They ask, "Do you hate your parents?" I see it sometimes on social media. A mom posts about making her 20-year-old son pay rent to learn financial responsibility. Frontal attacks spin up pretty quickly about what a horrible, evil woman this is who obviously hates her kid.

I get that the overall financial picture is different today, making it much harder for young people to go out on their own without help, and I don't want to discount that. But back then, for me, my mom really got it right.

Her rigid position on paying my own way was a huge motivator for me. I wanted beautiful things. I wanted to go places and do stuff. And it was up to me to make it happen.

The Stone Pony

2.15

W hen I graduated, my grades qualified me for an interview at Bell Labs in New Jersey. In its day, Bell Labs was one of the most exciting and important research facilities in the world. Its research created the fundamental technology (transistors) that allows computers to sit on our wrists instead of filling a warehouse.

I worked there as an engineer in the robotics research department during the birth of AI—an absolute dream job for any engineering graduate. Well, almost any.

As it turned out, I wasn't good at it, and I didn't enjoy any part of it. I hated being an engineer. This situation gave my internal critic a good start on my professional inadequacies:

You blew it. You chose so wrong. This is the only thing you are trained to do now. You are going to be stuck in engineering, miserable forever. You are so stupid for having ended up here. You got your whole life wrong. There are no other options for you.

As you are here in the future with me now, you know I didn't stay an engineer. But even though I hated the work, my time at Bell Labs was weird and wonderful, and it opened unexpected portals to my future. One was access to the emerging technology of digital music, which led to the invention of CD players—which led to me studying everything about it and wanting to buy a real stereo with a CD player myself.

And since I had made some progress on my post-thyroid weight loss, I was no longer in hiding—never wanting to go anywhere, always feeling ill, and hating all my clothes. So, one day I decided to put on my new jeans and cute leather jacket and use my Bell Labs expertise in digital music to go shopping for my stereo.

I had unknowingly stepped into one of those high-end audiophile stores. Compared to anything I had ever seen before, this place was like a science fiction set, with spotlights highlighting museum-worthy pieces. Gigantic speakers stood all around, looming aggressively.

Three men stood behind the front counter, silent, staring at me. Finally, one of them spoke. "If you are looking for the laundromat or the Chinese restaurant, those are next door."

It seemed that a woman had never entered this place alone before.

"I'm interested in looking at CD players."

They remained silent, as though aliens had abducted them but left their bodies standing there.

After a long pause, I added, "Do you sell CD players?"

"Yes," one of them mumbled stiffly. Still, they just stood there.

"OK. Soooo," I said, searching for any conversational path, "what is the price range of your CD players?"

"Two hundred to four thousand dollars." Back to silence.

"That is quite a big range. Could you explain why that is?"

No response.

I sighed, then continued. "Is the difference that some have more sophisticated digital-to-analog converters? Do they have a higher resolution of error correction? Do they have a better response over a bigger dynamic range?" Then I pulled some CDs out of my bag and said, "Could I listen to these?"

Their mouths dropped open.

At this point, one man stepped forward and boldly said, "I'll handle this."

He took me from room to room, playing music for me on various systems and speakers, teaching me how to listen critically. It was fascinating to hear the differences.

There came a point when I thought, "I'm really having fun, but I've been here a long time, and I'm not ready to buy anything." I was feeling a little awkward and said, "I hope I'm not taking up too much of your time. Do you need to spend time with other customers?"

He answered, "The store has been closed for forty-five minutes. I've stopped selling audio equipment—I've been working on a date. How am I doing?"

I have never, before or since, met someone as into music as Ross was. Music was the main focus in his life—more than family, career, hobbies, or causes. He knew every bit of new music that was ever released and was also well versed in opera, classical, and anything else that made a sound.

I believe he might have been the first person in the US to have a Sony Walkman. For those of you who are too young to remember, the Sony Walkman was the first portable device you could carry around with you to listen to your music—on cassette tapes. It fit in your pocket and ran on AA batteries. So, with his Walkman, Ross was able to take his music with him during every moment of his life—which he did.

One day, we were in San Francisco together. Ross at 35 was like a cross between Mick Jagger, the "Mayhem" character from the car insurance commercials, and the most enthusiastic Walmart greeter on the planet. Ross was *a lot*.

At one point, we sat down on a park bench and a homeless guy came and sat next to us. He was drinking Schlitz Malt Liquor out of a paper bag. I know that it was specifically Schlitz Malt Liquor because Ross asked him, "Hey, what are you drinkin'?" Ross would enthusiastically and with total openness talk to absolutely anyone. He would sing in full voice in line at the grocery store. I always marveled at his joyfulness, his extroversion and warm ease with people. *All* people.

Anyway, this homeless guy started carrying on about how beautiful Ross was. Ross was beaming. But then the guy started asking for money.

Ross never gave money to people on the street. But, being as chatty as he was, Ross said, "What do you need the money for?" The guy then said, "Batteries. The batteries in my Walkman died and I miss listening to music."

Well, this was the one thing that could reach Ross's heart and turn him around. So he reached into his pocket and pulled out not his wallet but two AA batteries, and he handed them over with a smile.

Ross was, on paper, my parents' worst nightmare. I was 20 and he was 33, and at any moment, you could never be sure if he was an alcoholic or a drug addict. He straddled that edge precariously. He had the mannerisms of someone high on cocaine whether or not he was high on cocaine. His resting state was raging exuberance.

We dated for three years. Ross was my first serious relationship.

When I had graduated from college and was working as an engineer, I was a very disciplined (uptight), socially awkward, rule-following nerd. Then I started dating Ross.

Ross came into my world and took my neatly organized perspective on life and scrambled its tidy lines and boxes until it looked and felt like spin art. Every day was like WHAM! What's happening now?

For my nervous system, it was like going from a reading a book in a big stuffed chair in a cozy corner to being dropped out of a helicopter into a raging underground party in Bangkok.

I never knew if a day with Ross would mean a lovely bike ride, a dark seedy bar, bingo with the seniors in the church basement, tickets to the New York Opera at Lincoln Center, a neighborhood school's second grade play, or not doing drugs in a group of people doing drugs, panicked the police would show up and single me out for arrest and my life would be ruined forever.

There was this one midnight when Ross left me standing outside the Stone Pony, a bar in Asbury Park, NJ, for a Tower of Power concert, while he went inside to find someone to pay $20 to let me use her ID to get in. *I'm standing alone outside a bar a midnight. This is crazy enough— but breaking the law to get into a club?* I was aghast and terrified. In fact, "aghast and terrified" describes my internal state for much of my time with Ross.

Ross dressed up for a friend's wedding.

Ross never mistreated me—but he was always being Ross. And "being Ross" was just a super intense sensory overload for me, all the time. But all the craziness, the parties, and the sometimes-illegal behaviors I deemed reckless and irresponsible awakened me to things that happen in the real world, where normal people have fun instead of studying at home and working all the time. Don't get me wrong, I didn't actually have the fun myself. I just nervously observed others doing it. Let's face it, I was still me.

But learning how to be with Ross out in the world, with his constant and vivid chaos and the crazy situations he would put me in, helped me break out of my oh-so-serious, studious, safely closed-off mode of living where virtually every social interaction caused me stress, panic, or pain.

And with this, Ross helped me create a few millimeters of space where I could tolerate the unknown. The world no longer terrified me all the time. After that, it was only about half the time.

In addition to the crazy stuff, Ross and I had a gentle and deep heart connection. We would get coffee from Dunkin' Donuts and go to the marina and watch the boats for hours, where we'd have wonderful conversations and listen to music. He got me into biking again, the one athletic activity I was actually pretty competent at as a kid but lost interest in through high school and college. We snuggled up to watch movies. We had a goldfish named Milton. Even my parents eventually came to love Ross.

I cannot imagine how I would have survived the crazy challenges that were to come in my career—and life—if it were not for Ross.

Ross's chaotic brand of exposure therapy better prepared my nervous system to be out in the world at large. And it came just in time, as a bit of magic then happened in my life.

I got a call from a recruiter representing a Silicon Valley tech company. He told me he was looking for an engineer who could demo products and answer technical questions focused on electronic design during the sales process. In that moment, I learned that there was such a job as "sales engineer," and I got an interview for the job.

My life was not over! I was not going to be stuck as an engineer forever. I had a way out.

So here I was at 22, on the very cusp of my career—all potential and no experience.

And now, we are going to take this super eager, naive, insecure young woman out of her familiar, small, brown world and drop her into Silicon Valley. What could go wrong?

Part 3

Sorry, I Was on Mute

—

"Courage does not always roar. Sometimes courage is the quiet voice at the end of the day saying, 'I will try again tomorrow.'"

—Mary Anne Radmacher

Worst embarrassment ever

3.1

I was in a small utilitarian room, with about 15 men in plaid shirts with pocket protectors sitting at desks and on tables and file cabinets—all of which seemed to be at a higher level than I was, kind of like an amphitheater built of crappy office furniture. I was sitting at the bottom, center stage, at the computer ready to do a demo. I felt very small.

This was the official start of my career in Silicon Valley. It was only my second demo in my new job as sales engineer after my two-week training period. This was the real thing now. The show was on the road, and the stakes felt very high.

I had been trained on only one of our two products. The salespeople had been instructed not to schedule demos for me on the second more specialized, printed circuit board design product until I got trained.

I started the demo.

"We don't need that product. We just want to see your printed circuit board product."

I looked at the sales rep. Our eyes met with a knowing glance. I expected him to say, "I'm sorry for the misunderstanding, but we're not prepared to show you that today. We'll need to reschedule."

Then he said, "Patty, show them what they want to see."

I just couldn't believe it. He knew I couldn't do it.

My heart was pounding. But as ever, I was feeling very duty bound, and I was clearly on my own.

"Uh . . . OK. I can *show* you the product, but I'm not prepared to do a demo. I'm new and haven't been trained on this product yet."

I clicked on the product icon, and then there we all were, staring at an image of a printed circuit board on the screen. That was it. That was all I had. I had no idea how to actually do anything with the product other than point to it on the screen. I was still hoping the sales rep would save me—but he was silent. He chose to make this my embarrassment instead of his.

Then immediately came an avalanche of questions from the engineers in the room.

"How do you edit multilevel traces?"

"How do you handle internal vias?"

"How many levels of heat sinks do you support?"

It just kept coming. I must have said, "I don't know, I'll have to find out and get back to you" at least 30 times. It was excruciating. I was so embarrassed.

I didn't know the answer to a single one of their questions. I didn't even *understand* their questions. I knew nothing about traces or vias or heat sinks. I was out of moves.

Then it came . . . my worst nightmare.

One of the customers said to the salesperson in a frustrated, angry tone, "Why did you bring *her*? She doesn't know anything!"

She doesn't know anything.

Even my internal critic was paralyzed at this moment, having nothing worse it could possibly add. This was as bad as it could get.

I was *so* humiliated. And I was heartbroken at my lack of ability and utter failure in this moment. I packed up my computer, and we left.

This was a huge injury to my confidence and credibility. I was the new sales engineer, and I had made a fool of myself. I went home a failure that night. I was embarrassed and afraid of losing my new job and ruining my whole life.

But you know what happened the next day?

I didn't die.

But I risked being known forever after as "the girl who can't demo that product." So once again, I made a decision. I decided that instead of backing away in fear and shame, I would change the story that was being told about me.

The next day, I found the product manager for the printed circuit board product and asked him, "Can you please explain to me what all of these questions mean? Why are these questions important to the client? How do I answer them? And how do I demonstrate those answers in the product?"

I was determined to not let the embarrassment of failure stick to me or stop me. I was going to figure out what excellence looked like and keep trying until I got there.

Which I did.

By taking matters into my own hands and getting help from the expert, within two weeks, I was in high demand to demo the printed circuit board product.

I could have chosen to avoid ever being humiliated like that again by just not putting myself out there anymore. But that strategy would have stalled my career. Some of the other sales engineers refused to demo that product *ever*, and they got away with it. The sales team worked around them. I did not get that luxury.

Turning this miserable experience into a success revealed a secret passageway that propelled me forward for the rest of my career: ***Don't avoid being judged. Seek it out. Only after being tested will you truly learn what it takes to be excellent.***

This strategy also came in handy for surviving new embarrassments yet to come.

Things that can actually kill you

3.2

My flight had landed after midnight. I was in upstate nowhere to do a client demo. Once I left the terminal, I found myself in an enormous parking lot, completely alone, and in the dark. I was still in my twenties, nervous and clueless about being out in the world on my own—especially in the dark. I walked and walked, hearing only the clack-clack-clack of my high heels echoing into the pitch-black void. I was desperately searching for my rental car. And I was scared. It was really creepy. *If the serial killer lurched out of the darkness now, no one would ever know.*

My nervous system is always on high alert (pre-meltdown) in the dark. At this moment, it was telling me:

Step 1. Avoid death in the parking lot.
Step 2. Avoid death by driving in the dark.
Step 3. Avoid death by getting hopelessly lost.
Summary: Avoid death.

I finally found my car. And it started. Thank God.

At this time, pre–mobile phones and GPS, I had only a list of written directions, a paper map, and a flashlight. That was the personal technology packing list in those days. Due to my terrible sense of direction, I got lost a lot on these demo trips, even in the daytime.

And when I'm lost out in the world somewhere, I get panicky and overwhelmed, and I feel embarrassed and stupid because normal people don't get lost this easily, and they don't turn into such a crumbling pile of nerves when they do. And that triggers my real, bigger fear, which is being lost away from home forever with no possible chance of return.

I missed an exit.

I drove and drove and drove into the darkness. My fear was clawing its way from my stomach to my throat. I began to panic. *What am I going to do? I have no idea where I am. I have no idea how to find my way. I can't do this. This really is the moment I will get lost away from home forever.*

But I managed to not die that night. I got to my hotel at about 3am—even though it was only an hour away from the airport—having gotten in a good two hours of extra panic before my 6:00am start time the next morning.

It was enormously draining to get so lost and so scared so regularly. And sometimes it got weird.

At the age of 24, I was sent to the National Security Agency (NSA), the top-secret, high-tech, government agency that protects the US from spies, communication breaches, and general security threats, to install software and do product training. I drove up to a gate (in daylight), but it was the wrong gate, obviously, as I am never in the right place on the first try.

"You are in the wrong place," said the guard.

I thought, *That's OK, I'm just impressed with myself for finding the site at all. He can tell me where I need to go.*

"Can you tell me—"

"YOU ARE IN THE WRONG PLACE," he repeated, pulling his jacket back and showing me the very large gun on his hip.

"But can you just—"

He interrupted again, and in a more serious tone—as if you could get more serious than showing a clueless person a large firearm.

"YOU ARE IN THE WRONG PLACE."

I backed up, hoping that there were none of those medieval tire exploding gadgets like at the car rental return if you go in reverse. I wandered around some more, wondering which would be the wrong turn I would take where I would actually get shot.

When I finally got to the right place, I entered a tiny lobby with a giant security scanner and received a visitor's badge. A lobby guard walked me down a long, drab hallway into a room full of men, then left. Before we got started, I asked, "Can I please use the ladies' room?"

No one knew where it was. There were no ladies there.

One of them agreed to help me find it. He clipped on a badge with a big *E* on it for (E)scort. My badge had a giant *V* on it for (V)isitor, but I couldn't help thinking it could just as well have stood for (V)agina, this place was so entirely male. He walked me to the very edge of the door to the ladies' room, then waited across the hall while I was inside.

When I came out, the cameras, I guess, saw that my (V)agina badge was too far away from his (E)scort badge and all hell broke loose. Lights started flashing, alarms blared, and voices came out of the ceiling saying, "Do not move or we will need to take action . . ."

I guess this is the place where I get shot.

My escort and I reunited in enough of an embrace to satisfy the cameras. Then we walked, shoulder to shoulder to avoid any more screaming hallways, to an outbuilding that I was told was magnetically shielded to prevent any kind of communication signal from entering or exiting. My host set me up at the computer to install the software and then said, "I'll be back within the hour." And then he locked me in all by myself.

One hour went by.

Two hours went by.

Three hours went by.

I am in a building that is purposefully blocked from all forms of communication—including screaming. There was nothing I could do. I was locked in. *At least in the beer ticket booth at Action Park, I could scream.*

Four hours went by.

No one is coming for me . . .

I am going to die here, alone, lost far away from home forever . . . wearing my (V)agina badge.

Five hours went by.

I had no plan. Not that a plan could have actually helped me. Because this building was designed to prevent people much smarter than I am from all forms of communicating. I reviewed my assets. I had a granola bar in my bag. End of asset list. I figured that at some point, an entry guard would see that I never signed out and would launch a five-alarm manhunt to track me down. And then someone would arrive to shoot me.

Before I could fully spin up this scenario in my mind, I heard the lock on the door click, and someone came in—unarmed.

As it turned out, my host, upon leaving me there, had had a dental emergency and left and never returned. It wasn't until he got home much later that he remembered he had left me stranded in the locked building, and called someone to retrieve me.

As I flew home on a very late flight—a result of having been imprisoned in a top-secret, magnetically shielded room for hours, I thought about how I could not survive the craziness of this job if Ross had not thrown me regularly into the weird, scary, and unexpected. This sales engineering job was like the Action Park of a technology career. It often felt like I was being shot out of the side of a mountain with a 20-foot drop into a cold pond.

I was sitting in the very back row of the airplane. By the time the drink service got to me, I was dying to order my Diet Coke, but I had a new thought. You know what might be even better than Diet Coke?

Vodka.

I had never been a drinker in college. I enjoyed a cocktail at home with my parents now and then, but at school, I was too busy struggling with engineering classes to discover college drinking. Now, in my mid-20s, I had to fling my timid, ill-equipped, always-lost self out into the abyss every week, into dark parking lots and scary rooms, with new people judging me every day and creepy clients asking me to spend the weekend with them. So I finally turned to drinking on airplanes.

And it helped.

Business results vs. the woman card

3.3

Six months into this sales engineering job, I was talking to Barb, the one other female sales engineer who had been with the company for a long time. She told me we were both getting paid the same salary—and that it was 30 percent less than the male sales engineers' salaries.

It was time for my performance review. I had never had a performance review before, and I wasn't sure how these things were supposed to go. But I do know when something is not fair. I thought I should bring up the low pay, but I wasn't sure how.

I went to the conference room to meet with the two executives doing my review. One was tall and dashing, and the other was wiry with curly red hair. They both told me I was doing a great job.

So, I decided to just ask. "I understand that I am getting paid 30 percent less than my peers. Why is that?"

"Well, we can't pay you as much because you are new here."

I thought, *That doesn't seem right. For one thing, Barb has been here longer than all of us, and she still has the same low salary as me. But more importantly. I'm actually doing a bigger job than my higher-paid peers. It's not fair to pay me less for more work.*

I didn't even stop to think. Fairness is a big trigger for me, with little to no gray area, and this disconnect caused me to blurt out, "That's not fair."

The two men looked surprised.

I was pretty surprised myself! I wasn't exactly sure how to follow that up, but I felt confident in the truth of my statement.

"What's not fair?" the one with the curly hair said in a patronizing tone.

His disrespect felt yucky, but I focused on keeping my insides from turning to liquid and clung to my sense of fairness.

I was at a major fork in the road of my career, though I didn't realize it at the time. One path was: "It's not fair that you are paying the women less." The other was, "It's not fair that you are paying me less for doing a bigger job."

It was not a conscious decision, but I took the second path because it was the one I could see most clearly at the time. So, I said to these two scary men:

"Well, it's true, I am new here, but you are not cutting me any slack for being new. I am demoing all the products—many of my peers are not. My sales manager left the company, so not only am I responsible for demos, but I am sent in alone to visit clients and close sales deals by myself, without a sales rep. None of my peers are doing that. I've developed marketing alliances and business plans with partners. My peers aren't doing that either. I don't understand why my being new has any bearing on my pay when I am successfully doing a much bigger job than the others are doing, and I'm doing it well right now, even though I am new here. Why is my bigger job worth less? It seems like if anything, my doing all this extra stuff so well should be worth more."

Again, they looked surprised. And again, I was pretty surprised myself!

I had found and used my voice.

I was beginning to understand that as timid and uncertain as I can be socially, when something is not fair, my voice finds me. I just can't help myself—I can't not say something. I speak up. It's almost automatic.

They gave me a raise.

The next day, I got a call from Barb. She said, "Thanks, Patty, for getting us both a raise." I guess my speech must have shamed them into giving her a raise too.

But even with our raises, we were still being paid less than the guys.

So, back to the fork in the road. If I had used the "it's not fair you are paying the women less" approach, it wouldn't have worked. And it would have labeled me as a complainer and been a liability to my career.

But choosing the totally founded business case, and focusing on how my role differed from that of my peers, I was much harder to dismiss. It was a much stronger argument.

So from this moment on, I decided that I would not cry foul when I thought I was being treated differently because I was a woman, and I didn't waste time even wondering if that was the reason. Instead, I always made good business cases for myself that focused on excellence—because that's what worked.

Did I have to be *more* excellent than the men to get the same consideration and earnings? Probably. But I didn't waste energy worrying about that either. Instead, I stayed focused on creating the most value for the company, and I wasn't shy about pointing out what that value should be worth.

"NO"

3.4

One of the most discouraging phases in my career was when I was trying to get myself promoted from my job as a sales engineer on the road all the time, to a product marketing position at headquarters which I deemed to be both more strategic and less death defying.

Respect for my capabilities in my career was hard to come by especially at the beginning. I knew that I was ready for a promotion, but the people handing out the promotions did not seem to see it that way.

The product marketing jobs I wanted said you needed five years of product marketing experience. I had zero years of product marketing experience.

Mom said, "Patty, how can you go for that job? You don't have five years of experience."

I told my mom, "They don't know that."

I actually did have plenty of experience. I knew I could do the job because I had already been doing lots of product marketing stuff in my sales engineer role. It just wasn't an official title on my resume.

So I went for these bigger jobs over and over again—and I got turned down over and over again.

One time I took two days off of work to travel to an interview for a product marketing job I was really excited about. I was pinned to the window on the tiny regional jet by the guy in 5B with giant legs and massive shoulders.

The inability to move my arms or legs made me think about growing up in our tiny house where you also couldn't move. Family togetherness was not optional—because our house was just not big enough to afford any family apart-ness. Our cramped living room housed our one TV. There was one tiny bathroom for all four of us. That was a lot of hair. Privacy was not a thing. And my bedroom was so small you had to walk sideways along the bed—my room had the vibe of not even having a floor.

Every minute of life included the presence of someone else, and it required negotiation to use the bathroom, or to watch your show, or to situate your schoolbooks and your limbs.

As I closed my eyes and the turbulence started bouncing our little plane along, I thought about how this simple lack of personal space trained me to negotiate, and my thoughts moved from my upcoming job interview to negotiating my biggest childhood dream. It was for my dad to build a shelf-like platform in my room—like an upper bunk bed to raise my mattress up so I could put a desk underneath. So, after dinner one night, I brought my parents into my room. We wedged in shoulder to shoulder between my bed and the wall as I started my pitch.

I was like a mini general contractor. "Mom and Dad, as you can see, there is no space for me to work in my room. And as you know, I have so many important things to work on for school, and all those art projects, which I have to do in the kitchen, in everyone's way. But I have come up with a great idea. Dad could raise the bed . . . so we could fit a desk underneath . . . and it won't cost anything, as Dad has the stuff to do it in the garage."

I was pitching my little heart out, thinking of how solid my case was. The thought of inventing space for a desk under my bed made me swoon. As ideas go, this was an unquestionably amazing one! I was going to get a space to work!

Then Mom simply said, "No," and they walked out.

It was a gut punch. After catching my breath, I thought, *They think I'm just a silly kid. My idea, my most amazing idea in the world—they didn't even consider it.*

When I asked again later, I got, "I told you no. It's not a proper thing to do in a bedroom."

I got the same response when I wanted glow-in-the-dark stars on my ceiling. "Not a proper thing to do in a bedroom."

Not a proper thing to do in a bedroom? What could possibly not be proper about glow-in-the-dark stars on the ceiling in a kid's bedroom?

I argued for my amazing bunk bed for years, but my parents never relented. I argued for lots of things as a kid. But between Mom's rules, my parents not having any extra money, and not having enough usable space in our home, I often didn't get what I wanted. But I got a different gift—I developed the ability to *argue*. My parents always said, "You should be lawyer when you grow up."

Still on the plane, with the giant dude blocking my view of the rest of the universe, I thought about how much *interviewing* is like *arguing your case*. I felt super prepared for this interview. And also, since this was a company I had worked with for some months as a business partner, they already knew me. In fact, they were the ones who had asked me to interview. I was a shoo-in. I was finally going to get my promotion to product marketing.

The next day, the interviews went great. They asked me how I would solve various product marketing issues, and I responded with concrete plans—things I knew would work, because I had done them already in my current role. I had real, relevant marketing experience and great ideas to grow their business.

At the end of all the interviews, the general manager said, "I'd like to offer you the job of sales engineer."

I was confused. "But I have been interviewing here for the product marketing job, not a sales engineer job. That's the job I already have."

"Oh, I was never going to give you the product marketing job. But I want you to join our team because the sales guys like having you around."

As I flew home after turning down the sales manager's offer to be the new office toy for the men, I thought about my childhood. It was the bunk bed/desk combo all over again. I had original, high-value ideas that would really work, but no one was interested in hearing them from me—because I was a little girl who no one took seriously.

And now, as a grown woman in the workplace, I was being treated exactly the same way.

The experience paradox

3.5

After my plane landed, I walked through the airport and headed to my car. I was so frustrated. I had prepared a great strategy for them (which, by the way, they went on to use) and gotten my hopes up, only to burn two vacation days on that pointless interview. I realized I had a long road ahead if the men around me only saw me as a plaything.

I was grumpy about going back to my sales engineering job the next day, because this disappointing quest made me think about Mitch. Last week, he had come to our office to see a product demo. Mitch was a skinny guy with stringy hair and a purple shirt. I started the demo as the sales manager finished the introductions and left me alone in the room with Mitch.

The one and only photo I have of me doing a demo as a sales engineer

I began, "I understand you are looking for a solution to this problem. I can show you an idea that has worked for other clients."

"That won't work for me."

"Why is that?"

"There's no way you have an answer to my problem."

"OK, maybe I don't understand your issue fully. Can you tell me more about your situation?"

"You wouldn't understand. It would be pointless to explain it to you."

"Yes, I believe I would. Please tell me more about what you need to accomplish."

"No, I don't want to waste my time. I'll come back another day when I can talk to someone else who knows what they are talking about. You can show me the demo if you want, though."

I really wanted to get out of that room, but my boss would have been upset if I did not complete the demo.

Later that day, a phone call came in for me.

"Patty, it's Mitch."

What on earth could he be calling for?

"Hi, Patty. I enjoyed meeting you earlier today in the demo."

My brain seized up. *That's how you act when you enjoy meeting someone?*

I didn't say anything.

"I am calling to see if you'll go out with me."

WTF?

As I drove home, I thought about that sales manager and Mitch and their collective disregard for my value. *My career feels so hard. It feels like I'm always swimming upstream. No one can even conceive that I could be capable. Or, even worse, they seem to think I am weird or wrong by even trying to be smart. They are just blocking me.*

But I could feel little patty, in her unrelenting way, telling me, "Don't give up. This is another time make the decision to keep going."

I decided that getting discouraged at how unfair it was that they were more interested in my boobs than my brain wasn't going to do me any good. I needed to keep trying. *I DO have product marketing experience. I just need to make people believe that my experience is relevant even though I haven't had the official title.*

By the way, this is a secret passageway I refer to in my book *RISE* as the Experience Paradox: **You can't get the job without the experience, but you can get the experience without the job.** It's ultimately how I earned every promotion in my career. I did not wait to be directed or given permission to do more than my current job. I just set out on my own to collect the experience I would need for my new job—before I was in it—so I could take that experience to the interview. So whenever someone said to me, "You don't have enough experience," I could say, "Yes, I do. You may not see the title on my resume, but let me crush you with stories about all my experience."

Stick with it

3.6

I finally crawled into bed near 1:00am, too wound up to sleep.

After that failed interview, I desperately wanted to call in sick the next day (or year). I was so tired. And when I am tired I want to give up. My exhausted brain kept jumping around from that interview, to how little sleep I would get, to when I would encounter another Mitch, when it suddenly landed on high school.

It was the beginning of my freshman year when I made the fateful decision to join the drill team. I know, this sounds alarmingly unlike me, being a peer-group, social, school thing in the crucible that was high school for me, but it was during the brief moment in time before the mean girls had decided to torture me and before the thyroid problem that took me down.

I had been seduced by the team captain's inspired choreography to Chuck Mangione. (You haven't lived until you've heard a small-town high school marching band play Chuck Mangione.) So when I was presented my uniform of a royal blue polyester miniskirt, white logo sweater, and pom-poms, I felt excited to join the team. Chuck Mangione, watch out—here I come!

What I did not foresee, however, was having to sit outside in the bleachers during the football games in the below-zero, icy New Jersey winter with bare legs and no coat. Only at the first frigid game did I learn it was actually forbidden to wear a coat.

I found that I could gut my way through the first quarter, but then the biting cold would start to sink into my bones, and before I knew it, I was freezing my pom-poms off. A slice of searing wind would cut through me, and I would cry, not because I was upset about it (which I was) but because I have a body that just cries automatically when I'm stupidly cold. And although the drill team was not the cheerleading squad, crying was still distinctly off-brand.

During the last three quarters of the games, I suffered miserably, and I was constantly in trouble with the coach (who was wearing a big coat) for not being perky enough while doing my best not to die.

"Mom, can I please quit drill team?"

"Nope. You chose to sign up. You can't quit."

"But it's terrible. The coach won't let—"

"You know the rule. You have to stick with it till the season is finished. You don't have to join again next year."

That was it. Mom's "stick with it" rule.

If Kerry or I ever joined an activity, no matter what happened, we had to ride out our decision for a full cycle. This was nonnegotiable. And it could be brutal if you chose badly. I assume this was another inescapable side effect of my Slovenian grandparents' ridiculous fortitude.

As I thought about suiting up and going to work again the next morning, I wondered, Did I survive Mom's rules because I was extra sturdy to begin with? Or did I survive the world's challenges because Mom's rules made me sturdy?

Would I still have become a CEO if Mom had let me quit drill team? I'm not sure, but I can effectively draw a direct line connecting Mom's "stick with it" rule with my ability to hang in there and not tap out too soon when I was uncomfortable or things got really hard or annoying at work.

As I finally started to fall asleep, I could feel little patty telling me, "Don't give up. You need go back there." She was reminding me in her unrelenting way that if I want to stay in the room, it's going to be uncomfortable sometimes.

"Stop bothering me"

3.7

I interviewed for many product marketing jobs without success, but, finally, finally, *finally*, I got promoted. I was 25. And this job came with a relocation from New Jersey to California.

Little patty was astonished by California. California had palm trees. And citrus trees! And bougainvillea plants! California had ocean cliffs and fog that squeezed itself into valleys like the creature from *The Blob*. California had surfing and observatories. California was the most exotic place in the whole world.

I was proud of myself for pushing through the NOs and surviving all the crazy, scary situations I had been put in in my sales engineer job without running away. I had won this promotion with the experience *I'd gotten for myself before* I was in the job.

Getting promoted and moving to California was a huge deal for me. And what was really great was that my big sister Kerry had already moved there.

Kerry and I had been in separate orbits for many years since high school and college. We didn't know each other very well in our current versions.

One night, on an interview trip to San Jose for this job, I went directly from the airport to a bar to meet Kerry and her boyfriend. She had told him, "I have to warn you, my sister is not fun. She's kind of dull and very serious about work. And she doesn't drink."

After the hugs, I sat down at the bar. The bartender approached. "What'll you have?"

"A dry Stoli martini, up, with olives."

Kerry about fell off her stool.

This moment was the beginning of our deep friendship to come—which absolutely involved cocktails.

Starting my new job as a product manager in Silicon Valley, I set off to understand what the customers were buying so I could work with the engineering team to build those features into the product.

I asked the sales VP to go over the sales forecast with me.

He just said, "No."

I was startled by this. I needed this information to do my job. I kept asking, and for weeks, he kept refusing. "This is confidential information. There is no reason for me to ever share this information with you. Stop bothering me."

"No" is one thing, but "Stop bothering me" little patty feels in her bones: *Ew. Go away. You're weird.*

And if being blocked by the sales VP wasn't bad enough, I kept asking the engineering manager when their meetings happened so I could attend. And he kept telling me, "You can't come to our meetings. We don't need to share any engineering information with you."

Let's take stock. My new product marketing job was to map the things *customers want* to the things *engineers build.*

The sales VP won't share any customer information with me. And the engineers won't talk to me about the product they are building.

This is going to be a short career.

I began to panic. *I can't do my job without this information. What am I going to do?*

So, I decided to talk to my big sister.

One afternoon, sitting in Kerry's kitchen, I said, "I have finally gotten promoted, but now I'm afraid I am going fail because no one will talk to me.

Kerry said, "You'll figure it out. Here's a margarita." My big sister always had high expectations of me. High expectations feel good. And she always had a cocktail ready.

Kerry had pioneered a spiritual practice in our family she called "eat, drink, and be merry." Whatever is ailing or troubling you, whether physical, mental, or emotional, the cure: Enjoy good food and drink and laugh with your people.

I'm not trying to be anyone's spiritual guide (or medical advisor) here, but Kerry and I have come to believe—and perhaps the credit goes to our mix of Slovenian and Italian heritages and hardworking immigrant grandparents who never missed a cocktail hour—that it's very healing to have a cocktail together and laugh for an hour.

I felt much better after administering the "eat, drink, and be merry" protocol with Kerry, and thought, "I will go back to work and persist. I will get into those conversations. They can't ignore me forever."

As I drove away from Kerry's house, I felt a warm rush of affection and appreciation for my family. They are a great source of positive energy in my life. And there is no one more positive than my dad.

George!!

3.8

Everyone was always so happy to see my father.

People of all ages and walks of life. Other people's children, no matter how shy they normally were, would instantly ditch their parents and run, beaming, to get close to him. Timid infants would jump out of their mothers' arms to get held by my dad.

Dad had this warmth and positivity superpower that made him the most engaging and memorable person in the room. Everyone loved George.

I marveled at how my father walked through the world with such ease and natural ability to connect with people. And it was an ongoing source of amazement to watch him use his superpowers to talk his way into pretty much anything.

Like, at one point, my dad became friends with the general manager of the conference business at the Playboy Club about 45 minutes away. Yes, it's kind of mind-bending that there was a Playboy Club so close to our sleepy town where nothing happened. Starting when I was 13, my family would regularly go there for dinners and shows as guests of my dad's friend.

My dad was able to parlay his friendship with the conference manager into visiting the Playboy Club multiple days a week and using all the amenities—the pool, the spa, the golf club—for free. He would pull his car up to the front entrance, throw his keys to the valet, and say, "Put it over there, I'll just be a couple of hours." He would talk to absolutely everybody, and everyone loved him. After months of this, everyone there treated "Mr. A." like a VIP.

My dad's general manager friend sometimes got me weird weekend jobs at the conference center. I worked overnight to set up a convention for hairdressers and worked as a runner (the person who fetches and schleps) for NBC at a televised bowling tournament. These were good jobs, but like all jobs in those days, they involved getting hit on by older men.

As a teenage girl, I was learning to build that inner scaffolding that allows you to maintain your composure when you are embarrassed and a little scared when men who are older and a lot bigger than you tease you, or grope you, or ask you to take a shower with them. I was learning that this is what the work world was like.

But back to my dad. A few years later, his GM friend left the company. Slowly, all the management changed. Then all the workers changed. Eventually, there was not a single person left from the old guard who knew my father. We all felt bad that he wouldn't be able to go there anymore.

But that's not the way George saw it. He just kept pulling up and throwing his keys with a friendly greeting to the valet (who had no idea who he was). One day, he was at the bar, and the new general manager of the facility sat down next to him and said, "Hi, Mr. A. Welcome back. It's always great to have you here. But I have a question for you. Do you mind if I ask you what exactly it is that you do here?"

My dad answered, "I'm not at liberty to say."

And he continued to use the place for free for years to follow!

Back at work, sitting at my desk, building a sculpture out of paper clips in my cube office, I thought about how the sales VP and the engineering team were still not talking to me. I knew I needed to find and use my voice at work in a much bigger and more impactful way than I had been doing.

While I don't have a tenth of the guts or social finesse that my dad does to talk my way into what I want, I decided to follow in his footsteps in my own way. I needed to stop focusing on not being welcome in these conversations and be more like Dad. I just needed to smile and make it happen.

Why should we listen to you?

3.9

I walked into the sales VP's office uninvited.

He was sitting at his desk and did not look up.

"It's clear you don't want to give me any information about your customers," I interrupted.

He looked up but did not speak. He looked annoyed, sternly tapping the point of his expensive fountain pen on his notes, like he was thinking, "Haven't I made it clear you are not welcome? Why are you still here, bothering me?"

I smiled at him. Just like Dad.

I continued, "That's interesting. Because if you were willing to share with me what you are trying to sell, I could see what your biggest customers want to buy, and I could prioritize those features to appear in the product sooner. That would help you close your biggest deals faster. But suit yourself. If you don't want to share this information, I'll just guess."

He was stunned. He put his pen down. "Uh . . . can you really do that?"

"Yes, that's my job." *You'd know that, you big jerk, if you'd have given me the time of day!*

I smiled at him again, just like Dad. "I'd like to work together with you on the forecast so we can both succeed, but you don't want to give me any information, so I'm stuck." I started to walk out.

He stopped me. "OK, I guess I can share *some* information about the forecast."

We finally started talking and working together. And with actual information about the customers, I was able to help him close some deals faster.

After a few weeks, he would come into the office all animated, like, "Hey, Patty! I want to tell you what happened with this big customer because I think you can help me." He began insisting on reviewing the full sales forecast with me weekly. I had won him over. He smiled at me now too. *Thanks, Dad.*

With this success under my belt, a couple of weeks later, I decided to barge into the engineering meeting I'd been forbidden to attend.

I was stared down by the group of 15 engineers (all men) tightly packed into a room. They were very annoyed by my unwelcome intrusion.

"Can I get five minutes of your time?"

"Well, you've already interrupted us. What do you want?"

They looked so mean, but I smiled anyway, as though I was welcome there.

"I'm hoping you can help me." A useful opener I also learned from Dad. "We need to make a small change to our product in the next version."

"*No.*"

"Why not?"

"Because we don't want to."

"It's a very small change. Why won't you consider it?"

"We don't need to listen to you."

"But it's very important."

"Why should we listen to you?"

"Because I'm the product manager. It's my job to define what goes into the—"

I didn't even get to finish that sentence. The fact that directing what would get built into the product was part of my job description meant nothing to them.

Then came their final blow:

"What makes you think you are so much smarter than all of us?" They all sat back smugly with their arms crossed over their chests.

By now, I was feeling very small and outmatched. But once again, I needed to get my own chair and shove it into the circle before the music stopped. I needed to stay in that room.

I smiled again and replied, "I don't think I'm smarter than all of you. I certainly hope I'm not! I'm counting on you to be brilliant in engineering the product. But let me ask you this. I talked to fifty of our paying customers in the past month and all of them asked for this feature. What makes you think *you* are smarter than fifty of our paying customers?"

They fell silent.

I learned at that moment that I couldn't rely solely on my opinion against the opinion of someone in charge. My opinion had no real power. But I realized that if I could add the voices of other stakeholders to my voice, it wouldn't just be my opinion against theirs anymore.

It was the opinion of 50 customers against 15 engineers. It was easy for them to shut *me* down, but they couldn't shut down the voices of 50 paying customers.

This was a pretty nifty secret passageway: ***Make your voice bigger.***

When it's only your opinion against theirs, your voice is just too small. But if you can bring an army of other credible voices to join yours, it's much harder for them to ignore you.

Being intentionally excluded from important conversations that were necessary to do my job was a tough pill to swallow. But I had to keep reminding myself that walking away frustrated and offended wouldn't solve anything.

Ultimately, the engineers made the change I was asking for. They eventually allowed, then even required me to come to their meetings. And after months of my working to get them to respect that I had value to offer, they actually asked for my help to design the new user interface from the ground up—work we did together that I led, and we were all really proud of.

This was a moment of great joy in my career: working with these brilliant engineers to make something really good from the ground up and building relationships that made us all smile.

I was learning that I was able to find and use my voice when it really mattered, when I needed to achieve something specific. But there were still other types of random social situations at work that rendered me wordless and mortified . . .

Not tonight

3.10

I found myself standing, with a sinking heart, at the entrance to a room full of strangers. I had been a product marketing manager for a few years now, and tonight was one of those networking events where I was supposed to meet potential customers.

As I stood there on my own, I thought about how I had talked my way into a raise, and how I had convinced the sales VP and the engineering team to talk to me. When there was a clear objective—particularly if something was not fair—my voice just came.

But there I stood, dreading to cross the threshold into a sea of strangers and small talk.

I got a glass of wine, then picked my way around the perimeter, looking for a point of entry. Everyone was already locked into conversation circles. I thought, *They all know each other, and I am on the outside. When I approach a circle, they will close up the gaps and shut me out. They are going to think I am weird.*

After a couple of laps, I took my glass of wine and hid behind a row of potted plants. I was trying miserably to look less mortified than I was.

Peering out through the foliage, I noticed that others seemed quite capable of doing whatever this networking thing was. They smiled knowingly as they talked to each other. They seemed so relaxed.

I really would like to connect with them. But I just can't find a way to get myself into these conversations. Why is this so hard?

My thoughts swung back to Mom and Dad and my lifetime of practice arguing them into the ground about things I thought were unfair or things I couldn't have.

But alas, networking is not arguing. Networking is socializing. And socializing is terrifying to little patty. And when socializing is the goal, adult Patty just stands there alone behind the ficus tree with her glass of wine.

My internal critic popped up:

YOU ARE HOPELESS. HOW HARD IT IS TO JUST TALK TO PEOPLE? LOOK AT THEM ALL. THEY ARE ALL SO RELAXED AND ENJOYING THEIR CONVERSATIONS. WHAT'S WRONG WITH YOU?

Not wanting to give in to my internal critic, I tentatively executed another lap. I approached some conversation circles, pausing briefly, but failed to wedge myself into any of them. The sturdy part of little patty kept me showing up to things, but the shy part was still entirely scared of a peer group.

I knew in my heart that my social timidity would not serve me in my ambitions to grow my career. I so wished I could be more like Dad in these situations, that I could have just a crumb of his incredible ease with people. Dad was one of those extroverts who thought networking events were fun.

I was determined to figure out how to become more confident about socializing with random strangers, but alas, I was not going to do it tonight. Tonight, I felt doomed.

Accepting defeat, I crossed the room a couple of times, trying to look purposeful so anyone expecting me to be there saw that I was there, and then I left as soon as possible. I was thoroughly exhausted, even though I hadn't talked to anyone.

I took my glass of wine back to my hotel room with a plate of networking cheese cubes, put on soft shorts and a T-shirt, and sat in the bed to watch a rerun of *Star Trek: The Next Generation* while assessing the quality of the comforter.

As I went to sleep that night, I was thinking about how difficult my job often felt—but that I would go back again tomorrow, like I always did. I thought about how my family shaped my stubborn refusal to quit hard things, and I giggled to myself about one moment in particular . . .

No drama

3.11

Kerry and I had just gotten home from school to find Dad in the living room with the most massive surprise of our lives to date. Our first color TV!

We all sat and stared with wonder as Dad turned it on and coaxed the picture into focus by wiggling the metal antenna.

The very first thing—the *very first* thing—that came into focus on the screen of our new color TV was the black-and-white beginning of the movie *The Wizard of Oz*.

"Jesus Christ! What the hell?" Dad was upset. This sort of undirected outburst was as upset as Dad ever got. Yelling was virtually nonexistent in our home. But after all that anticipation, there we were, still watching a black-and-white TV, silently transmitting to one another our fallen hopes.

Then, after the tornado, Dorothy woke up in Oz.

And at that moment, when her world changed, our world changed too. Not only is that the scene when the movie suddenly switches from black and white to color; it's probably one of the most deliberately colorful movie scenes ever constructed. "Toto, we're not in black-and-white anymore," we telepathically conveyed to each other as we sat there with our mouths open in amazement.

When I searched my mind for the most crazy, fraught, alarming, dramatic thing that ever happened in our home, the story about the color TV and the crazy coincidence of the black-and-white beginning of the Wizard of OZ was all I could come up with.

We did not have drama. Which meant that I could come home to a place where I never needed to worry about my physical or emotional safety. The adults who were supposed to take care of me took care of me without fail.

When I tell others about my family life growing up, they are incredulous. "You mean your parents stayed together? No one was a drug addict? No alcoholics? They were nice to you the whole time? The police never came to your house? No guilt trips? No scary fighting? Nobody beat you up? Really? Can that really happen?"

It took me decades to appreciate that a drama-free home is not typical—and to understand the enormous advantage that gave me.

I saw an article recently that described growing up in a drama-free home as a type of unrecognized generational wealth. I can't agree more. I was very fortunate.

Every day little patty came home broken down by the humiliations and indignities of the school world, her very safe, drama-free home gave her the opportunity to rebuild herself. She could start each new day with a full tank.

On top of that, Mom averted another type of drama by always drilling into us that it was very specifically *not* important to be pretty. If we ever became interested in looking pretty, it wasn't forbidden, but any efforts in the pretty department would be immediately minimized by the idea that *what's important is that you are smart.*

How to get sexually harassed without damaging your career

3.12

It would be incomplete to talk about building a career in a work world created and dominated by men without mentioning the hands and penises.

One night, after a team dinner in a beach condo where we were all staying for an offsite meeting, I was sitting on the floor with my boss. Everyone else had just left, but my boss stayed behind so we could chat about our customers and our work priorities for the next week.

Then he started kissing me.

It wasn't exactly scary, but it was certainly unexpected. In that first moment, I was neither kissing him back nor pulling away. I was still trying to form my first real thought about what was happening—because it was so sudden. Then he stopped abruptly. I guess he realized it was a really stupid thing to be doing. He said sorry. And then he left.

The problem for me was not that moment itself. It was the next day when he would not look at me or talk to me. He talked to everyone else on the team, but he totally ignored me.

Now, this was the scary part. *I am being eliminated from the conversations where everything happens. Past experience has taught me well:*

I have to stay in the conversation. I have to stay in the room. I have to advocate for myself.

By lunchtime, I couldn't take it anymore. I walked up to him and said, "OK. What happened last night shouldn't have, but there's no problem for me or for you. But today, you are avoiding me. You are not talking to me. I will have a big problem if you let what happened change the way you treat me and you cut me off from important work conversations because you are uncomfortable."

It was so interesting to me that even though he had started it, he was older, and he was my boss, I had to be the one to make sure *he* was not uncomfortable so *my* career would not be damaged.

I decided then and there that I was not going to let actual harassment from men end my career.

Ever since I was 13, there was always a steady stream of men conveying with their creepy gazes, words, hands, and erections that my body was available for their entertainment—in school, at sports events, at parties, at the supermarket, and at the doctor. And not surprisingly, all those things that happened out in the world also happened at work. When I was in my 20s, men at work trying to kiss me and get their hands inside my clothes was a pretty regular occurrence.

But when I was coming up in my career, there was not even such a thing as "sexual harassment." Of course, it happened all the time—there just wasn't a name for it and no recognition that anything was wrong with it when it happened.

As a woman, you were a solitary player in a huge ecosystem of men. If you were uncomfortable with a man's behavior toward you sexually, it was entirely your own problem. Here were the available options:

1. Fight back. Speak up. Report it to the authorities to get support. Just kidding. That was not an actual option back then. There were no authorities. There was no one who cared. If you spoke up you would be a lone voice shouting into the wind, and if anyone heard

you at all, they would wonder what you were complaining about. After all, you decided to be an intruder in their world—it was just part of the deal you signed up for.

2. Hide. You could leave entirely. Or you could a find a new job that was out of his path. But to get away from him often meant taking a lesser job and giving up on your career aspirations. So you disappear. He stays.

3. Maneuver and endure. Stay in it. Protect your physical safety. Tolerate the uncomfortable, demeaning behaviors, and don't let it make you angry or depressed.

4. Be excellent. *So excellent* that they can't deny your value, even while they are trying to grab your butt.

It was very clear. As a woman, your career is disposable. His is not.

To stay in the room, you basically needed to figure out how to be sexually harassed without damaging HIS career.

Boundaries

3.13

Once again, I was inspired by my clever big sister. Kerry was in the workforce five years ahead of me, fresh out of college and working for one of the big consulting firms. She was beautiful—tall and stylish, with long, flowing hair and young, happy energy.

Every time she walked into one of the glass-walled offices on the first floor, the phone would ring. When she picked it up, she would hear a man's voice. "I can see you. Talk to me, I want to listen to your voice."

All of the partner offices were on the second floor, and they all had glass walls too. It was a partner who was stalking her. She would find notes and sometimes money from him in her locker. It got so bad that she was afraid to walk to her car at night.

There was literally no one she could go to for help. There was no HR. Her only practical option was to go to a partner, but that was not a real option because all the partners were men, and one of them was the problem. She had no idea who it was. What if she guessed wrong? Would any of them believe her anyway? Or even if they did believe her, would they do anything about it? If anything, the company would protect the partner, and she would be fired for causing trouble.

But it was just getting too scary. She needed to find a way to keep herself safe and keep her job.

Then, to protect herself, Kerry made one of the most brilliant 5D chess moves ever. With no formal channels to pursue help, she decided to tell the whole story to the gossipy receptionist.

Well, that did the trick! Once word spread like wildfire, the stalking stopped in a day.

She never had to pit herself against the machinery that would have fired her. And she never was pegged as a complainer. She was safe, and her career continued unscathed.

When Should You Speak Up?

Professional women today still tell me they go through a mental flow chart when they get unwelcome sexual advances at work: How serious was it? How scared am I? Who was it? How powerful is he? Is he a manager, peer, or client? What is the potential cost to my career of calling it out? Is it worth it?

Because too often, even today, if the woman speaks up, she disappears, not him. I decided it was important to really know who I was and set clear boundaries.

Is It Dangerous or Just Annoying?

I was in my early 30s when I defined my boundaries as the line between "dangerous" and "just annoying." If a man physically threatens me or withholds a promotion based on sex, that's dangerous. And I must address it. I must protect myself. I must act or leave.

But if it's disrespectful behavior, such as suggestive comments or handsy greetings, labeling those things as "just annoying" takes away their power to hurt me. I can look at the man like *I have the power* and think, *You are an idiot. I should not be uncomfortable about your behavior—you should. You should be ashamed of yourself.* And then I just move on.

But it's tricky. It's not always clear what might be dangerous. And annoying situations can turn dangerous later. This is the life of a woman—we are constantly trying to figure out if it's dangerous. It's exhausting.

In a perfect world, every bad act would be brought to justice. But I was not in that world. So, I did my best to put as many things as possible into the "annoying" category, because it was impractical not to—it wouldn't have made a difference anyway, and there was just not enough energy in my soul to confront every bad behavior.

Silicon Valley

3.14

The prevalent work culture in Silicon Valley says that working like a maniac and sacrificing your well-being is not only necessary but also really cool. To me, it always felt like a cage fight to see who could work the hardest and craziest hours. Burnout was admired.

In my product marketing roles, I came to feel that I was just not cool enough for Silicon Valley. I did not think that sacrificing my health and my personal life to work at a job in a leading-edge tech company was cool.

But everyone around me seemed to like this deal: You get to join a company with a mythical mission that will change the world. So you do it for a low salary, compared to a "boring job" at a bigger company, because you're going to get a giant stock payout later. You'd be stupid not to take this deal. And you get to disappoint your family with things like mandatory 1am volleyball staff meetings on Saturdays, because it's all so cool.

I did not fit in this world. I found every bit of this crazy burnout game baffling because most people never got the big payout.

I was out of sync with my peers yet again.

I went home every day feeling like my humanity—and everyone else's—was being disregarded. I once mentioned the idea of a life outside of work to a colleague. He winced, like someone was going to appear out of nowhere to stab him in the neck for even hearing the idea. "A life? Are you kidding? Geez . . . don't say that out loud!"

It was clear that wanting a healthy life was for the weak and uncompetitive and those disloyal and uncommitted to the mission.

So, I would keep my mouth shut, mostly, and try to preserve my weekends for recovery so I didn't get sick.

One day, at a special team-building meeting, the leaders were asking everybody this question: "At breakfast, are you the chicken or the pig?" The punch line was that the chicken is *involved*, but the pig is *committed*.

People exclaimed in brainwashed obedience, "I want to be the pig!"

I just sat there thinking, *Seriously? This is idiotic. The pig dies. Its resources are consumed one time and then it's used up. Wouldn't it be more valuable to the business to take good care of the chickens so you can have nice, plentiful eggs forever? To maximize the value someone could contribute over and over again instead of killing them off?*

I kept my mouth shut and walked away. In reality, there was always a long line of people signing up for these jobs, so companies didn't need to worry about taking good care of their employees.

I don't belong here.

As I sat in my cube after this stupid pig discussion, I thought, no company should make you trade your health for their profits.

So, why did I stay? Why didn't I look for a more comfortable job?

Well, this was the job that I was in, and I was good at it, even though I felt so out of place in every way.

And I still wanted what they were having—a self-directed life and the earning potential that comes from a career. And there was good career potential here. And little patty had racked up lots of experience feeling weird and unwelcome and focusing on excellence instead of discomfort. So I could take it. And I was learning a lot, which was always my idea of fun anyway.

Get a script

3.15

One day, as I was going about my business as a product marketing manager, I ran into the CEO in the coffee room. Cue brain stall, freeway pileup, awkward silence. I left without even getting coffee.

I walked back to my desk feeling like a stupid failure, thinking, *I need to do better. I never again want to stand there silently not knowing what to do when I meet an important person. I want to be able to have normal work conversations with executives without feeling like I am going to die.*

My internal critic likes to dig in on this one:

YOUR CAREER IS NEVER GOING TO AMOUNT TO ANYTHING BECAUSE YOU TURN INTO SUCH A SILENT WEIRDO IN SO MANY SIMPLE SOCIAL SITUATIONS. JUST GIVE UP NOW. DON'T KEEP EMBARRASSING YOURSELF.

I was going to need to figure out how to find my voice in uncomfortable situations.

When I got back to my office with no coffee, I thought back to a time near the very beginning of my career when one of my peers—another 20-something female—and I found ourselves being introduced to a big, scary VIP. He was very tall and impressive. We were standing in a grand ballroom in front of the first row of seats in the auditorium. I froze. I had no idea what to say or do, so I mumbled, "Uh, hi," then just stood there, having nothing else to say.

As my peer was introduced, she smiled, shook the VIP's hand, and calmly said, "Hello. How are you today?"

I was startled by her mastery. *WOW! That's really good. I wish I could do that!*

So looking into my empty coffee mug, I decided, *The next time I find myself face-to-face with a scary, important person, I will not lament that I have nothing brilliant to say. Instead, I will do exactly what my colleague did when meeting that VIP. I will smile, shake their hand, and say, "Hello. How are you today?" I can do what she did—because I will use her exact script.*

Was I embarrassed that I didn't know how to say hello without a script? Yes. But it didn't matter. It was a practical solution. I can do practical. I can follow what works.

I had locked in my very first script: "Hello, I'm Patty. How are you today?" And every time I used it, you know what happened? They started talking to me! There was no silence—except from my internal critic. *Wow! With a script, I can silence my internal critic!*

Emboldened by my new superpower, I decided to make a list of all the situations that made me uncomfortable, then set myself on a scavenger hunt for scripts to deal with them so I could always be prepared.

I'd say to a colleague, "What do you do when you meet the CEO in the coffee room unexpectedly?"

They'd answer, "I have a chat."

"No, I mean: What do you *say*, specifically? What are some things you can say when you chat with the CEO? I don't know how to chat with the CEO. I need to know."

I became an avid student of people who seemed at ease with others, and I snatched up their scripts—which gave me a voice when I couldn't find my own.

People sometimes thought I was weird for asking, but I persisted. I was always collecting scripts.

This turned into a super potent secret passageway for me: ***You don't have to feel awkward and without words if you simply prepare a script for uncomfortable situations ahead of time.***

Because having a script made life so much better, I expanded my hunt for scripts to accomplish all kinds of different, important things, not just social niceties.

"What do you say when you need to give someone bad news?"

"What do you say when you disagree with your boss?"

"What do you say when an employee is not meeting expectations?"

Over time (like, after 1,000 tries and a couple of decades), I actually became comfortable and quite good at meeting new people. Sometimes, it is even pleasant and fun.

But I would not have had that breakthrough in my twenties if I had not first given myself the *permission to be prepared* by collecting scripts instead of simply disqualifying myself up front because I was not a "natural" with people.

So, I rewrote my internal program to say, "My awkwardness does not disqualify me. It's OK that I need to prepare. It's OK that I use a script." I will never be embarrassed *a second time*. Because next time, I will be prepared.

When I coach others now, I always try to provide a specific script for what they could say to follow my advice. Because the confidence to act is in the script. It's the script that enables them to actually do the difficult thing, just like it always did for me.

Working to enjoy my life

3.16

Not everybody at work was annoying. And though the men in power could make my life uncomfortable and my internal critic had lots of material to test my insecurities with, work was also where I started to find my people.

I have always loved smart, funny people—and the nerdier, the better. And tech companies in Silicon Valley had plenty of those people on offer. I made some good friends, one at a time, introvert style—and they liked me back. And I loved spending time with Kerry now that we were living close by.

In a mind-blowing development, Kerry got her scuba diving certification. *Scuba diving?* I could not fit scuba diving into any context in my universe. People from New Jersey don't go scuba diving.

When I asked her why on earth she was doing this, she said, "I want to go on a scuba diving vacation with my boyfriend."

But as it turned out, when I started dating a guy at work and he was going on a scuba diving vacation with friends, he told me, "You can't come. It's a small island and there's nothing to do there other than scuba dive, and I don't want to feel guilty about you being bored while I am diving."

A little cold, but honest—and practical. I wasn't upset, but I thought, "Huh—the only way to have a social life in California is to be a scuba diver." I actually believed I had no other option if I wanted to make friends. So I got my scuba certification too.

The moment of my scuba certification with my buddy Tim in Monterey, CA.

Little patty had always been searching her heart out in her small, brown world for beauty that would truly amaze her, and with scuba diving, she hit the mother lode. It turned out that scuba diving in the tropics was the most exotic, beautiful, amazing thing ever.

I found a whole new, impossibly colorful and bizarre world underneath the surface of the ocean where I was met with all sorts of alien life forms, spectacularly designed fish, and fantastical creatures, all going about their business with their own plans and homes and commutes. It's truly magnificent and expansive. In the deep water, I can fly—well, at least hover weightless—over mountains and canyons and cliffs. It's staggering and joyful. Despite my initial horror about the idea, scuba diving has become a lifelong passion and brought new, good friends into my life.

With the winnings from my Silicon Valley job, in addition to tropical scuba diving vacations, I bought my first condo. I was enjoying my life outside of work. I went cycling on the weekends. I painted pictures, I sang, I shopped for shoes with Kerry and Mom, and I hosted house parties with drinks and food and dancing in the kitchen to the Rolling Stones.

I was following in little patty's path. She knew the world outside was unwelcoming and scary, but home was the good, happy, safe place. So, I always made sure that my own home was my happy place where I could relax and recover. I made it pretty and shared it with friends. I think that's one of the reasons why having a beautiful house was always so important to me: If home was reliably safe and lovely and full of laughter, I could endure whatever the outside world (or Silicon Valley) threw at me.

One of my new work friends was a man who I started to spend a lot of time with outside of work. He was the smartest person I have ever known—an MIT engineering graduate. He was super funny and talented, and we got along great. We dated for about three years, then moved in together.

We were two happy introverts who would come home at night and recover from the workday by eating dinner and watching a movie on the sofa.

We pooled our assets and bought a bigger, fancier condo, and ultimately, we got married. He was a good partner and a good man.

Secret passageways

3.17

Little patty gifted me the idea of secret passageways early on when she decided to combat being bullied with being a good student. And she still gifts me that bubble-letter level of excitement each time I find a new one.

Little patty showed me that you can find secret passageways simply by paying attention. She paid attention to everything around her, both as a matter of survival and because she had a need to learn as much as possible about everything.

I know I have found a secret passageway when an on-the-spot insight enables me to understand or do something that felt impossible the moment before. It feels big and wonderful.

I also know it's a secret passageway when I can feel the change happening inside me. It's like plugging in a new skill pack in a video game: *Now I know exactly how to do this. And I don't need to learn it twice. And I will do it this new way forever. And I will share this secret with the world!*

I tend to seek out secret passageways because I am quick to say, "This is just too much trouble." I am unwilling to just muscle my way through a bunch of hard work that doesn't seem worth it. The feeling of pointless struggle ignites a combination of practicality and laziness in me that compels me to find an easier way.

Also, I am just unwilling to fail alone—what I learned in college. Relying solely on my own limited knowledge and abilities is a losing strategy. So I *always* get help. Because the easiest way to find an amazing secret passageway is to simply ask someone else where it is . . .

Help really helps!

3.18

When I was 19 and dating Ross, he took me to meet his sister, Susan, and her family. First off, I was blown away by their house. It was very big and luscious. It had marble floors. It had high ceilings. It had a big, fancy kitchen. It had curvy, cushiony furniture and plush carpets. I wandered around in awe, mentally waving my arms around to take in the enormity of the indoor space (and when no one was looking, I really did wave my arms around). I was overcome. I want a big, beautiful house like this someday . . .

And then I met Al.

Al was Susan's husband—Ross's brother in-law. Al was a robust, joyful, and intense Italian man. His energy was part elite athlete and part teddy bear. I learned that he had worked at very high levels in industry and government. He was currently running his own management and investment company. When Al talked about business, I was spellbound. I thought, *I will never know as much about anything as Al knows about business.*

When Al met me, I was nowhere yet in my career—I was still an engineer at Bell Labs. But he must have spotted potential in eager super-student Patty, because he took it upon himself to be my mentor.

I had no idea what a mentor even was at that point in my life. But what I experienced from Al, in a very real way, was high expectations. I thought, *Wow—someone this amazing is interested in pushing me to be bigger than I am because he believes in me!*

Once Al became my mentor, I could go to him with any question or problem in my work or life and he would always help me.

So many people act like they would rather stick needles into their eyeballs than have to admit that they don't know something and ask for help. Even though I was constantly worried about my credibility, it never occurred to me that asking for help would damage it. Whenever I have asked help from teachers, mentors, or anybody, it was never like they were thinking, "Oh, poor Patty, she is weak or unqualified because she doesn't know this." On the contrary, their reaction when they saw me using their help was more like, "Wow, look at her go!"

I never felt that I had the luxury of pretending to know things. If the choice is between pretending to be smart by not asking, but never learning how to do the thing, and getting the help that allows me to do the thing really well—there is no choice. My credibility kept growing because I kept *doing* bigger and more valuable things—which I only learned how to do by asking for help.

I can never repay Al, not just for his belief in me and his decades of help, but for reinforcing so strongly for me the very foundational secret passageway to find the most success. ***Always ask for help. Because help really helps.***

Are you bragging or complaining?

3.19

I was sitting in a conference room for a staff meeting with our new CEO, Jim Davis. I didn't know exactly what happened to the old CEO (that's Silicon Valley for you), but he was gone, and we had a new one now, and here he was.

At the time, I was still a product marketing manager at the startup company where I had finally managed to get the VP of sales and the engineering team to talk to me.

It was 9:04am. when someone casually strolled into Jim's meeting.

"You're late. GET OUT. And close the door behind you," Jim barked. We were all startled.

The person said, "But I need to be here to—"

"This meeting started at 9:00. It's 9:04. You are late. You can't come in if you are late. GET OUT."

"But—"

"What part of 'YOU'RE LATE, GET OUT' did you not understand?"

We all sat perfectly still and didn't speak. This was way different from the ambivalent lateness we were all used to.

(No one was ever late to one of Jim's meetings again.)

Jim was a mountain of a man, six foot six, a square head upon a square torso—an imposing monolith. His face showed the ravages of being shot down three times as a helicopter pilot in Vietnam. Since Jim saw every day of being alive after that as a bonus, he felt no need for unproductive social niceties.

Straightforward doesn't even begin to describe his no-nonsense manner. Let me phrase this another way: Jim could be scary.

At the time, I was the product marketing manager, one person in a marketing team of six. One day, after returning from a client visit, I learned that Jim had cut the size of the company in half and cut the marketing organization down to one person. Me. I was now the whole marketing team—one person with six jobs.

Jim Davis's publicity photo at the time that I first met him

But on that day, duty bound as ever, I did not question the viability of my new gig as a whole marketing organization. I just got to work doing everybody's job.

After doing the work of six people for a while, I believed that I deserved a raise. In my mind, this was a straightforward and practical request. So, I went into Jim's office and sat down. "I am working very hard. There is too much work for one person to do," I said, completing the sentence in my mind: *since you fired everyone except for me.*

He replied, "Are you bragging or are you complaining?" That was one of his gems whenever people expressed discomfort with a work task.

"Would you consider giving me a raise? I'm doing a lot."

"I don't need to pay you more. I could fire you and replace you for less."

That was it. That was the whole conversation.

I walked back to my cube and slumped into my chair. As I started doodling an infinite pile of swirls on a Post-it note, I considered . . .

1. He could *not* replace everything I am doing for less. If he believes that, then I am not communicating well enough what I actually do. I am, once again, just shouldering an impossible workload and silently trying to not die from it.

2. If I want more money, I need to increase not just the actual value of my job but the *perceived* value so he can't say that again. I need to show that what I am doing is worth more money to the company than what I am being paid.

That was probably the most potent secret passageway that I have used forever after to argue for my worth:

Your pay has nothing to do with you—it's only about what the job you are doing is worth to your company. It's never personal. If you want a raise, define and do a more valuable job, and negotiate your pay based on that.

With Jim's no-nonsense leadership, our struggling startup lived to fight another day. At that company, by showing my value clearly, I went from being a groveling product marketing manager to, troublingly, a whole marketing organization, then ultimately to be promoted to the VP of marketing—with a raise and business cards and everything.

And then Jim left. He went to a big technology company—Hewlett-Packard (HP).

Some months later, the phone rang . . .

It was Jim. He was recruiting me to work for him. As it turned out, in Jim, I had a rigorous supporter.

I wouldn't have seen that job opening in a million years, and they would never have considered me for it at all if Jim hadn't said, "We need to talk to Patty Azzarello."

As time went on, Jim would become a strong mentor and advocate for me. His support for me kept increasing, his expectations of me got higher and higher, and he continued to open doors for me.

I want to be super clear about this. I would have received exactly none of the breakthroughs I experienced in my career and life without help from mentors, especially Jim and Al.

Jim was like a walking jukebox of wisdom, always ready with a nugget to share no matter what the situation:

"You have to have the first meeting before you can have the second meeting."

"Rob the train first. Then divide up the loot."

"Successful companies are the ones who can afford their mistakes."

"People, Process, Profit—in that order."

While Jim's gruff straightforwardness could seem scary, he was never a bully. He was a leader who truly cared about people.

What I came to learn about Jim was that his whole intention for being at work was to help people develop as humans and in their careers. And I was a big recipient of that effort. So many of the insights I built my success (and sanity) on were things I initially learned from Jim. So many of the scripts that helped me find my voice were given to me directly by Jim.

My internal critic *hated* Jim. It was always telling me, YOU SUCK, YOU SHOULDN'T TRY THIS, YOU'RE NOT GOOD ENOUGH, while Jim, the giant in the room with the booming, high expectations, would say, "You need to think bigger. You can do this, and I will help you."

My first mentor, Al, guided me to never sacrifice my values for my job while I was growing my career. But Al was never part of my corporate world. There, it was Jim who protected me from adversaries and helped me navigate my corporate career for decades.

I can never thank them enough. They both changed my life profoundly for the better in ways I never could have seen coming.

In the end, I never did resolve the disconnect of how I was going to survive my career in Silicon Valley, where I just didn't fit. I hung in there uncomfortably until Jim scooped me out of the unknown ranks of a small startup and opened the door for me to step into the executive world by recruiting me into HP in Colorado—a large, very stable, old tech company, which the Silicon Valley dudes made sure to let me know was *very* uncool.

Part 4

Staying in the Room

"The most common way people give up their power is by thinking they don't have any."

—Alice Walker

Big sky

4.1

I had landed on another planet. Colorado was nothing like anywhere I had ever been. The sky really did seem bigger. I had never understood that expression before actually standing in the Rocky Mountains and looking up. Even the air felt different—because it was. There is less air up there. It makes you dizzy.

Living at a mile high with less oxygen was not the only thing I needed to get used to. Career wise, I found myself quite suddenly in a big organization within a gigantic company. I felt lost in the buildings and in my nervous system.

For the first month, the company set me up in a rental house, whose prior tenant was a very popular 20-something man named Dan whose friends didn't seem to know he had moved away. I knew his name was Dan because a rowdy group of young, drunk men would come and shout his name and beat on my picture window every night. I would take my cat and retreat to the bedroom and hide until they finally gave up on finding Dan.

I had moved to Colorado to work for Jim in my first big leadership role. I really wanted to do everything right, but to be honest, the fact that at age 29, I had a job leading an engineering organization of more than 100 people was mind-blowing. I had a good sense of what I needed to accomplish with the product and the customers, but I did not have a concrete plan for what should happen next Tuesday. And I had a hundred people waiting for me to do something. I felt in over my head. And I was scared.

Every cell in my body felt unsettled.

I went to Jim.

I was very fortunate that Jim was both my manager and my mentor. I could always ask him the most basic questions about my job without fear of getting fired for not knowing how to do my job.

"I'm not sure where to start."

Jim replied, "Talk to everyone. Then you'll know what to do."

He meant that literally. So, I spent the first two weeks of my new leadership job doing nothing but one-on-one meetings. A hundred of them. This was an unusual way to start a job, but with Jim's support to do it, I got the chance to ask every single person at every level in my new team, "What is working and not working here? What do you need me to know?"

If I had talked only to my managers, as was my original plan (and everyone had expected me to do), I would have totally missed all the dirt—the stuff most important to my success in my new role. Because in these conversations, I learned that people were really pissed off and discouraged. We had poor communication, a couple of bullies, warring tribes, expensive projects with no success in sight, lots of doubts and disagreements, and angry, disengaged salespeople.

And much to my relief, after these 100 conversations, I was no longer scared. In fact, I felt smart and capable.

Using Jim's advice to talk to everyone had given me a superpower. Not only did I now have a solid plan for precisely what I needed to do; *I also had a hundred people who were motivated to help me do it because I took the time to listen to them.*

Talk about a secret passageway! *If you want to inspire your team to support your plans, respect them enough to seek their opinions first.*

Everything in my environment was so new that I was paying attention like my life depended on it. And one of the things I noticed was that none of my peers were doing this kind of listening. It seemed like they were just shooting in the dark. They, too, had broken, confused organizations, but they were not fixing them. They were just carrying on the status quo. By really listening, I was so far ahead of the game it felt like I was cheating.

But this important insight brought me face-to-face with a hard truth: My organization was broken, so I needed to change it.

I knew I needed to build a new management team, and Jim agreed, but I had never done such a thing before. This would require a whole new gauntlet of decisions and responsibilities. (And all of this I would need to implement with less oxygen than I was used to.)

Once again, I was so lucky that Jim was there for me. He showed me countless secret passageways about personal leadership, and about building and leading high-performing teams. (I later put pretty much all of these secret passageways in my books, *RISE* and *MOVE*, because I wanted every leader to receive the benefit of Jim's wisdom.)

So, with Jim's support, I built a new leadership team and reorganized the group.

Fast-forward, I did well. The team had come together. We were fixing things. We set clear goals and we were doing great delivering on them.

Over the next couple of months, I started developing a friendship with one of the guys I had hired on my new team—Jacek. He preferred to go by "Jack" at work. Our friendship grew out of working on important things together (which is how I make friends as an introvert), and we started spending time together outside of work.

Jack liked to show off the nature in Colorado, and since I was clueless about my new planet, he invited me to go cycling with him on the weekends.

Having moved there a few months ahead of my husband, it seemed like a great way to get a guided tour of my new town and speed up my acclimation to the high altitude.

Most people didn't care about our friendship, but some insisted that it was inappropriate and believed that Jack got special privileges at work because of it.

If you were to ask him if he got preferred treatment from me, he would just laugh . . . or sigh. He got the "privilege" of the ugliest piles of work I could find, over and over again, because he was so capable. He was the kind of person who, whenever I handed him a big, hairy problem, took ahold of it and immediately smoothed it out and made it smaller—even before leaving my office. (Others, by contrast, would expand a problem, then set it on fire and hand it back to me.)

Jack had an uncanny ability to find straightforward solutions to complicated issues, and to get people to stop debating and start doing. I was never worried about anything I delegated to Jack. And he helped me be a better leader too, by communicating very clearly what people needed from me when I missed it. Even the people who didn't like my friendship with Jack benefited from it because it made me a better leader for them too.

But here's the thing. There is no issue with being friends with an employee unless you let the friendship interfere with your judgement. If you were my friend, you got no free passes at work. I held you accountable for deadlines and mistakes the same way as everyone else. I always hired the best person for the job. If you, my friend, were not the best person for the job, I did not give you the job. As long as I was consistent, it never became an actual problem, though some people still grumbled sometimes.

I was good at my job, but that was not going to be enough to succeed, as there were many more challenges to my reputation and credibility yet to come . . .

Fraud and drinks

4.2

I will say that I got a lot right with this new team. I was learning how to build and lead a highly capable and motivated team, with the help and support of the highly capable people themselves. I love spending time with brilliant people, so I liked this part of my job very much.

But I was still always looking over my shoulder, worried that I was going to get found out somehow—that I shouldn't have this job. I could overhear the gossip about me:

"She looks so young."

"No one under 35 could have this job."

"I would be so angry if they gave this job to someone younger than 35. That wouldn't be fair."

I was so desperate to hide the fact that I was only 29—something I believed in my core would destroy my credibility and get me fired if it were found out. It was not cool to be young and in charge (and female) in those days. And I could feel how closely I was being watched and judged.

My internal critic assured me daily, YOU'RE WORRIED ABOUT BEING TOO YOUNG TO HAVE THIS JOB BECAUSE YOU ARE WAY TOO YOUNG. THEY ARE GOING TO FIND OUT THAT YOU DON'T HAVE ENOUGH EXPERIENCE, AND NO ONE WILL RESPECT YOU, AND YOU WILL LOSE YOUR JOB AND NO ONE WILL EVER GIVE YOU ANOTHER ONE.

One evening after work, I took my new team out for drinks. The waiter came and everyone placed their orders. When he got to me, I said, "I'll have a glass of white wine," and I continued the conversation with my team.

The waiter interrupted: "Can I see your ID, please?"

Time stopped. I was mortified. No one spoke. Everyone became fascinated by their water glasses, knowing the question of my age was off limits. It felt like an explosion had gone off. That waiter sent a shock wave into my group that I was not sure I could ever recover from.

I did my best to keep a straight face, though my heart was pounding and I probably turned a different color. I fumbled to get my ID out of my bag, and I did my best to continue what I had been saying as if it hadn't happened. It was never spoken of again.

Invisible

4.3

After a year in my first big job, I went into my meeting with Jim to hear the news of my first big raise. I had accepted a very low starting salary to get in the door, and Jim had agreed to adjust it after a year of solid performance.

With the support of the team I had built, I had done so much more than anyone expected: We fixed the quality issues, we created a much shorter and repeatable development process, which (even though that does not sound so exciting) was a big, friggin' business-saving deal, and I personally got us out of the pit of despair with the sales force and customers. I knew Jim recognized and appreciated my work. So I was super excited for our conversation.

"So, what is my raise?" I asked, feeling very proud of my accomplishments.

"I'm sorry, but I can't give you a raise."

I was stunned. *How can that be? After everything I have done?*

He continued, "I tried to get you 15 percent, but nobody knows you."

My brain just could not take this in. *Nobody knows me? What does that have to do with my raise?*

Almost choking on my words, I replied, "What do you mean, nobody knows me?"

He explained that he was not the only one who had a say in my raise, and that he, too, had been caught off guard that he couldn't just give me a raise on his own. It had to be approved by a committee—and the committee didn't have the faintest idea who I was.

As I sat there, dumbfounded, Jim said to me, "You need to start developing your network with higher-level executives across the company."

I was still numb, but I thought, *OK, how many things are wrong with that sentence?*

Why doesn't my work stand on its own? That doesn't seem fair.

I am not a networker.

Why on earth would big executives want to network with me?

Where would I even start?

I am wildly uncomfortable with this.

Jim said, "I can't advocate for you if no one knows you. I'm going to try to go back and get you 5 percent now and try for more later. But so we don't land here again, here are 10 people I want you to meet. Schedule meetings with them. Tell them I sent you."

I was learning the hard way that your work results and your personal reputation are two very different things. And that you need to manage both of them *on purpose.*

Not getting a raise even after such extraordinary outcomes was the first time I really got smacked in the head by that lesson.

The importance of understanding your reputation is a huge theme in my book *RISE*, where I share how to navigate this reality:

1. You can't succeed if you are invisible, and

2. You need to make yourself visible, but not be annoying.

So off I went. It was a strange and unsettling process to repeatedly come face-to-face with an important executive I didn't know, not have a real reason for being there, and struggle to have a meaningful conversation. But I did as Jim told me.

And some very interesting things happened.

The good men

4.4

It's a simple fact that straight, white men have owned the vast majority of the power and wealth in the world for a very long time—and still do. If any of the rest of us want to participate in that machinery that runs the world, we need to accept that we are starting from the outside and find a way in.

My work environment felt in many ways like another closed circle of people having a conversation that didn't open up to let me in when I walked up.

There Were Always Good Men

Instead of being angry about this fact of life, I decided to see what would happen if I just asked these men who controlled the machinery if they would tell me how it works and let me in.

So, I just started asking, "If I want to get in the room, get included in the important conversations, get a promotion, what do I need to do?"

And you know what? They told me.

Jim's advice that I needed to not be invisible was one of the most valuable secret passageways of my whole career.

The mission he sent me on to network with executives made me super uncomfortable—but with that direction, he was not only telling me how to get in but providing the treasure map.

And after about a year of these awkward encounters with Jim's list of the 10 executives I must meet, I found myself seated across a desk from Bill Russell. Bill was a top executive. He seemed very poised, and I was braced for yet another uncomfortable meeting. But Bill was friendlier than the others. He made me feel welcome. He asked about my career goals.

I thought, *Oh, he seems inclined to help me. I should ask him for advice.* So I said, "I'm focused on doing a great job for Jim, but I'm also interested to learn: How does one get on the short list of people who are considered for a general manager position here?"

He seemed amused by my question. He asked me, "Do you have a mentor in the company?"

I stumbled a bit, talking about Jim being a great mentor, but thinking that Bill probably meant someone outside my organization at a high level. So, I finally said, "No. Will you be my mentor?"

He seemed surprised. He laughed. "Did you come here to ask me that?"

"No, but since you brought it up, I wasn't going to pass up the opportunity to ask."

Bill must have liked that answer. He said yes.

When Bill agreed to be my mentor, I wasn't sure exactly what that meant, but just three weeks later, he called. There was a job opening to run a global marketing department for a computer business. And Bill told the hiring manager, "You need to talk to Patty Azzarello."

I was stunned. Bill had opened a huge door for me. And damn, was Jim right about the networking and not being invisible! Because Bill Russell was about to change my life.

I never would have even *seen* this job opening on my own. And if I won the job, it would be a big promotion and an enormous leap forward in my career. I would be leading a huge team on a global scale.

So, as it turned out, I had asked Bill where the secret passageway was, and not only did he tell me, but he held the door open for me.

Throughout my whole career, I would find good men like Jim and Bill who were happy to help me—who treated me kindly and had high expectations. And all I needed to do was ask for their help.

So, How Did I Find These Good Men?

To find the right mentors, I had to get out of my own limited, introverted way of thinking and kiss a lot of frogs. After Jim's initial networking challenge, I got in the habit of asking smart people at work for help—lots of them, all the time. Some of those conversations were awkward and some of them were great. I always followed up on the great ones.

After a few great conversations, some of these people became my mentors even though they didn't know it. If they were smart and willing to talk to me and I always learned from them—they became my secret mentor. They never needed to know.

But sometimes I would try to close the deal for real. I would say, "I find our conversations so valuable that I'm beginning to think of you as a mentor. Would it be OK with you if we made these conversations a more regular thing, and I got on your calendar for half an hour every month?"

I have only done this a handful of times in my career, when it felt authentically right (and not like an awkward marriage proposal), but everyone I asked said yes.

For every big promotion in my career, one of these mentors helped me find, prepare for, or gain access to it in some way. Every big step forward I made was supported if not outright architected by my mentors.

And all of them were men.

It was quite surprising to me that I could just ask them, "How does this machinery work, and how do I get in?" and they told me the secrets and let me in. And there was never even a hint of any kind of sexual advances or expectations from them. The good men just helped.

I Got the Interview

At Bill's insistence, the hiring manager begrudgingly added me to the candidate list. I think he was hoping for someone who looked more like him.

In the end, the interview team chose me. I won the big, global marketing job.

I was 31.

And I was *terrified*.

Flying flash cards

4.5

As my start date approached, I thought about how I would be leading hundreds of people all over the world, along with my peers, in a massive effort to turn around a failing computer business that was losing $50M each quarter when I got there. This was a huge job. Of course, my internal critic popped up.

YOU'VE NEVER LED A GLOBAL TEAM. YOU ARE NEVER GOING TO GET ALL THESE PEOPLE ALL OVER THE WORLD TO FOLLOW YOU AS THEIR LEADER. YOU ARE IRRELEVANT TO THEM. THEY DON'T KNOW YOU. THEY WILL JUST IGNORE YOU. REMEMBER WHAT HAPPENED THE FIRST TIME YOU TRIED TO LEAD?

My internal critic could get surgical and could not resist a good childhood trauma.

I was four, and my kindergarten teacher decided to leave the room and put me in charge. Yes, she put a four-year-old in charge of a room full of five-year-olds. Her parting comment was, "Patty, I want you to create a flash card game for the group." Then she was gone.

Again, what were the adults thinking back then?

But I have to say, in that moment, I was so excited to have been chosen for leadership. *I get to create a flash card learning game and share it with the whole class!* I could feel the gravity of this responsibility, and it was thrilling.

I carefully spread out all the picture cards on the tables and eagerly handed out all the letter cards. "OK, the game is to match the letter on your card to the picture card that begins with your letter." I demonstrated by placing the *H* card on the horse picture.

I was reveling in my own cleverness as I held the *CH* card for myself with the idea that as the exercise wound down, I would, with a flourish, place it masterfully on the cherries—and everyone would gasp in amazement at my advanced knowledge. Yeah, I really thought that. I actually believed that this mob of five-year-olds would be impressed with my competence and grateful for such a fun learning experience. (I am still that same person who thinks learning is more fun than fun.)

Well, as you can imagine, without a teacher in the room, as soon as I finished my very earnest briefing, flash cards were flung into the air. There was running. Tables were knocked over and chairs were thrown. There was screaming. I remember seeing underwear.

The flash cards cascaded to the ground like confetti.

I stood there numbly, still holding the *CH* card. I was crushed.

Then the teacher came back in.

When she saw the chaos, she yelled at me for not maintaining control of the room. And I absorbed that failure as my own.

Now here I was in this new job, and I was worried. This job was so much bigger and more complicated than anything I had ever done before. I was way in over my head. I did *not* want to fail, but I felt so overwhelmed I couldn't even think straight.

If we were going to get the business turned around, I was going to need to lead in a way that would get people on board with my plans. My internal critic was really on a roll now . . .

IT'S GOING TO BE LIKE THE FLASH CARDS ALL OVER AGAIN. YOU WILL BE ALL ALONE WITH YOUR GREAT STRATEGY. NO ONE IS GOING TO FOLLOW YOU. YOU WILL FAIL AT YOUR FIRST BIG EXECUTIVE JOB AND IT WILL CRUSH YOU.

It startled me a little to think that the seed of such an important leadership secret passageway had been planted that day when I was four years old:

Just because you are excited about your great strategy, it doesn't mean that others will automatically want to follow your great strategy.

I had to find a way to succeed as the leader of this big organization. *How am I going to get a team of people spread out all over the world to WANT TO HELP ME turn this failing business around?*

You are not that important

4.6

In the first few months of my new job, everything was a firestorm of urgency and chaos.

The mountain of work and the problems attacking me from every angle were never ending. Every day, I was scheduled solid from 7:00am to 7:00pm, and people still wanted me to do breakfast meetings, dinners, and late-night conference calls. I wasn't sure how I would survive the pace.

One afternoon, I was sitting with my executive coach (thank God I had an executive coach), holding my head in my hands. "I'm overwhelmed."

"Patty, you need to schedule time to think," she told me.

What an unreasonable, ridiculous luxury that would be. Is she insane? That's impossible. There is no time to schedule anything. She doesn't understand the severity of my situation.

"Patty, it's never going to get better unless you have time to think."

While I agreed that having time to consider problems and options in a state of calm would be a dream, I kept insisting it was just impossible to make that happen.

I showed her my schedule and how packed it was. She looked it over and said:

"Schedule time to think."

I showed her again, pointing more vigorously, thinking she didn't really get quite how busy I was . . . and she said:

"Schedule time to think."

Before I could object again, she finally said, "Patty, you are just not that important."

OK. Mind blown.

That was the slap in the face that I needed to break my addiction to being too busy. I had to stop that line of thinking that goes: If all these people can't live without me that must mean I am very important. Because as it turns out I was about to learn a vital secret passage way that would carry me through the rest of my career:

Busy does not equal important.

At my coach's insistence, I nervously canceled a couple of things and scheduled two hours on my calendar just to think.

But when I tried to honor that blocked-off time, I could feel the judgment and disapproval. "Why is Patty unavailable? This is unacceptable!" I was not sure I would survive the awkwardness. Will people decide I am not an effective leader if I am not available every waking moment?

But as it turned out, other than a few early grumbles, there was no mutiny, and nothing came crashing down in these two hours I gave myself each week. In fact, everything got better. My coach had been right to push me. With more focused brain power, I was able to figure out how to make progress on the most important stuff and eliminate chaotic stuff that was keeping us all too busy in the first place.

Scheduling time to think not only made me smarter and more prepared to lead; it made me feel strong and healthy instead of stressed out and crumbling under the pressure. Jim always said that as an executive, taking care of yourself as a human is one of the most important things you can do. Now I understood that.

To get this business turned around, I again used his "talk to everybody" approach to figure out how to put a new strategy and a new management team in place.

And I hired Jack again to lead an especially challenging part of this new chaos.

Here is a lifesaving secret passageway: ***Hire people as smart as you (or smarter) who you can really trust to delegate big things to.***

Jack never let me down.

I was finding, again, that asking everyone for their input made them inclined to follow me. Despite my internal critic's endless chatter that no one would accept me as their leader (and feeding me images of flying flash cards), I found that by really listening and showing respect, I was able to motivate people all over the world to stay on board with me and the new strategy, on what felt at the beginning like a sinking ship.

Working with my new team and my amazing peers, we turned the business around. In one year, we went from losing $50M per quarter to being profitable. I was very proud of both surviving and winning, and I was incredibly grateful to all the wonderful people I worked with and what we accomplished together.

I had thought (hoped) that each new success would make me feel different on the inside, like a more confident, accomplished, deserving-of-the-position kind of person, but alas, I was still the same me. Success alone does not chase away all the insecurities . . .

Moon shot

4.7

I was sitting in the cafeteria at a round table of 10 people at a celebration with ice cream. We had pulled off the biggest turnaround in the history of the company. It was a lively atmosphere and everyone was in a good mood—except for me. Because it just so happened to be the anniversary of the first moon landing, and everyone at my table was sharing their profound experiences and memories.

I was panicked. *Oh, crap. I don't have a moon story.*

As the conversation moved around the table, I was frantically trying to come up with a moon story—or a plausible reason for why I didn't have a moon story. By the way, there is no plausible reason for not having a story about the first moon landing if you were alive and conscious at the time. At that moment, people were not doing other things. It was the biggest event in the world, and the whole world stopped to watch it—together. *Everyone* had a moon story.

The real reason I didn't have a moon story—because I was only three at the time—was the one thing I couldn't say. I frantically thought through other possible explanations, *travel, illness, coma* . . . but none of them worked.

Now, the conversation was two people away from me. *Check mate . . . This is the moment I will be outed for being way too young to have this job. What am I going to do?*

So, I got up and hid in the bathroom.

As I sat in the stall with my head in my hands, connecting the points of my patent leather pumps, I flashed back to right before I started kindergarten. When I walked out of my room that morning, I had been expecting to lie on the sofa with Mom to watch *Sesame Street*, one my favorite things in the world to do. But instead, Mom and Dad sat me down at the kitchen table. That moment had a super weird vibe, almost like a meeting. But we didn't have meetings in my family—and I was only four. What was going on?

Mom said in a foreboding tone, "We know you want to start school in a couple of weeks, but . . ."

A bolt of doom shot through me. *What?! Are they about to tell me I can't start school this year? If I can't start school, I'll die!* I started to cry.

In an eerie, official-sounding tone, Dad continued, "The law in our state says that you have to be five years old by October 1 to go to kindergarten. Your birthday is October 8. They won't let you start school until next year."

My brain was caving in. *A year? I've already waited soooooo long, and now you are telling me I have to wait another year? That's forever. I can't wait a year!*

My parents looked at me. Then Mom looked at Dad and said, "She can already read. We cannot keep her out of school for a whole year because her birthday is a week late. She's gonna burn the house down."

They needed a solution.

And then Dad proceeded to tell me about our family's secret crime.

"We have done something against the law, and we did it so that you can go to school. We had a lawyer friend create a false birth certificate that shows September 29 as your birthday. We can submit the false certificate to the school, so you'll be able to start in a couple of weeks."

I wasn't sure whether to stop crying or cry harder.

They continued, "But you cannot tell *anyone* that your birthday is October 8. *No one* can know your real birthday. If you tell anyone the truth, we could all get in big trouble. We need you to pretend that your birthday is September 29th, OK? Or, if you want, you can wait a year to start school."

Well, obviously, I was not going to wait. I agreed to lie about my birthday. But it felt scary. I was breaking a law. What if I messed up and let the real date slip out?

What happens to you if you break a law? Would my parents go to jail? What would I do if my parents were in jail? Would I go to jail? Would I get held back a year? Would I be kicked out of school entirely?

If anyone found out my true birthday, my whole future could collapse.

As I sat there on the toilet in my suit, without a moon story, I thought, *I have been lying about my age as though my life depended on it since I was four years old.*

I kept thinking, *If they know how young you are, you can't do what you want. You will be disqualified. Being too young is a dream killer.*

Eventually, I left the bathroom and returned to the party. I sat at a different table, making sure to choose one without an age-revealing topic.

Pretending to be 40

Ease and grace

4.8

One afternoon, I was sitting on the bright orange bench in the hallway near the company coffee shop with Jim. He was grilling me about my future. Jim always showed me how high expectations felt: great, but also heavy, and often scary.

I wrapped my fingers around my coffee cup, trying to extract some extra life force from the heat. I told Jim that I wanted to get promoted to the next level.

Jim said, "You are ready for a bigger role in terms of your accomplishments, but you lack the necessary gravitas."

"What do you mean?"

"You need to show up in a way that will make others know and respect that you are the one in charge."

Ever searching for a good script, I asked, "What does that look like? How would I do that?"

What he gave me was not quite a script but a sort of formula to follow. It included things like: Walk into the middle of the room. Don't lurk at the edge. Greet people as they come in. Have intentional things to say about the business. Never appear overwhelmed and panicked. Don't cancel things at the last minute. Always appear calm and in control of your business.

And to my relief, I thought, *OK, this is different from the ugly, aggressive, acting-like-a-big-shot stuff I officially denounced when I decided that I wasn't going to make enemies.*

He continued, "People need to know you are the one in charge, even before you say anything—so you need to conduct yourself with ease and grace."

There it was.

Ease and grace.

I knew in my bones that I was severely lacking in the ease and grace department. I was more in the always-trying-too-hard, uncool, awkward camp.

As I left my meeting with Jim and headed back to my office, I pondered Jim's advice. *What inaccessible-to-an-introvert sorcery was going to be required for me to conjure up ease and grace? That seems like rock star stuff.*

5 points, 2 ideas, and 3 questions

4.9

Here I come with my very intentional stride and my very neutral French manicure, with my hair pulled back tightly in a granny bun, in my black suit, high heels, and understated, quality jewelry. For many years, that was my Patty-at-work-pretending-to-be-40 uniform.

I still did not have a clue about ease and grace, but you'd find me well prepared for any meeting, with the first words out of my mouth being some very serious and efficient form of "Here are my 5 points, 2 ideas, and 3 questions." Then I would have an entirely business-focused conversation, say thank you, then make an immediate exit.

That was the formula: Get right to it. Be all business. Make my escape.

Why did I need to make this efficient escape?

Well, there were a few things at play for me. First, it was just basic awkward, nervous, introvert stuff. Why would I invite any unnecessary conversation or, God forbid, small talk? That would just be painful.

Add to that the eternal echo of little patty in the background, reminding me that if I try to be friendly at all, they'll be, like, "Ew, why are you talking to me? You're weird. Get away from me." (Alas, even after decades of evidence that this doesn't actually happen, my default mode is still to never risk opening myself up to that kind of rejection.)

Also, very serious, all-business Patty thought, *Getting right to the point is a good thing, isn't it? People are super busy; not wasting their time shows respect. I'm scoring extra points for being so efficient with their time, right?*

Particularly with bigger executives, I would just nervously, abruptly start the meeting thinking, *Tigers, you will not be getting your snack today. I will be efficient. I'll be OK if I stay very serious, stick to business, and get everything absolutely right. If I don't leave any room for them to react to what I am saying, they can't attack me.*

This was me doing what most young women do to be taken seriously at work—being very serious.

But let's be clear. What this very serious, all-business, 5-points-2 ideas-and-3-questions act is—is survival.

What it is *not*—is ease and grace.

Connection

4.10

Being so businesslike all the time to manage my reputation and credibility so carefully seemed my only option. Which required hiding my humanity. Which was a recipe for feeling lonely at work.

But as it turned out, after about eight years of marriage, I was feeling lonely at home too. My career kept advancing, but our marriage did not. It felt like our connection had been weakening, not strengthening. We were not getting along great anymore.

One time, I had been working three months straight of late nights preparing for a big event. Each night, I would wait for everyone to leave the office. Then I would change into shorts and a T-shirt, microwave a Lean Cuisine, open a Diet Pepsi, and settle in for another four hours of work.

I tried my best to share what I was doing with my husband and make sure he knew that this was temporary, that I would be back and fully present with him after the event. He didn't seem to care much either way.

All that hard work culminated in a four-day offsite event, where my efforts paid off big-time. My team and I hit it out of the park. After the last day, I dragged myself home feeling thoroughly exhausted and also triumphant. My husband knew that this was the big week and this was the big final day.

As I crossed the threshold into my home, I was craving a hero's welcome. I had an immense need to celebrate and collapse in equal parts.

He was watching TV.

There was no special dinner. There was no dinner.

There was no hug.

There was no celebration.

There was no acknowledgment of what I had accomplished.

It was just Thursday.

I made my own dinner.

I so longed to be able to go home and—just like when I crawled into bed with Mom after a bad day at school—to have someone who was interested in my day and wanted to talk to me.

Instead, every day, I went from feeling unanchored and always at risk at work to feeling ungrounded and very much alone at home too.

I was earning all the money to support our life. I did not resent that—being the duty-bound worker that I was. That was just part of my identity, and it was our stated agreement, and it truly didn't bother me. But it bothered him.

I want to be very clear that he was a good man.

The reason our marriage failed was not because of what might seem like the obvious reason—that I was too invested in my career to prioritize the effort to support a healthy relationship. I was all in.

Let me rephrase that: Tireless, super-student Patty was all in for putting the time and effort into maintaining a meaningful relationship.

So when our connection started breaking down, I tried very hard to improve it. And, ever the good worker, I really thought I could do the relationship work for both of us.

I could not.

Also, my professional life was getting bigger and more public at an accelerated rate. But he was settling into a desire for a smaller, more private life, which was his right. We had a good, loving, fun, authentic start, but we just could not make it around the corner together.

He was always kind to me, but I needed an enthusiastic teammate. I needed someone to notice how much I was growing—and to be happy about it.

After the divorce (that I initiated), being on my own let me expand into the person I needed to be. For me, being out in the world alone was far less lonely than being in a relationship with someone who didn't really see me.

And though I can't speak for him, he and my mom remained friendly, and it seemed to her that he also started thriving more without me—which made me very happy to know.

Power struggle

4.11

Having been promoted to the global marketing role, I was invited to attend a high-level annual meeting with the top 100 executives across the company. The invitation alone felt like getting a gold star. But as soon as I stepped foot into Grand Ballroom/Salon C on the Mezzanine level of the conference center, I got nervous.

As I walked around the room among the towering conversation circles of men, I couldn't help but feel that they seemed so important and powerful (and tall). I felt particularly small in that room. A very specific worry started to brew:

I don't feel powerful and important.

Am I supposed to?

Is feeling powerful and important a key part of having a job at this level?

Am I not doing my job right?

Or . . . am I just supposed to act *powerful and important so other people* think *I'm powerful and important?*

I was confused. I had finally gotten in the room. But dammit, my internal critic also got in the room.

YOU ARE NOT LIKE THEM. EVEN YOU CAN SEE THAT. THIS JOB IS WAY TOO BIG FOR YOU. YOU'LL NEVER PULL OFF "POWERFUL AND IMPORTANT."

I *really* wanted to be good at my job—and at the same time, I definitely didn't want to act like a big shot. I would often find myself doing the psychological equivalent of checking all my limbs: *Well, I still don't feel powerful, but at least I'm still here. I must be doing something right. Or at least I'm not getting it wrong enough to get bounced out of the room just yet.*

I have to say, even in my biggest roles, where I had actual power at my fingertips—thousands of employees under my watch, millions of dollars of budget to manage, billions of dollars of revenue to keep growing—I never felt personally powerful. Mostly, I felt crushing responsibility.

It was clear to me that my job was to manage the *power of the role.* None of that big stuff was a reflection of me personally. It wasn't my power. I thought, *Just because I am in this big role, that does not make me a superior life form.*

I kept wondering, though: Was *feeling* powerful part of the ease-and-grace thing? I just didn't know.

A couple of weeks later, I was at a client's office on Long Island. In the small conference room were the VP of technology—a large, dominant type—one of his direct reports I'll call Seth, and me. The VP told me, "The reason we are having this problem is that Seth makes stupid mistakes. He's not good at his job. No one listens to Seth. He screws everything up."

Seth looked small and mortified. Little patty knew exactly what this felt like. I was cringing and heartbroken for him. I had worked with Seth on prior occasions, and I knew that Seth knew way more about the technology, the industry, and the matter at hand than this VP. The problem was not Seth.

But later, when the VP walked me out and we ran into *his* boss in the lobby—this dominant bully instantly changed into a cowering suck-up. I was even more appalled by his behavior in the presence of his own boss—it made his big, tough-guy bullying of Seth even more despicable.

Watching this weird, creepy transformation, a new thought started to brew: *Wait a minute. If I am still the same insecure little kid on the inside, afraid that no one will like me, standing alone in the cafeteria holding my lunch tray, this asshole probably is too.*

And once I saw it, I couldn't unsee it.

Forever after leaving that lobby, whenever I see a big, scary man acting like a powerful bully, I see the hurt little boy, as plain as day. I can't *not* see it. I want to reach over and gently squeeze his forearm and say, "Awww . . . did somebody steal your ball? Did your father yell at you for crying about it? Poor thing."

Seeing the big bullies as fragile little boys was my first step toward understanding that there was a better way to show up as a leader than "powerful." And with this insight, when I got bullied at work, I could more easily just step aside and let the aggression roll by instead of being crushed by it.

Mom had given me the secret passageway for keeping my self-esteem intact with bullies. I have used her advice for the entirety of my career and life: **Bullies need to make you feel worse than they feel. It's always about them. It's never about you.**

Once I saw these aggressive men as their own scared version of little Kevin or little Bobby, struggling with their own human frailties, I was no longer worried that they were innately gifted with a kind of power that I didn't have. It made me stop worrying once and for all about feeling or even acting powerful.

While little patty was still scared of personal rejection herself, she was never going to let me treat anyone else without respect. She would keep pushing me toward my goals, but *acting more powerful than others was never going to be on my path to ease and grace.* I would find another way.

Year of the Snake

4.12

After a couple of years in this big global marketing role, I went for another promotion. This one would make me a general manager for the first time.

I was 33. If I got this job, I would be the youngest general manager at the company in modern history. Once again, I won the job. And once again, I was terrified. And this job required me to relocate from Colorado back to California.

As I was preparing to step into my new GM role, I got ambushed. There were three ladies—my executive coach, a media coach, and an HR consultant—who all, independently of one another, told me some version of the following: "Patty, when you get to your new job, give up the act! You do not need to act so businesslike all the time."

The idea of taking this advice felt like losing a limb.

But the ladies persisted. "Really. I have seen you when you are too tired to maintain that facade. Because when it fails, and the less formal you shines through, you are actually *more* credible and impressive. Be that person."

I knew that as a young woman stepping into a general manager job, I was about to be scrutinized by more eyes than ever before. How I was perceived would play a huge role in my ability to do the job at all, and in my ultimate success or failure. So, I had a choice to make. I could:

- Stick with the buttoned-up, all-business act that had been keeping me alive so far. Or . . .
- Show up as a less formal person at work for the first time ever.

But could I really abandon my carefully managed identity? Wouldn't that destroy all the years of credibility I had worked so hard to build up? And there was still my young age to contend with. Little patty still worried. *Will I go to jail for hiding my true age if I get caught?*

At 33, I was now 10 to 15 years younger than many of my peers and even some of my direct reports—so, more than ever, I was frantically feeling the need to hide my age. I wasn't getting older as fast as my jobs were getting bigger.

A couple of weeks before I started this new GM job, I was at a Chinese restaurant in Boston with a group of leaders from the company. We were chatting and laughing when I looked down at my place mat and froze.

Oh no . . . it's the Chinese zodiac.

My eyes locked onto the 12-year lists of birth years next to each animal. I was desperately hoping that no one would want to talk about it.

But now everyone was looking down finding their animal.

And then it began . . .

"I'm a rat."

"Me too."

"I'm a dragon."

"I'm a monkey."

My age was a topic of great curiosity and concern to everyone around me, but everyone also knew I did not talk about my age *ever*.

But there was a new guy there.

"Patty, which one are you?" he asked casually.

Everyone looked at me, waiting for my response.

If I revealed that I was a snake, that would mean I was either 9, 21, 33, 45, or 57.

When they realize I am only 33, word will spread across the world by tomorrow morning. I am going to lose my GM job before I even start. I won't be trusted to lead this organization, and I won't be considered for a promotion for decades. I will be forever bounced out of the room. THIS is the moment when it all comes crashing down. I am going to be taken out by a place mat.

So, I got up and hid in the bathroom.

NOT uncomfortable

4.13

So many things about my job made me uncomfortable. So why did I choose this path in the first place? And why on earth did I stay? The statute of limitations on Mom's "stick with it" rule was long past.

Well, it all started when I was in college. I saw a guy graduate with an engineering degree, and then he immediately bought a condo. Wow! That became my whole life plan at age 16—*if I can graduate the engineering program, I can afford to buy a condo.*

So, at the beginning, I embarked on my career with no other specific end point in mind. And without a defined goal, over the years, I just ended up following an ever-advancing trail of gold stars and higher pay—and I upgraded my condo.

But as time went on, I was discovering that I was really good at leading organizations. And that's what I enjoyed most about my work. So, that became my direction. I wanted to lead.

With this idea of leadership in mind, I officially named a goal: *I want to be a CEO of a public company.* This goal pulled me forward for many years.

And to be honest, another reason I stuck with my uncomfortable career path was that I was just not bold or creative enough to see any other possible career options for me. I was on a leadership track in a tech career. And leading was what I was good at. So I just kept going on the track I was on. Like the Alpine Slide. You are already on the track. Just try not to die.

Was it hard and uncomfortable? Yes.

There were all the rooms of dismissive men where I needed to assert my existence, all the new technology products and markets I needed to learn, all the business deals and maneuvers I needed to lead, and, of course, all the closed conversation circles I had to break into. So much of my work was really uncomfortable.

But, as it turned out, I was also really good at being uncomfortable. Little patty had trained me well.

Whenever I would hesitate, she would say, "You need to go in."

"But I'm scared. I'm not sure I can do it."

"You do know that your fears are all in your head, right? People actually told *me*, 'I hate you,' and I still went in. Don't be a wimp. Focus on the work and just pretend that you are not uncomfortable, like I did."

Little patty had given me a way forward. Being uncomfortable does not disqualify me. It just presents me with a choice.

When I feel uncomfortable, I can choose to have a meltdown in front of the intimidating audience or the big executive, or I can just *pretend* that I'm OK.

That was the secret passageway—***You can just pretend. You can just pretend that you are NOT uncomfortable—because—and here is the big news—NO ONE IS CHECKING.***

There are no confidence police who will show up and say, "We know you are not confident, so you are not allowed to act like you are. You should be all tentative and nervous and weird. This show of confidence is a violation. We're dragging you off to jail for acting like you're doing fine."

The truth is that every time I got a big promotion, I was terrified on the inside, but what people saw on the outside was someone fairly poised and smiling, maybe even impressive.

If you saw me on a stage, or in a meeting, or at an event—same thing. I would appear calm, and project confidence. Sometimes, that confidence was because I actually was comfortable and confident. But other times, it was just that I looked OK on the outside even when I felt like liquid on the inside.

I think this should be written into the job description of every executive position: Ability to pretend that you are not uncomfortable.

Is she still here?

4.14

While there were always good men who cared about me and helped me, they were not in all the rooms I needed to be in. There was also a steady rotation of men who were disrespectful and dismissive of me and tried to shut me out. They made it clear that I was not welcome and only begrudgingly tolerated my presence.

There were plenty of times when I felt really discouraged and tempted to give up, when I felt so clearly that I was not wanted or valued, but—I just kept coming back.

People always want to know: What is this mysterious source of my resilience? To be honest, it's not a very complicated answer. *I got used to feeling uncomfortable, and I refused to get chased away.*

I kept being annoyingly competent. I kept injecting surprisingly valuable work and insights whether anyone wanted me there or not.

After a while, the men seemed kind of puzzled by the fact that they hadn't shaken me off yet—like they were thinking, "Wow, she's still here? How can she still be here?"

I realized that a secret passageway for resilience is simply: *Just refuse to go away.*

Laughter

4.15

One night after my work as a busy executive, I walked into my parents' house in my standard suited-up uniform. When my travel brought me to their town, I always stayed with them. I kicked off my heels and fell onto the sofa. Mom knew I needed an introvert reset. I closed my eyes for 10 minutes.

When my eyes opened, my dad was standing there with a smile and a Manhattan. Cocktail hour began. I did not move from the sofa for hours. Later, Dad delivered directly to my lap a huge bowl of pasta with lentils, which, according to the ancient Italian secret, was at least half olive oil. This evening was better than going to a spa.

My parents were always nurturing in every way you need parents to take care of you. But what I remember most about growing up in our home is how much we laughed. There were really no days without laughter in our home.

Mom was a genius at creating fun moments for our family. When I was little, before she hurt her back, Mom made up a game where she threw 4 million marbles on the living room floor and gave us all a cup—Dad too. You had to turn the cup upside down and crawl around, sliding it along the floor. The objective was to coax as many marbles under the rim of the cup as possible in the allotted time. The more marbles you collected, the more that would fall out when you lifted the rim to try to get more in.

The four of us ended up lying on the industrial carpeting (which, I have to admit, made an ideal playing surface), laughing so hard our stomachs hurt. It was such a stupid but weirdly compelling game. Mom called it—and I believe this was the best part of all—"Marble Cupway."

As we became adults, the laughter kept coming. Mom and Dad were fun. Really fun. And man, could they throw a cocktail party. Mom would invent crazy games for adults too. She had a real knack for games that would

Mom and Dad, purveyors of laughter

make people laugh. Sometimes the laughter was so loud I thought the police might show up. Mom and Dad showed me that when you host a party at your house, it is way better to be fun than fancy. I never clean up after my guests during a party. We make a mess. We relax. We laugh.

Sharing joy with people in my home has become one of the best parts of my life and always makes me grateful to Mom and Dad.

Whatever challenges and indignities I needed to face in my career, both as a human and as a woman—because of my family, I knew that having a sense of humor was the best way to keep going. It worked so much better than leaning in to disappointments or looking for reasons to be offended.

When I think of the enormous gift of laughter in my home, the resilience and self-worth it infused into my life can be largely summed up by how I felt playing Marble Cupway with my family on our tiny living room floor.

Loose hair

4.16

I t begins . . .

It was my first day in my new job as the general manager of a global financial software business. I walked into the room with high hopes and loose hair.

It was time to take the less buttoned-up version of myself on the road, even though I still found that idea terrifying. *Remember: I need to just pretend that I am not uncomfortable.*

As I scanned my badge at the door, I felt my hair swish behind me. It startled me. I thought about how this was the first time at work that I had ever unleashed the neatly pulled-back granny bun I had clung to in-my-20s/pretending-to-be-40 years. I even allowed myself colored nail polish. Colored nail polish, for God's sake! Things were getting crazy.

I got introduced to several people that morning. Thinking, *Be like dad,* I smiled and did not jump straight to business. It felt weird. *But so far so good. No one is running away from me.*

I was then greeted by the highest-ranking member of my new team, who appeared to be 15 years older than me. This was the highest-stakes introduction so far.

I smiled, shook his hand, and casually said, (using my prewritten script for meeting a scary, important person) "Hello. How are you today?" desperately hoping my less formal demeanor would not make the world implode.

I followed this guy into his office, and he offered me a scotch.

Hmmm. So I take my hair down and smile, and the first thing that happens is that I get offered a scotch at 11 in the morning?

"Thanks, maybe later."

I had no idea where my new, loose-hair persona would lead me, but as I met each of my new team members, I continued to smile and say, "Hello. How are you today?" I also joked and laughed a bit with people. I thought about how this all felt so wildly inappropriate and careless compared to my past practice of getting right to my clear and businesslike 5 points, 2 ideas, and 3 questions.

OH MY GOD. YOU'VE GONE TOO FAR THIS TIME. YOU CAN'T BE THEIR GM. LOOK AT THEM. THEY ARE ALL SO MUCH OLDER AND MORE EXPERIENCED THAN YOU. AND *NOW* YOU ARE GOING TO DROP THE BUTTONED-UP ACT? ARE YOU KIDDING ME? YOU ARE THE YOUNGEST GM IN THE ENTIRE COMPANY—AND A GIRL. IS NOW REALLY THE TIME FOR AN EXPERIMENT? THIS IS GOING TO BE A TRAIN WRECK!

I couldn't stop thinking about the risk.

What was going to happen?

Would people laugh at me?

Was I so ill-equipped that everyone would just ignore me and go about their business as though no one had even stepped into the role as their manager? Like with the flash cards?

Would I get fired my first day?

Would it feel like one of those dreams where you end up at work in your underwear?

I was braced for some unknown horror each time I smiled and said hello, but as it turned out, no one was running screaming from the building—there was no major, external, apocalyptic shock wave matching the one that was happening at the core of my identity.

In most conversations we smiled and laughed a bit, and then, we still got to the important business pretty quickly. No harm done. *I think.*

This was a huge job. As I got on my feet in this new role, I realized that once again, I needed to restructure the management team and the organization. Once again I had a big, hairy product problem to be managed, and once again, I hired Jack, with another promotion. This time, I asked him to relocate his family to California from his beloved mountains in Colorado. He said yes. His family was not happy at the time, and his little girls hated me—until they grew up and started fulfilling lives in LA and San Francisco. Now they all blame me for their happiness.

Over the first few months, I was starting to feel pretty good about my credibility in this GM role, once again with help and support from the very capable team I built.

The tremendous crater in my gut had seemed to close up. And since no one was laughing at me, or excluding me from anything, or saying, "Ew, go away," even little patty finally relaxed, and I stuck with my less formal approach. And I was actually feeling more comfortable than ever in this big role.

But you never know what other weird, fresh hell will come up to further challenge your credibility . . .

The fall

4.17

I was speaking on a stage in a dark room in front of about 2,000 customers. The only light in the room was the projection of my slides on the back wall. I was in the middle of my talk.

"What I want to emphasize is the importance of having a system that can adapt to unexpected inputs."

I walked back to point at the screen, continuing, "To avoid the expensive error that normally happens, the right system should—"

And at that moment, I simply disappeared. Gone. And then the audience heard a blunt thud.

What I had not realized was that the stage had been set up about 30 inches in front of the screen, but it was so dark that I could not see the gap. So I stepped right off—into the abyss. One moment I was making a vigorous point, and the next I was lying beneath the stage. I couldn't move or think. Some number of microseconds (or days) later, I couldn't tell which—my brain switched back on.

I have just fallen off a stage and rolled underneath it. I am lying on the floor. I can't see anything. It's really dark under here. And last I remember, there were a lot of people out there . . . are they still there?

In real-world time, several seconds had gone by during which the audience heard nothing. I was doing an inventory of my extremities to ensure that I had not paralyzed myself. Apparently, several people from the audience had leaped to their feet and were about to come rescue me, but then everyone heard, "rumble, rumble, rumble" from my lapel microphone and a very small and quiet voice saying, "I'm OK . . ."

Finally, I stood up. I was visible, but waist deep between the back edge of the platform and the screen behind it. Still stunned, I thought, *I need to get back up and keep going.* But I didn't walk around to the front of the platform and climb the four steps like a normal person. Instead, I hoisted myself onto the stage from the back, like a seal lumbering out of the water to flop onto a rock.

I regained my standing position and brushed off my black suit, which was absolutely covered with dust bunnies. As I emerged from the cloud, I thought, *I am embarrassed as hell, but I need to do something. Just name this for what it is and own it.*

I limped to the podium, smiled, and said, "It's a great pleasure that I get to share one of my true career highlights with so many people." I got a round of applause, presumably for not dying, but also, presumably, for staying present without nervousness or apology. Since my reaction was relaxed, everyone else could relax.

This was an odd way to discover some ease and grace, but there it was. *In an embarrassing moment, don't pretend it didn't happen. Just relax and be human.*

Then I hung on to the podium for dear life and finished the last 30 minutes of my presentation on one foot. I had just sprained my ankle in front of 2,000 people.

Embarrassment always sucks, but it's just not optional when you are moving forward in life. You simply can't get everything right. If you try to avoid embarrassment, you also end up avoiding success—avoiding life. You end up avoiding the very things that bring you all the amazing stuff you want.

Little patty reminds me all the time that amazing is likely to be ungraceful at first.

Ditch the fear: Work in your gifts

4.18

I had been a GM for more than a year now. But my age wasn't the only thing that had me worried about my credibility almost daily. I was a technology business leader—and I hated technology.

I was always looking over my shoulder, worried everyone would find out how unqualified I really was.

My internal critic would practically sing to me about it every day.

YOU ARE ONLY PRETENDING TO BE INTERESTED IN TECHNOLOGY. AND EVERYONE IS GOING TO FIND OUT. NO ONE WILL RESPECT YOU WHEN THEY LEARN HOW NOT TECHNICAL YOU ARE. YOU WILL NEVER GET AWAY WITH THIS.

One day, after a particularly technical meeting, I retreated to my office and thought about how I had gotten fired from the first job I ever had. When I was 13, I became the piano accompanist for a children's dance school. Think of a mob of five-year-olds running around in tap shoes. My piano playing was to be the organizing force to get them to tap away in synchronicity. But there was one key problem—I was not a good piano player!

I guess I was channeling my Slovenian grandfather when I said, "Sure I can do that," even though I knew I wasn't qualified. I have no idea how I even got the job. I could get by, but only just. I had to white-knuckle my way through. If I missed a beat, the whole class missed a beat.

I swear, this job was more stressful than being a CEO.

Being in a job you are not qualified for is terrible. You spend every moment trying your hardest while at the same time knowing you are failing. Sitting on that piano bench with all ears on me, I was constantly afraid of getting in trouble for being bad at my job.

And ultimately, I did. I was fired and replaced with someone who could actually play the piano. Though it stung for super-student Patty to be incompetent, and it was embarrassing to be fired, it was a also relief to have been taken out of a job I sucked at. But life went on for me and the mob of little dancers.

In my role as a technology business leader, I needed to white-knuckle my way through many technology-focused situations and contribute where I could. I did OK, but I always felt I was at risk of being out of sync, a beat behind everyone else—just like a bad piano player.

I was *always* worried about not being good enough.

For the record, here's a list of things I suck at:
- Playing the piano
- Being a technology guru
- Being a financial analyst
- Actually, anything in the finance department
- Reviewing dense detail of any kind
- Playing volleyball
- Actually, anything involving hitting a moving ball

But eventually, something shifted for me. I got some wonderful coaching that helped me stop worrying about what I was bad at and start focusing on what I was good at. And I finally came to realize that there was a lot more to being a great technology business leader than technology. For example—leadership.

I started to observe something very interesting watching my peers. While they were brilliant at the things I struggled with, like being technology experts or being able to hit a ball—their organizations were a mess! And more importantly, they were not delivering on their brilliant strategies. Their people were throwing the flash cards in the air—their teams were not aligned or motivated or executing.

I finally realized, *Wait—that's what I do! I don't need to be the technology visionary who thinks of the strategy. I need to be the one to make sure we actually implement it. I can focus on my unique strengths and be even more successful.*

Up to this point, I had been failing to appreciate my own natural strengths. Because when you are good at something, it just feels easy—so it doesn't seem very impressive. But when I saw people doing things with ease that I am bad at, I would always think, *Wow, that's amazing!*

I had to learn to accept that when others observed me using my natural strengths with ease, they were also looking at me and thinking, *Wow, that's amazing!*

As soon as I started leaning into my own unique strengths, I did not feel scared in my job anymore. This one shift was life-changing for me. It made *everything* better.

Because stepping out of fear is a beautiful thing. And I also discovered that it's super useful for achieving ease and grace when you stop worrying and suffering all the time.

My career and my confidence soared. My well of enthusiasm for life was refilled.

Once I made this change, even my mom said to me, "Patty, it's strange, but you actually seem to like your job now."

By letting go of my fears about having weak spots and focusing instead on being a great leader, I found a secret passageway that seemed more like cheating than ever before. I had found a giant shortcut. ***You don't need to be good at everything. Know what you are good at, and do THAT. Delegate the things you suck at.***

And I thought, as long as I don't try to get a job that relies entirely on skills I lack, like technology visionary or financial analyst, I'll be OK. And it's not too difficult to just avoid volleyball entirely.

Don't disqualify yourself

4.19

A fter two years in my first GM role, my true dream job opened up. It was the GM position of a much larger business—a $1B network management software business that employed more than 3,000 people internationally, plus a huge network of partner companies all over the globe. If it hadn't been a subsidiary business of HP, it would have been the 14th largest software company in the world. In other words, this was a BIG job.

I was 35.

My internal critic stopped me dead in my tracks.

DO NOT PROCEED. YOU'RE *WAY* TOO YOUNG TO HAVE A JOB THAT BIG. YOU'RE STILL TOO YOUNG TO EVEN HAVE THE JOB YOU HAVE NOW. THERE IS NO WAY YOU ARE READY FOR THIS. AND WHEN YOU FAIL AT GOING AFTER YOUR DREAM JOB, IT WILL BREAK YOU FOREVER.

This time, I agreed with my internal critic. This was just too big for me right now. I wasn't ready.

I remember thinking, *Someday, that's exactly the kind of job that I want. But not now. Someday . . .*

So, I decided I would just keep my head down, focus on being a great GM in my current job, and wait for another big job to become available later.

Jim pounced. "Patty, why haven't you put your hat in the ring for this job?"

"Are you crazy? I'm not ready."

Then Jim showed me the list of the other candidates (all male) who were going for this job.

I was stunned. *OMG, are you kidding me? None of these men have any general management experience—and they are going after THIS job? If they think they are qualified, I can at least interview.*

I recalled the secret passageway I learned from that disastrous "she doesn't know anything" printed circuit board demo. *Patty, remember: Put yourself out there to get judged. Even if it doesn't go well, you'll learn what excellence looks like for next time—and either way, you won't die.*

Later in my career, as the hiring manager for big jobs, I have heard experienced women say, "Oh, I'm flattered, but I'm not ready for that job. It requires ten skills, and I only have strong experience in five of them, a little in the other two, but for the last three, I have no experience at all."

Women have a tendency to talk about themselves as though they are trying to impress you with the exacting precision they can use to describe their shortcomings. While men I knew to have far less experience than the women (even if the job description required breastfeeding) would simply say, "I'm your man. Sign me up!"

So, I got myself into the interview . . .

The hiring manager said, "What makes you think you are qualified for this job? You have no experience at all in network management."

This was the moment when I needed to stay in it, even though I was dying on the inside.

I did my best to resist becoming defensive, trying to make stuff up about network management, and babbling like an idiot.

OK. Deep breath. *That's actually true. I have no experience in network management.*

Then, I recalled my college scholarship interview, and how I'd learned that when you are uncomfortable, the best way to get unblocked is by stating the authentic truth of the situation.

So I got my strengths in clear focus, and that gave me the confidence to tell the truth.

"That is correct. I have no network management experience. But you have three thousand people here who are experts in network management. You don't need another one. What you need is *me*. You need me because you have a business that is losing market share in a growing market. It's lacking a coherent strategy, and you have an ineffective organization structure, which is competing against itself internally. That is why you are not winning. I'm here to build and lead the right team to execute a clear and winning strategy. That's what I do. That's what you need. That's why you need me."

Part of any successful interview is managing your energy. Instead of presenting yourself like you are in a tryout, tentatively and defensively, like, "Do you think I can do this?"—you need to lean forward and energetically convey, as if you are already in the job, "You KNOW I can do this."

When I left that interview, I was in a sort of shock . . .

That was a big swing! And I was reeling from it.

And yes, of course, I went and hid in the bathroom. This was one benefit of there being so few women around. You could always get some solitude in the ladies' room.

This time, I went to a nicer bathroom and sat on the little sofa bench—a material upgrade from my toilet-based hiding of days past—to ponder my situation. *That was friggin' scary. But I did it. I'm really glad I did it. If I don't get the job, at least I was not the one to disqualify myself.*

Let me shout this secret passageway in all caps to drown out my internal critic:

SCARED DOES NOT EQUAL DISQUALIFIED.

Never disqualify yourself just because you are scared.

Go for it, then let *others* be the ones to disqualify you. No matter what happens, you will always learn something important.

I think about my Slovenian grandfather, who just kept putting himself out there for jobs he was *actually NOT qualified for* and getting fired over and over again until he finally found one where he stuck the landing. His whole life was a shining example of never disqualifying yourself.

But in this instance, I had disqualified myself. And I had almost failed to show up for the biggest breakthrough of my entire career. It was my mentors who brought me back into the game. Having mentors to help you combat your internal critic is a beautiful thing.

And . . . OMG.

I got the job.

Glass cliff

4.20

This was a great job. It wasn't one of those glass cliff jobs . . .

Have you heard of the glass cliff? It's kind of like the glass ceiling in that it's used to describe why women don't reach the top positions.

But the glass cliff is about giving the ugliest jobs with a high likelihood of failure to women instead of men, because women's careers don't matter. Another version of this that I see with women executives is that while the men around her get promoted, they just keep piling all the big, ugly work onto her until she dies or just gives up and goes away.

For a man, it would be, "Heaven forbid a failure damages *his* important career"—but if it's a woman who crashes and burns, there is no sense of loss. The system doesn't care. Women are not considered part of the permanent setup. While men are seen as dutifully building their important careers, women's careers are seen as non-vital.

I had been given more than my fair share of glass cliff jobs and big, ugly piles of work that I just gutted my way through, duty bound as I have been since the beer ticket booth incident at Action Park—do an excellent job no matter what.

But there was a secret passageway for me here about how I was able to advance my career so quickly. It was to take the glass cliff jobs on purpose. *Go for the ugly, higher-level jobs that you would not otherwise win if the top men were competing for them.*

I competed for several highly desired executive jobs, and I did not win them because the men with the better networks and flashier careers got them.

But the less appealing (though still big) jobs the top men didn't want, I jumped on. I could make huge leaps forward where having less experience didn't matter as much, because the competition was lighter, and no one cared if I failed. But I didn't fail. My success again seemed to leave them scratching their heads and thinking, "How can she still be here?"

I also learned that the ugly jobs accelerated my experience faster than the sexier jobs could. In an ugly, struggling business, *you* need to make really hard decisions and scary trade-offs, and do big, difficult stuff compared to a business that is just growing no matter what you personally do or don't do.

All of my glass cliff jobs let me compete for bigger roles sooner and gave me the deep experience I would need to go after my dream job. Which was not a glass cliff job. Which I was now in.

And having just started my new dream job, more than ever before, I was in big rooms, big negotiations, big presentations, big deals, and big networks. Initially, all of that was wildly uncomfortable.

If I'm honest, I was not confident that I was ready for it. My internal critic was having a field day:

YEAH, YOU TALKED A GOOD GAME IN THE INTERVIEW, BUT YOU KNOW YOU ARE NOT QUALIFIED FOR A JOB THIS BIG. YOU FOOLED EVERYONE. AND NOW YOU ARE FEELING WOR-RIED ABOUT IT BECAUSE YOU SHOULD BE. BECAUSE YOU ARE A FRAUD. AND THEY ARE ALL GOING TO FIND OUT.

Imposter!

4.21

I went to see Jim in a panic. I found him waiting for me in a small conference room. My enormous briefcase hit the chair next to me with a potent thud. He was calmly sitting there with a coffee and no briefcase. *How do people not carry their work around with them all the time?*

I sat down and proceeded to have my meltdown.

"I am in over my head and I'm not sure what to do. I'm talking to everyone like you taught me, but it's not working this time. It's all just too big. I keep talking to people and groups all over the world and every conversation reveals new issues and problems. Nothing is repeating. I can't get my head around it, and I'm afraid I am going to lose my job."

Jim just sat there calmly. *Isn't he seeing the disaster that is me unfolding before his very eyes?*

"Patty, stop worrying. New is stressful. New is supposed to be stressful. There is no way around that. Your job right now is to cope. Just think about what a mess it would be for them if you walked away. What they need from you right now is to come back to work again tomorrow. I promise you, in a few weeks, all of this complexity will snap into focus and you'll know what to do."

Jim was revealing another secret passageway:

In a new, challenging situation, don't underestimate the value of just coping.

That was a huge gift. And wow, who knew? I have actually been on the right track my whole career by simply refusing to quit—by not getting chased away.

I would never have come to the idea on my own that coping was part of the value, especially in my nervous-breakdown state. Having a good mentor in moments of panic is a lifesaver. But in that room, on that day, Jim also offered another executive insight that hit me like a lightning bolt: "Patty, *all executives are frauds. Everyone is bluffing.*

"No executive can know everything they need to know about their job. It's impossible. It's just too big. *At some point, we are all bluffing. That's part of the job.* You just have to cope."

Well, I felt like I had just been given the keys to the kingdom.

I have imposter syndrome. So do you. So does everyone else on the planet who is trying something new or bigger. I began to see it as a sign of doing something right instead of doing something wrong. As a human, we have only two options for avoiding imposter syndrome: never try anything new, or—be a psychopath.

I still had moments when I felt so overwhelmed and discouraged and insecure that I wanted to flee. But then I replayed Jim's voice in my head. *Patty, just cope. Just come back again tomorrow. In a few weeks it will all snap into focus.*

Jim was right. About six weeks later, I could see the big picture. I could see the way forward. But before that happened, a different massive confidence crisis was looming right around the corner . . .

Really not ready

4.22

Only five weeks into this big dream job, I needed to give the keynote talk at our annual customer conference.

I was to take the stage and speak to an audience of a few thousand of our biggest customers, partners, industry analysts, and members of the press, along with key people in my new team from across the world— all of whom were waiting to hear from *me* about the future of network management.

Let's pause for a moment to take stock. This was my fifth week on the job—a network management job for which five weeks earlier I had exactly no network management experience—and now I've been tasked with inspiring the whole network management universe to have confidence in *me* as their new leader.

I have never felt so *not ready* to do something in my whole life. It felt like the biggest spotlight in the world was beaming directly at me, highlighting my shortcomings and impending epic failure.

To prepare for this event (calamity), I got a lot of help from my team, who created the content of the presentation for me. Every free waking moment for the two weeks leading up to the conference, I studied and practiced this new content. This was not my normal process. Normally, I know the material, and I am super comfortable on a stage. But since the content was all completely new to me, I had no choice but to study hard and even have notes in my hand during the talk. I have never used notes before or since.

The day came. The auditorium was full. It was approaching showtime. My internal critic and my intestines were locked in a duel over who could be more discouraging. Ten minutes before I was to take the stage, I went into the bathroom. How I wish I could have stayed hidden in there.

My internal critic was just about to fully spin up, to make sure I really knew this was going to be a disaster, but as I was leaving the stall, I somehow smashed my hand in the door. The pain split through me like lightning. My hand was on fire.

But a small miracle was gifted to me in that moment. With that shock, all of my manic nervousness exited my body. My internal critic was silenced. I was still scared, but now at least I was calm.

I took the stage.

Everyone was waiting.

I had won my dream job, but this was the moment to either solidify myself as the leader, or fumble and fail on that stage in a mortifying way that would end my career. The stakes had never felt this high.

As I faced the audience, blinded by the spotlight but knowing they were all there, I thought, Patty, you know the content is good because your team created it. They helped you. You have notes that you are holding in your throbbing, smashed-in-the-bathroom-stall hand, which has miraculously calmed your nerves. You know you are good on a stage. Trust that. One more breath. One more step.

So, I delivered that keynote to all the most important people in my world at the time.

And . . .

The crowd did not throw their flash cards in the air and knock over the tables in their zeal to abandon me as their leader.

I had been able to use my engaging stage presence to make up for my lack of deep subject mastery.

I didn't embarrass myself or my team.

I did fine.

I am not being modest. It was only fine. I know this because the next year, when I gave the keynote at the very same event—this time being way more experienced and having my own knowledge and opinions about the future of network management—many people said, "Wow, that was amazing! You seemed so much more relaxed up there than you were last year."

I was equally proud of both performances.

You have to ask

4.23

My mentor Bill Russell, who had opened doors to other jobs for me in the past, was now my boss. I walked into the small conference room where he was waiting for me and closed the door behind me.

I was nervous because I was going to make what felt like a wildly big ask. And I was doing my best to pretend to not be uncomfortable.

Because I'd started so young and gotten promoted so quickly, I was always paid the lowest possible salary for my job level. Which often meant that I was paid far less than the people who worked for me.

That was never truer than now, in my job running the $1B software business, where some of my team made double my salary. I decided it was finally time to negotiate my pay to be more in line with the size of the job I was doing.

I told Bill, "I am at the very bottom of the pay curve, and I am doing a very big job. I want to propose a set of even bigger performance objectives and commitments for myself for the coming year." I slid a copy of the list across the table to him. Then came the ask: "If I meet these specific goals, in a year, will you give me a 20 percent raise?" (This pay increase would move me from the *bottom* of the *bottom* rung on the pay curve to the *top* of the *bottom* rung on the pay curve. I really was being underpaid.)

I waited.

My heart was pounding . . .

Then he said, "OK, that's fair."

I was thrilled. But, when the meeting was over, I still went and hid in the bathroom for a while to recover from that. That was big.

Fast forward to the end of that year.

I had done really well and met all of the goals we had agreed on. It was time to get the big news—and the big raise.

Once again, Bill and I sat together in the same small conference room to review my performance:

"I grew market share by 15 percent."

"Yes, well done."

"I have resolved all the conflicting product lines and increased the revenue."

I continued down our pre-agreed list of objectives to get his confirmation of my success.

"Thank you, Patty. You have done a great job."

Then we just sat there in silence. I felt like I had moved the world, having over delivered on every measure. I was waiting for him to give me my raise, but he wasn't saying anything.

Did he forget? Is he not saying anything because he changed his mind and didn't tell me? Did the company disapprove and he doesn't want to tell me he couldn't get it done?

He just stayed silent.

Damn, I need to break this silence with another very uncomfortable conversation.

"Um . . . in our last discussion, we agreed that if I accomplished these things you would give me a 20 percent raise. Is that happening?"

"No."

Now I was either dying on the inside or ready to crumble into tears, I was angry. This was not OK. We had an agreement.

As I reached for my notes from our last conversation, preparing to confront him, he said, "I am giving you a 30 percent raise."

Then with a smile on his face, he said, "But if you didn't ask me about it, I was going to give you 5 percent."

I was stunned at the audaciousness of his game. I didn't love it. But he gave me a 30 percent raise. In reality, he more than came through, and he did a great thing for me. And once again I was learning how the world worked. You have to do the uncomfortable thing. You have to ask.

Confidence is an outcome

4.24

I was encouraging a colleague to press her manager for a promotion, which she so obviously deserved. "You have to ask," I said. "You have to show your value. Your boss doesn't see it."

"I can't do that. He already said he can't promote me."

"You have to have the conversation."

"But I would be uncomfortable doing that. He already told me no—I can't ask again. It's easier for you, Patty. I can't do it because I don't have your confidence."

There it is . . . "But Patty, it's easier for you. You have more confidence."

So, I told her my secret: "The way I deal with situations when I don't feel confident is to just pretend that I am not uncomfortable. That way, I can get through it."

She didn't believe me. She continued to ask me questions as if searching for a way to make the scary conversation less scary or find a different, less uncomfortable option. She wanted to feel more confident *before* doing the hard thing.

I can never tell anyone how to get the outcome without doing the hard thing, because that's not what I've ever done.

Pretending that I am not uncomfortable, while it allows me to take action on the scary thing, it is mostly for the observer. Kind of like needing to pretend you are not afraid of spiders for your kids (Not the smallest of reasons I didn't have kids). But my putting on a brave face does not take away my internal fear.

For me, it unfolds more like this:

I cannot imagine myself actually doing this thing—it's just too scary. It feels like standing at the edge of a cliff, needing to jump into the ocean. It might go OK, but it might go horribly wrong, and I am afraid that I might die of humiliation (or of actual death).

The mere idea of starting the scary conversation makes me feel nauseous and panicky, like I can't move, and that my face will melt off.

But I have no choice. I must do this thing.

So I take a breath, and I make myself stop thinking about the big picture. I just take the next step. Off the cliff. Something happens. I don't die.

So that's what "Patty, it's easier for you because you have more confidence" actually feels like on the inside, even though others might see me looking confident on the outside.

But I often get asked: "How do you actually get yourself to do the scary thing in the first place?"

Well, what little patty showed me was this: *When you feel scared or unwelcome, LEARN.*

Little patty kept going back into the fire every day at school so she could keep learning. Learning worked as a shield against the fear and pain of being bullied. Learning made her feel braver and happier—and that strategy still works for me.

When I do the scary thing despite my fear, one of two things happens. It goes well, and that is a success. Or I fail and am humiliated—but I don't die. And that is also a success—because I *learned* how to do it better for the next time. (And I didn't die.)

The practice of doing the uncomfortable thing and not dying from it is valuable. You get better at doing the thing itself—and you get better at the not dying part.

And after you do the uncomfortable thing many times, because you keep learning, it starts to feel easier, and sometimes it even becomes comfortable. Because all that swimming upstream is good exercise. It makes you stronger. So, over time, as I developed actual confidence, the need to pretend to be OK started to fade.

Whatever confidence I have was an *outcome of doing scary things* while scared, not an *inherent trait* I was gifted with.

If I had waited to feel confident first, *before* doing uncomfortable things, I never would have done anything.

Start from where you are standing

4.25

I was standing in the wings, waiting to go onstage. The producer of the TEDx event was standing behind me, gripping my shoulders with his hands and saying, "No matter what, you cannot go out on the stage until they are done clearing the musical equipment."

At this point, even though I already had a thriving executive career and had become practiced at dealing with confidence crises, the TEDx stage still felt like a really big deal. And sometimes all of my tools I use to deal with my anxiety fail, and I panic.

Like at this moment.

Because with a TED Talk, whatever you do out there—brilliant or humiliating—it will be on the internet forever, instantly searchable as YOUR TED TALK. As I stood there, watching the musical number, I was unable to move, both from general nerves and from being held firmly in place by the producer's grip on my shoulders.

Earlier that day, I had met the person who would introduce me to the audience. He had many sheets of paper with facts and stories about me, and he told me what an honor it was to introduce me and how he was looking forward to it. As he took the stage, I was curious what fun facts he would pull out of his large pile of notes.

But instead, he simply said, "It's my pleasure to introduce Patty Azzarello." That was it. It was over in a second. No data. No fun facts. No notes. And more notably—no taking up the necessary time to get the musical equipment cleared.

The producer intensified his grip and said, "You can't go out there yet."

The applause died down; Patty Azzarello did not appear. There were a few sad, lagging, lonely claps. Otherwise, just silence and a distinct absence of Patty Azzarello.

Finally, after what seemed like an eternity of silence, the last of the equipment was taken away. The producer moved his hands from my shoulders to the middle of my back and *pushed* me out onto the stage and said, "NOW!"

I felt as if I had just been shoved out of an airplane. I stumbled onto the stage in my heels. The audience and I were all a little stunned by my abrupt entrance.

The first moments of my talk were a bit rocky, but I managed to settle my nerves and avoid panic by doing two things, the first of which I had learned only the night before from a friend who trains firefighters.

My friend said, "If you are nervous about your TED talk tomorrow, just remember: Start from where you are standing. Trust your training." The stakes in his work are certainly much higher than anything I do. If I perform badly on a stage or in a meeting, no one dies.

I thought about his words and realized that wishing for the situation to be different is not useful. The situation is what it is. Stop worrying about the big picture and what could be different, and just *start from where you are standing.*

I completed my TEDx talk in reasonably relaxed form (and without falling off the stage). And one second after I got off the stage, before I could even start to judge my performance in my own mind or worry it wasn't good enough, my phone beeped with a text from Wendy that said: YOU

FUCKING CRUSHED THAT. Wendy had come to see my TEDx talk. She was still my biggest supporter.

The advice I'd gotten the night before gave me a new secret passageway to help me deal with any scary task. I say this to myself all the time now: ***Start from where you are standing. Trust your training.***

 Stop thinking too much about why the hard thing is scary and instead think more practically. You don't need to see all the steps up front. You just need to take the first one. Then just take the next breath. Take the next step.

One more breath. One more step.
 Repeat.

Don't forget to give yourself the promotion

4.26

On my one-year anniversary of falling off the stage, I spoke again at the very same event with largely the same audience in attendance. When I was introduced and stepped up onto the platform, instead of applause, I got laughter.

 The laughter didn't feel great. You just don't live down disappearing with a thud in the middle of your talk in front of 2,000 people.

 But this year, I had made a plan.

 I knew that I needed to change the story. I was not going to let myself be known as "the lady who fell off the stage" for all time. It was kind of like not letting that awful "she doesn't know anything" printed circuit board demo from so long ago define who I was.

After taking the stage, I said, "Before I get started, I decided to take some extra precautions this year." At that moment, three big guys in hard hats appeared and placed traffic cones on the four corners of the platform, then wrapped hazard tape around the cones—I was safely enclosed.

I got another laugh, but that laughter *did* feel great.

I was figuring out that if I could just gut out humiliation past the part where I want to die, I could give people new memories to substitute for the embarrassing ones.

More importantly, I was learning that I could be the writer of my own story. I could own how I choose to show up in my role as a leader.

I decided that my professional reputation would be based on my good-humored, competent, respectful leadership behaviors. If I stuck to that plan, those positive behaviors would overshadow any embarrassing moments along the way.

But even with racking up successes in this new giant job, I was still feeling very imposter-ish.

Once again, Mom came to the rescue. We had all met up for a vacation weekend in Carmel-by-the-Sea in California. Mom and Kerry and I were sitting on a bench, soaking up the sunshine, looking at the bright blue water and the glowing white sand beach.

Mom said, "You've come so far. Remember when you were a teenager and you were afraid to even make a phone call to schedule an eye doctor appointment?"

Kerry said, "Yeah, you were so shy back then. How are you even doing this?"

I thought for a moment. "I like what I am doing, but I am so young, and there is so much I don't know. My new team and my business are both doing really well. I just wish I could feel more confident about how I was seen in this big position. I still feel like an imposter."

Mom said, "Patty, for God's sake, they put you in charge of the fourteenth largest software company in the world. Is that not a big enough sign of how well you are regarded? What more do you need to believe you deserve to be there?"

"I guess . . ."

Then Dad came and sat on the bench with us, and we were all instantly laughing—a gift that endured for decades.

It felt really good to get this emotional boost from my family.

Over the next few weeks at work, I kept thinking about what Mom said, and I came to a ground-shifting realization.

Despite all the things that fueled my fear of getting bounced out of the room—the low expectations, being too young, not being technical enough, not having enough gravitas—I'd still gotten the promotion.

But now, I needed to truly believe that:

I deserve to be here.

I am allowed to fully occupy this role and feel confident in it.

I don't need to be tentative or act apologetic with my former peers that I got this promotion.

I can act with clarity in this role and fully own its authority. I can make the key decisions without second-guessing myself.

It was time to stop searching every room I found myself in for disapproval. I needed to just stop worrying about whether or not I belonged there and finally own up to the one secret passageway I had been afraid to take: ***Don't forget to give YOURSELF the promotion.***

I had to stop waiting to feel welcome. I needed *give myself the permission* to be in the room.

Part 5

Swimming Upstream

"The man on top of the mountain didn't fall there."

—Vince Lombardi

"Always keep a bottle of champagne in the fridge for special occasions. Sometimes the special occasion is that you've got a bottle of champagne in the fridge."

—Hester Browne

Swimming upstream

5.1

I was in a dark cave in chest-deep water. A giant waterfall was thundering just out of view, roaring so loudly I could feel it in my liver. That's where we were heading.

There were about 10 of us waiting along the inside wall of the cave, looking toward the opening ahead while the guide fussed with some ropes and other stuff. An athletic-looking woman near me took the words out of my mouth: "Can we try to swim to the waterfall?"

"Sure," he answered and smiled.

The two of us started swimming upstream. At first, it wasn't too bad, but as we got closer to the opening, the current became so strong that it just blew us right back to the group.

He laughed at us.

But by then, he was ready to start the tour. He swam upstream on a very slight diagonal course, where he quickly reached a handhold along the opposite edge. Then, one by one, he threw each of us a ring buoy to pull us across to the handhold. Once we got there, all we had to do was pick our way along the cave wall until we entered a vast open dome, where the current eased and we could finally relax and revel in the glorious waterfall.

I was so annoyed.

Here I was, literally swimming upstream against an impossible current, and there was literally a friggin' secret passageway: See that edge? Swim across—grab onto it. Then you can walk your way around and avoid the current.

The other woman and I could have easily swum across to the handhold on our own. But instead of saying, "No, we need to go as a group," which would have been reasonable, or instead of him telling us how to do it, he told us, "Go ahead," then laughed at us when we failed.

It occurred to me that this is what much of my life has felt like.

Riding on the rickety van back to the hotel, I closed my eyes. I thought about how although I got what I wanted in my life, it didn't happen without a lot of swimming upstream. And it didn't happen without people telling me, "Sure, give it a try," waiting for me to fail, and laughing at me when I did.

Later that night, with the sensation of the fierce countercurrent still fresh in my mind and body, I was sitting at the dive bar at the hotel, drinking a margarita. They were served up in thick, straight glasses of recycled glass. I approved.

I thought about how much effort I had ultimately invested in my life to become mentally and physically strong—to make myself fit enough to endure the energetic demands of my career—but also how no amount of mental fortitude, super-student energy, or ninja-level fitness would have allowed me to make my way upstream had I not been shown secret passageways along the way.

But I knew that as my jobs got bigger and more demanding, I needed to maximize every last crumb of my energy if I was to keep going.

It's kind of like a video game where the objective is to navigate various situations and preserve your life force by managing energy points.

You are presented with tasks and decisions where you will gain or lose energy, and to continue playing, you can never let your life force dip below a certain threshold. To succeed in this game, you have to be constantly aware and intentional about what you invest your precious life force in: what boosts your energy, what drains it, and what restores it. You need to pay constant attention: Which direction are the energy points flowing?

It has become very clear to me that my success in managing my life force has been a combination of both building strength and resilience *and* finding shortcuts.

And you know who showed me one of the most important shortcuts? Dad.

No one cares how hard you work

5.2

It was Take Your Daughter to Work Day. I was about nine. I was immediately compelled to climb into the unimaginably exotic, standard office swivel chair in the corner. As I sat, swinging my legs to make the chair move back and forth, I watched Dad stand over his desk and open his briefcase. He took out some blue papers. He put some of them on his desk, stapled the others to some white papers, put those in his briefcase, and then turned to me and said, "OK, now we go for coffee."

Wait! What just happened? I was just getting settled in this groovy chair to watch Dad work. Was that it?

I wasn't sure what "work" I observed that day, but I remember thinking that Dad seemed very sure of what he was doing. And I loved having coffee with Dad, so that was good too.

I had coffee with Dad before school almost every day starting around age seven. We would put a quarter inch of butter on a slice of white bread toast, score the middle of the toast with the knife so you could fold it neatly in half, and then dip it in our coffee. The toast would be both crunchy and mushy, and the butter would be both cold and soft. Heaven.

Right before we left the office, he ducked into the photocopy room, emerged with a package of paper, and handed it to me with a big smile on his face. I lived for when Dad would bring a home a whole ream of paper, and now I was getting it at the source! This was very exciting. Hugging the heavy block of paper tightly, I thought, *I can draw and fold and cut and color anything I want! And since I get the whole pack, still brand-new with its wrapper on, that means I also get the glossy white sheet of cardboard that comes on one end. I can make something super elegant with that!*

I recall so clearly, during that period of my little life, being very concerned that if Dad were to lose his job one day, he would not be able to bring home paper anymore.

On this day and throughout my childhood, my dad showed me that you could earn a living *and* enjoy your life outside of work. This was quite an Italian mode of living. You work to enjoy life. That's the only point of work. The only point of life is to enjoy life.

Dad's work allowed him to control his own schedule, and with that freedom, he was home for dinner at 5:30pm every single night of our lives. Dad was present for us in every sense of the word. While my mom was not well, Dad was on all our school trips with all the other moms.

It never seemed that my father worked very hard. But he must have been doing a good job because he was offered multiple promotions (all of which he refused because he did not want to mess up his pleasant life).

So, thinking about Dad, I thought, *While there is no chance that I will be anything other than an overachiever, why not be an overachiever with as little effort as possible? And why not make the whole point of being an overachiever to enjoy my life?*

Over the course of my career it became so clear to me that:

No one cares how hard you work. Your company can absorb an unlimited amount of work from you and not care about you.

This revealed a super important secret passageway: **No one other than you has any motivation whatsoever to make you less busy. Everyone else only benefits from your endless willingness to work.**

At my work, I realized that one else was going to make sure that I was OK. I am the one who needs to protect my life force and my soul and manage my energy points.

To do this, I developed a kind of highly productive laziness. It wasn't about avoiding work. I want to be clear about that. It was about choosing to do only important work and refusing to work endless hours on chaotic, repetitive, low-value tasks.

I had to figure out what was most important and do those things really well. So, I found ways to deliver high-value outcomes that people noticed—but to do them with less busywork. The fact that it took less effort did not make it less valuable. *You don't get promoted for how hard the work feels. Only the visible outcomes matter.* (This is a big theme in my book *RISE*.)

No one was directing me to work more selectively or efficiently. Everyone else would have been totally fine if I just killed myself working long hours on everything.

"Love your work" is bad advice (for me)

5.3

I'm really tired of movie stars and professional athletes and supermodels telling me that I must *love* my work. That idea never landed with me. In fact, I always felt a little bullied by it.

In reality, the people who have a true passion, actually know what it is, never get bored with it, and can make a good living at it represent such a small percentage of humanity that their opinion is just not relevant to me.

I don't love my work. And that's a really good thing for me.

I have observed that insisting people should love their work makes them suffer in two big ways. The first is when a person tries to make a living out of a hobby they love, and then they struggle to earn enough money, and so they ruin their hobby and don't enjoy their life. The second is when a person has a great job, earns plenty of money, lives a happy and interesting life, and loves their people and hobbies—but because they don't truly love their work (and famous people keep telling them they are supposed to), they walk around feeling like they are failing.

Don't get me wrong, I'm not suggesting it's OK to hate your work. Hating your job is like slow drip torture on your nervous system. Talk about energy points just gushing out in the game.

What I opted for was, instead of feeling pressured to love my work, I sought out work that I *liked*—work that offered me some of my favorite things that would feed me the energy points I needed to stay in the game.

Business leadership does that for me. It offers tons of opportunities for learning, being amazed, helping other people grow in their careers, and, of course, collecting gold stars for my achievements.

But do I *love* my work? No.

And the fact that I don't love it . . . well, that's what the money is for.

I don't expect to get paid to do the things I love: to go scuba diving, or to have lunch and wine in a sunny piazza in Italy, or to paint a picture, or to go for long walks in nature with friends. I love those things.

Work—I get paid for.

If I don't like my life, *that's* what's not OK. The goal is to work to earn enough money to feel safe and to enjoy my life. Money is never the end goal. *Enjoying life* is the important goal. (Thanks again, Dad and the Italians.)

Loot and joy

5.4

My dad was an insurance adjuster, so his work kept him on the road making new friends with people whose houses and cars had just been wrecked.

When a client's property needed to be replaced, the company took the damaged thing and stored it back at headquarters in the "contents room."

I'm not sure what was supposed to happen to the stuff after that, but let's just say my dad was no stranger to the contents room. And some of these contents would find their way into our home.

Once, we got an old-fashioned radio, the kind that looked like a piece of wooden furniture. It had flame marks on the top. Not flame marks as in a decal or the pattern of the wood grain—flame marks as in this radio had actually been on fire at some point.

The color TV (that we watched *The Wizard of Oz* on) was melted on one side. This TV was special, not just because of its survival skills but because it had an early version of a remote control. The remote had just one red button on it.

Kerry: "You have the remote—change the channel."

Me: "I'm trying. It's not working."

Kerry: "You need to rub it on your leg for a while to work up some static electricity."

Me: (dutifully rubbing the remote on my jeans) "OK, I'll try it again . . ."

It worked about 20 percent of the time. But made us laugh 100 percent of the time.

When I went to college, I took with me a contents room VCR that had been through both a fire and a flood. It later also survived an earthquake, after which it was crushed on one side and missing a part of the front panel. I made a Frankenstein-like circuit board repair with some crazy glue, wire, duct tape, and my soldering iron. It then continued to work fine until VCRs died as a species.

We ended up with all these weird things mostly because we had no money to buy new ones. And it was actually less difficult back then to be financially responsible because there were no credit cards. If you didn't have the cash, you simply didn't do the thing.

I wanted singing lessons.

No cash.

Kerry wanted to go skiing.

No cash.

Game over.

But I learned some important lessons about money by watching my mom manage the little money my family did have. Like, when I joined Girl Scouts, the family ate cheaper food for a few weeks to pay for it.

One time, Mom made us all go out to breakfast as one of her obligatory family outings. We all ordered a bagel and coffee. Dad ordered orange juice. Mom said, "You can't order orange juice."

"Why not?"

"We can't afford the orange juice."

Mom never needed to pretend we had more money than we had. That orange juice money went into a savings account, where she would put away some small amount every single week to make sure that there would be enough funds for mounds of Christmas presents and a one-week family vacation to the Jersey Shore. Every year. She never failed.

Here's what I learned about money and joy from Mom. And it has made my life materially better in every way.

1. Even if you don't have a lot of money, you can still have things you want if you regularly save some small amount of it.
2. Saved money can fund joyful, shared moments—which are truly important.

Thanks to Mom, I became an "I can't afford the orange juice" kind of saver, so I avoided a lavish lifestyle riddled with debt—which helped me preserve a gazillion energy points in the game. And I always have money for happy things, like vacations. And not once in my adult life have I ever skimped on a comforter.

Conserving energy was particularly important to me because I always felt like the baseline of physical energy I started out with was lower than everyone else's . . .

Not straight

5.5

I was on an Alp. Due to my aforementioned dismal sense of direction, I can't tell you which Alp, but I can tell you it was in either France or Switzerland or Italy. Kerry and I trekked through all three countries on our eight-day, 80-mile Tour du Mont Blanc hike. When we arrived at our hotel after the third day, Kerry went to the front desk to get ice. The receptionist asked, "Do you want the ice for your drink or your knees?" The answer: Both.

There was a moment, a few days into this expedition, when the trail disappeared and became a pile of boulders we needed to climb over. For some reason, in that moment, I panicked. I'm not sure anyone noticed, because this was not a particularly difficult or treacherous part of the trail. We had already walked about 40 miles over a few days, on routes with many more obviously death-defying, ninja-obstacles—steep technical terrain, narrow trail edges with infinite drop-offs, suspension bridges, abyss-adjacent ladders built into vertical rock faces—and on all of those, I was fine.

But for some reason, at this particular spot, which looked like nothing much, I was stuck. I had both hands on the ground. I started to cry. I couldn't move forward. I felt so stupid. The other hikers were all causally bopping along, gliding effortlessly around me up and over the top, like water around a stone, then heading down the other side without a second thought.

What was wrong with me? I had to move. The only other option would be to get rescued by an emergency helicopter—an idea not as far-fetched as you might think, as one person in our small party of eight had been taken off the mountain in the emergency helicopter in the very first hour on the first day of the trek.

That's the thing about disassociation from trauma—disassociation protects you from experiencing ongoing trauma. Disassociation really works—that is, until it doesn't. And for me, this moment on this trail was when it gave out.

I was 10. My parents and I walked into an orthopedist's office. We were there because I was walking funny, and the school nurse, after a 12-second examination, thought I might have scoliosis.

The doctor sat at his desk with his back to us, looking at some X-rays on the screen. He was finishing something up for another patient as he didn't greet us when we sat down. I remember looking up at the X-rays, thinking, *OMG. Whatever problems with scoliosis I'm here to deal with seem trivial compared to this poor person's deformed spine I am seeing on the screen.*

I couldn't stop looking at the X-rays, though. How to describe them? In the back-facing view, at the bottom part, there were no building blocks of vertebrae even visible. It looked more like a cloudy mass. Right above that, the spine twisted like a DNA spiral, then curved severely back and forth at the top. From the side view, at the lower cloudy part, you could see the individual discs, but instead of the spine going up vertically with a gentle curve in the lower back, it looked more like a right angle. The lower part was basically parallel to the floor—two of the discs looked like a number 11.

How can part of your spine, the thing that supports your whole body, go parallel to the floor? Can that person even move? Can they stand up at all? I was transfixed; it looked so strange. *What must that person's life be like? What would it feel like to have a spine like that?* I really wasn't that concerned about my own spine. I wasn't even sure why we were here. I didn't have any pain, and the school nurse was hardly an expert. But I really wanted to ask the doctor about *that* person.

Then he turned around and said hello. But instead of taking down the other patient's X-rays and putting mine up, he simply pointed and said, "Of most concern is this spot here . . ."

OMG—that's what it looks like inside of ME?

The world swallowed me up. The picture truly terrified me. My spine is a catastrophe! How can this be? What is going to happen to me?

At one point, in my parents quest to figure out what we should do, we ended up at a hotshot Park Avenue orthopedic surgeon in New York. He told us that in addition to the severe curves and the parallel-to-the-floor part, I had a third condition: a vertebra in my lower back was out of line. It was shoved forward, not quite in line with the others. The issue with this, he explained, was that any fall or bump could make this one vertebra slip further forward, sever my spine, and paralyze me.

He recommended a massive surgery.

The plan was to chisel several pieces of bone from my thigh—enough to put me in a leg cast—and then use that bone to fuse seven vertebrae to make me straight and to stabilize the one that could slip forward and paralyze me.

In addition to wearing a leg cast from crotch to knee, I would also be in a full-body cast. For a year.

The surgery was scheduled . . .

Outcast in a body cast

5.6

A fter the initial shock, I cannot remember a single feeling I had while waiting for this surgery.

Disassociation, baby.

Wendy on the other hand, seemed much more attuned to the situation and kept asking me, "Are you sure you are not going to die?"

I can only recall three practical thoughts from this pre-surgery period:

1. The way I understood it, a big impact, like a car crash or bad fall, would definitely paralyze me. But also, any jarring impact from normal life *could* paralyze me. The only viable ways to not be paralyzed were to never move again—or to have this surgery. As scary as the surgery seemed, I guess it felt less scary than the inevitability of being paralyzed upon any bump or stumble.

2. I could foresee that the recovery period would be an epic source of new opportunities to bully me. I would be an outcast in a body cast! That's not going to make things better.

3. How would I deal with a body cast in my life? It's already hard enough to buy clothes that fit. What will I wear? Will I even be able to walk with the cast on? Will I be in a wheelchair? How will I go to the bathroom?

No one was informing me about what I should expect. There was just a date on the calendar. The only thing I knew for sure was that if I didn't have this surgery, if I lost my footing and fell down, I could paralyze myself. The thought that I could paralyze myself was with me any time I was moving around. My lifelong fear of stumbling to my death was taking hold.

In the months leading up to the scheduled surgery date, my parents set us off on a quest for second . . . and seventeenth opinions. It was a lot of doctors.

We happened upon Dr. O' Leary, also in Manhattan. He was the orthopedist for the New York ballet at the time.

He said to us, "This girl has no pain. Why would you do such a massive surgery on a girl with no pain?"

He told us that he had ballet dancers who have this same (vertebra out of line) condition and they are fine. No special risk of paralysis. He said, as long as she doesn't have pain, why don't we just keep an eye on it?

So, the upshot of all this is:

1. I did not have a surgery that would most likely have wrecked my health and my life.

In fact, I recently googled the name of the doctor who recommend the surgery and found that he had been accused of doing too many unnecessary surgeries on young people.

I found a group chat about him. Other patients wrote that he told them, "You need the surgery, not because of the present state, but because of the future state. Your spinal curve will get worse, and it will compromise your heart and lungs, and then you will die." (I guess he'd escalated his fear tactics from paralysis to death.) Everyone who ended up having the surgery complained of severe pain and mobility issues for the rest of their lives.

Talk about dodging a bullet. My God. When I think about the three people who have had the biggest practical impact on the quality of my life, they are, in order, Mom, Dad, and Dr. O'Leary.

2. I stayed crooked.

I've since had occasions where I've met people who have seen my X-rays before meeting me, and the reactions are the same—kind of like mine was. When I walk in, they are stunned that I'm upright and walking without assistance. But it turns out I never had any real complications or bad pain. In fact, as an adult, I probably have less back pain than anyone I know.

3. I have weird posture and I walk with an awkward gait.

But I do my best to mostly pass as normal. I am good with this deal because I am so grateful for the mobility I possess *from having avoided that horrific and unnecessary surgery.*

OK, back to the Alps . . .

One thing about walking 80 miles for eight days is that when you are not on demanding technical terrain, there is quite a lot of time for chatting. And a big part of the discussion in our group was about each of our training programs and what physical challenges we each dealt with. Everyone had already noticed that I walk funny, so it made sense to tell them this story about the near miss with my back surgery.

Everyone in our group had observed that going uphill, I was like a machine, but going downhill, I was tentative and the slowest by leagues.

You are much more likely to fall when descending than climbing. So on these 80 miles, every descent required great thought, and careful placement of my feet and my walking poles. The mental load of each step down was exhausting.

But, after everyone had heard my orthopedic story, something became immediately obvious to them that had never even occurred to me. They said to me, "Patty, being told when you are 10 by a scary doctor that you will *paralyze yourself* if you simply fall down is not something you get over—ever."

Could that be true? Doesn't everyone feel danger when they walk down stairs? Anyone? No? Only me? The idea of being permanently timid about walking was hard to accept, because part of my identity is my ability to get over obstacles and keep moving forward. Did I never get over this one? Could this past trauma about paralyzing myself be why I have always been so shaky and ungraceful on my feet?

As we continued our walk and reached a lovely, wide, flat, and non-perilous path, I started to think that maybe that scary doctor and the even scarier impending surgery/paralysis threat had never fully cleared my amygdala. Because any time I face a downhill scenario of any kind—steps, escalator, trail, Alpine Slide—my nervous system simply feels peril.

So there I was, on my hands and knees, frozen, fighting back the tears. In that moment, I wasn't thinking about my back or being paralyzed. I was simply stuck. I was facing a patch of terrain that registered subconsciously as DANGER, and the *feeling of the trauma* overwhelmed me. Isn't it interesting how past trauma can stop you dead in your tracks and you don't even know why?

But I had a decision to make—call the helicopter or keep going.

So, I leaned upon my standard technique for when I am really scared of something I have to do. *Stop thinking about the big, scary picture and why it scares you. Start from where you are standing. Or in this case, crawling. Just take one more breath, take one more step. Repeat until your brain feels like you are out of harm's way.*

It only took about four steps. Then I was OK.

Weak and weird

5.7

When your spine does not hold you up well, it costs you a lot of energy points in the game.

My physical self-image settled in very early, and a very deep groove of my programming formed simply as: *I am awkward and weak.*

This story was supported by the fact that little patty was always the weakest and slowest and least athletic kid in her class. Then she was told by the scary doctor to be afraid to move or she could paralyze herself. So she stayed afraid to move.

The result of all that was that I scored a doctor's note to get me out of gym class for the rest of time and didn't exercise my body for more than 20 years. So adult Patty was weak too.

I needed to preserve my energy points with great care because everything made me tired. Especially things that involved standing. So, my physical weakness started impacting my executive career—which regularly required standing.

After speaking on a stage for an hour, I would be thinking, *I'm going to collapse if I don't sit down.* When people from the audience would immediately swarm me to ask me questions, I wanted to kill them. *How can you not let me sit down after all that?* I actually started asking my assistant to place a barstool near the stage exit so I could sit to answer questions at eye level because I simply couldn't stand anymore. The stool may have been weird, but it helped.

I spent a lot of my time at work being exhausted. As usual, I just gutted my way through it, thinking I had no choice.

But the mental and physical demands of my job just kept getting bigger. I was often afraid that I would fail at my career because I was just too physically weak.

It was becoming clear that I needed some kind of strategy to deal with my physical limitations—to either gain more energy points faster or lose fewer to begin with.

The mountain

5.8

One day, I was riding a bicycle up Trail Ridge Road in Colorado with Jack. We were heading up to 12,183 feet of altitude. (Given my story so far, this might seem surprising to you. It was surprising to me too.)

The computer on my bike measured my speed at 4.0mph—a snail's pace on a bike. When the air is thin at altitude, your body has less strength and ability to function. But I thought, *I'm about to fall over, either from a lack of forward momentum or from embarrassment. Mosquitos are just landing on me, absent any registerable wind speed to blow them off—tiny, winged hecklers, just sitting on my arms, mocking me.*

Let me try to speed up a bit. I turned the pedals a micron faster and my computer said 4.2mph. In a second, my heart rate spiked, I began to black out, and my legs and arms started shaking. *OK. 4.0mph it is.*

Jack is an intrepid outdoorsman and athlete. After we started biking together on our weekend sightseeing tours, he decided he was going to turn me into a proper cyclist. I had no idea what I was getting myself into. I was hoping we would do some more relaxed strolls on our bikes, culminating in coffee and a pastry. Instead, after a three-hour (felt like twenty-hour) climb in the mountains, I would find myself lying on the side of the road in exhaustion.

"You need to eat," he said.

"I can't do it," I said, staring at one of those old-fashioned power bars that had the consistency of bathtub caulk. I think choking those things down was more physically demanding than the ride itself.

I might have just slid into being a busy, unhealthy executive forever after, if it were not for Jack. He believed I could do more, and he seemed to know how important physical challenge was for my life—even though I didn't. So he always presented me with new, fresh tortures. And being a good student, I always followed him up all the hills. And in doing so, I got stronger and stronger, both physically and mentally—which turned out to be vital to managing my energy as my career got bigger and harder.

In another life-expanding area, Jack also taught me how to blow my nose without a tissue by pressing on one nostril and being very decisive about it so the snot comes out with enough velocity that it doesn't stick to your face. (My mom could not have been more horrified when I proudly told her of my new skill.)

And he also made me pee in ditches. Once, we were in the middle of a multi-hour ride when I needed to stop. He found a ditch on the side of a small highway. "Go down there, the cars won't see you."

One of the great injustices in the world is that men can pee easily with their clothes on, in a nonchalant standing position, with their backs to the world passing by. For a woman, there is nothing nonchalant about it. You need to lower your pants all the way to your ankles and squat so you don't pee on bike pants or your legs or your feet.

After I had picked my way carefully through the tall grass to the bottom of the ditch, I looked around to see what the traffic above was doing, trying to confirm that no one could see me. I pulled my bike shorts down, and as I lowered my butt toward the ground, suddenly, an Armageddon of 8 million giant grasshoppers erupted all around me. *OMG, they are jumping into my hair . . . and my shorts!* I ran up to the highway screaming, my shorts still down around my ankles until I could check that they were free of intruders, waving my arms in a frenzied dance to get them out of my hair.

We found a different ditch.

I finished the ride.

Jack and me during one of our rides in the mountains of Colorado

I never expected any of my achievements to come in the form of physical challenges. I had disqualified myself from such things.

In fact, I had broken my number one rule to never be the one to disqualify myself. I never broke this rule at work, but in my personal life, I had disqualified myself from being a physically capable person, without a second thought, for decades.

But thanks to my dear, benevolent tormenter, Jack, who believed in me, I dragged myself up mountain after mountain, and on 100-mile rides, and on climbs so steep I feared I would tip over backwards. Talk about making the world bigger for me. Those Colorado mountains are BIG. The scenery was inspiring even when my performance was not. Jack describes me as slow, stubborn, and patient. The accomplishment counted. No matter how painfully slow I climbed, I got the gold star.

A New Self-Image

The result of all this biking was that Jack gave me a gift that changed the course of my life at the most fundamental level. His steadily increasing challenges pushed me to change my self-image from weak to strong—stronger than average, even—and to believe that I was physically capable, despite my catastrophe of a spine. I was able to totally reprogram my internal story. This was the most important makeover of my life.

And with this new programming, I decided to explore what else I could do to become even stronger. I still had my crooked spine to deal with, but I decided I would no longer disqualify myself based on that. I would let a doctor disqualify me if they saw fit, but I would not disqualify myself anymore.

In my forties, I found a doctor I really trusted, and he told me that crooked spines age badly—meaning degeneration and fractures and pain. That put the fear of God in me. *I might not be paralyzed, but I could still become immobile and in pain as time went on.* But he also told me that all spines have curves that allow them to take impact, and my unique curves would adapt to athletic exercise and absorb impact in their own way. He gave me the green light to get fit with very few limitations.

So, in my own mind, I decided that in addition to biking, I would pursue a fitness strategy to create a sort of exoskeleton of muscles. If my bent nail of a spine wasn't going to hold me up in my old age, my muscles would take over. And my bones would stay strong too. I would counteract any degeneration with fitness. Or, to be more accurate, super-student Patty would be in charge of my fitness.

To achieve this goal, I began to work out with a personal trainer. Over the years, personal trainers have pushed me farther and farther. Now, in my 50s, I am an athlete. I am running and jumping and doing push-ups and pull-ups and lifting heavy things repeatedly.

I work out every day because I feel I have no choice. Staying fit was a game changer for me in every part of my life—especially in my work. Now, after an hour on the stage, I welcome audience members and their questions and conversations—and I do it on my feet! I can stand all day.

So, as it turns out, I—the slow, weak, and awkward one—am physically quite capable. I never saw *that* one coming. I am an order of magnitude stronger and fitter than I was in my 20s. I hiked 80 miles in the Alps, for God's sake!

Talk About Adding Energy Points!

Getting fit has done more for my energy, mental well-being, and confidence in my ability to keep swimming upstream than anything else I have ever done.

I owe a great debt to Jack for his belief in me.

But truth be told, as important and motivating as fitness is for me, and as much as I am committed to working on it every day because I know my life depends upon it, my favorite activity is still to lie down. I *love* to lie down. Sometimes I feel that I am genetically related to a sofa.

But I stay fit with that same little-patty, super-student diligence I have had since I was four—except for the days when all of that highfalutin diligence goes out the window.

The sofa and a bag of chips

5.9

It's a Saturday. I have failed the morning.

The alarm went off at 6:00am. I had intended to organize some stuff and run some errands, then dig into some work for a client. Instead, I hit the snooze button repeatedly until I finally dragged myself out of bed at 9:15. That's 3 hours and 15 minutes of hitting the snooze button.

I'm fuzzy as to what happened after that, but now it is somehow 11:45am, and I am on the sofa and I can't get up. And I am racked with guilt because I have so much stuff to do; I shouldn't just be lying here on the sofa.

My internal critic jumps on this:

IF YOU WERE AS COMPETENT AS YOU PRETEND TO BE, YOU WOULD BE MAKING PROGRESS TODAY. YOU SHOULD BE ASHAMED. YOU ARE SO LAZY. YOU SUCK.

All I can do is make more coffee and keep watching TV. I am wearing my crappiest sweat clothes. Hours go by. Another 236 brides have Said Yes to their Dress. Now it's 5:00pm and I am eating, with embarrassing gusto, something from the fluorescent-orange food group.

Levels of Sofa Acceptance

For a long time, these sofa crashes brought on not only guilt but an identity crisis. Because when I am productive on a project, I'm like a wood chipper. So, bad days were like—if I am not being productive, who *am* I even?

I would feel bad, and then I would feel bad about feeling bad.

I was embarrassed to tell people, "I don't feel well today." I would try and hide it from everyone in the world—except I couldn't fool Mom. If Mom called, I'd answer the phone:

"Hello."

"You don't feel good today."

Mom could tell in two syllables when I wasn't OK. And she always cared when my life felt difficult. She would tell me, "Patty, don't worry about it. I promise this will pass. You will be fine." I never believed her.

I also told my friend Melissa how embarrassed I was about these bad days. She said, "You are being ridiculous. You are a high-performance machine. A race car can't keep running at full capacity all the time without occasionally going into the shop for maintenance. You need the downtime. You need the Doritos. Not only shouldn't you feel guilty about it; you should schedule it."

After many years of shame about my crashes, I finally admitted that Mom and Melissa were right. It was a monumental shift for me to accept that it's OK to feel bad sometimes—and it doesn't mean I'm failing.

I had to accept that these fairly regular debilitating crashes, when I would feel unfocused and lazy and ill, were, for me, simply part of being a highly productive person. I had to admit that my super-productivity can't happen without my sofa.

I learned to tell myself at those moments, "The most important thing you can do today to be productive—truly, *THE MOST IMPORTANT THING YOU CAN DO TODAY TO BE PRODUCTIVE*—is to lie on the sofa and watch 47 episodes of *What Not to Wear*."

(Quick aside: I love me a makeover. You are still *you*, but you get help, and the help really helps—the story of my life. And this show even teaches people how to successfully shop for clothes, a task for which I still have PTSD.)

There was a somewhat tricky secret passageway I have needed to reluctantly come to accept:

Sometimes resilience really does look like lying on the sofa in the fetal position.

I now accept that resilience is not about always being strong or doing everything right so you don't get damaged in the first place. The world hurts everybody. Resilience is about being able to recover and add back energy points when you crash and your life force drops below the required level to continue the game.

When my nervous system gets overwhelmed, the only way I can recover is to be by myself and do nothing. With this awareness, though it took many years, I can now move more quickly through the phases of denial. I have even graduated from mere acceptance of these bad days to something more like *radical acceptance*—I have actually learned not just to enjoy these days, but to savor them.

Sometimes, instead of cooking dinner, I'll eat Doritos and drink bourbon. And I do it not just without guilt but with pleasure. Thus I have achieved an even more advanced level than radical acceptance, which I call *hedonistic acceptance*.

And here's a surprising plot twist for an overachiever: Without the guilt, recovery is way more effective. *Wait . . . am I now overachieving on resting?*

It's funny—no matter how much I worry that I might want to revel too long on the sofa in the hedonism stage, and that I'll descend into overindulgent madness and nacho cheese dust, I don't actually end up spending many days at a time there. Usually it takes just a day or two of being horizontal, and then I am renewed. I regain my energy and enthusiasm and can get on with it. Life force restored. Energy points back in the account.

It's kind of like doing a cleanse—but with chips and bourbon.

Straight and strong

5.10

The same doctor who cleared me to exercise like an athlete, once did the geometry on my X-rays and told me that if my spine were straight,

I'd be 4.5 inches taller. Wow—4.5 inches taller! What would that be like?

If I could be granted any experience for one day, I would choose to live in the body of a strong, athletic man in his prime. The first thing that implies to me: a straight spine. I think the world would look and feel totally different from a wondrous 4.5 inches up—not to mention seeing things straight on, with no twist in my alignment.

I could, for that day, revel in the extraordinary feeling of equal weight in both of my feet. I would finally be able to achieve the elusive yoga corpse pose (lying on the floor flat on your back with your legs straight, which for me might as well be a Cirque du Soleil maneuver). I would embrace and delight in the earth's gravity with a sense of stability and certainty in my core that I can't even conceive of. I would be beyond fascinated to experience that.

But to have a straight spine *and* be as strong as an athletic man—now, that would be truly exhilarating.

Since I am always searching for ways to improve my strength and build my energy reserves, it follows that my chosen experience would be about strength. But why an athletic man and not an athletic woman? Men tell me how, growing up, there came a day when they realized they could pick up the equivalent of their body weight and throw it across the room. I am in awe of that thought. I really am kind of obsessed with (and jealous about) what having that kind of strength would feel like.

If I got to live as a man for a day, sure, the gender and sex aspects would be interesting—but in reality, I think I would just spend the whole day knocking on people's doors and saying, "Can I pick up your refrigerator?"

I have no curiosity in my body at all to know what it feels like to have a baby, but I do want to pick up a man and throw him across the room.

Vacation time

5.11

While it's vital that I know how to recover my energy when it is spent, it's not enough to simply get back to neutral when I am down. I need to refuel my *enthusiasm* so I can have extra energy points in reserve for those moments when life gets hard by surprise.

That's where vacations come in.

Every year for many years, I went to the same remote island in the Bahamas for a week of scuba diving.

In addition to the beauty and amazement that scuba diving offers, I think another reason why I enjoy it so much is because it's the only time in my life, while floating weightless, my body totally supported by the water, that I am absolutely, 100 percent subconsciously free of the fear of falling and paralyzing myself—and it's also 100 percent free of small talk.

On vacation, people often ask me, "What do you do for work, Patty?"

My answer is consistent: "I don't talk about work while I'm on vacation."

"But can't you just tell me what you do?"

"I don't mean to be rude, but I don't talk about work while I'm on vacation." They still think I am rude, but I don't care.

I am desperate for this vacation. I get so little vacation time, and it's precious. This is my opportunity to rebuild my life force. I do not want to talk about work, because then work takes up space in my vacation. If I say anything, you will start asking me questions, and it will take up even more space, not just now but throughout the week whenever you have new questions for me. Each question will get me thinking about my work, and that will drain energy points.

To gain even more energy points, my vacation strategy also included making it clear that I would be unavailable. Before I left, I told everyone: "You can reach me if there is an emergency, but it's kind of tough to connect. Here is the number for the main office in the US. They can contact the island by fax. Then I can try to call you back between 6:00 and 9:00pm Eastern Time. To call, I need to walk half a mile to the boat dock, where there is a phone booth with no door, that has an old-fashioned kitchen wall phone nailed to a board. To make the call, I pick up the phone, and sometimes an international operator will answer. There is no schedule for when operators are actually there, so it might take a couple of days for me to connect. And the whole endeavor involves getting eaten alive by mosquitos."

This story about the old phone at the dock—which was true—cut off communication for a week. Over time, the technology evolved. But even after the island got a brand-new cell tower and full high-speed internet capability, I never changed my story about the mosquito-ravaged phone booth. My vacation time was protected.

By the way, this communication lapse was also good for my team. By covering for me, they grew in their roles. My boss got to know the high performers I left in charge. A great delegating strategy is to simply be unavailable sometimes.

People ask me, "Weren't you afraid your boss would think you were not valuable and your people could replace you?"

"No. That's the whole point. If your people can replace you, that means you are ready to be promoted. And you become known for building a high-performing team. If no one can replace you, you're seen as a weaker leader, and you are stuck."

Keeping yourself too important to go on vacation is not a winning strategy for you, your team, or your company. And my unavailability while on vacation also gave everyone on my team permission to be unavailable on their own vacations when it was their turn.

After more than ten years of visiting this same island, I was well into my executive career when one of the dive masters and I were sitting in the shallows at a glorious white sand beach, gazing at the gorgeous expanse of Caribbean ocean that shimmered like opals. The energy points were absorbing into me with every breath as I ran my fingers through the silky sand.

He said, "I know you don't like to talk about work, but can I ask—Do you actually work? Do you have a career?"

I laughed. "Yes, and yes."

"Did you go to college?"

"Yes."

"What did you study?"

"Electronic engineering."

His face changed into someone I didn't know. And then he said in disbelief, "But that must mean . . . that must mean . . . that you're *smart*."

Well then! I have been so good at being on vacation that someone who has observed me on vacation for *ten years* was staggered to discover that I was smart! I call that a vacationing success. The energy points flooded the account with bells and flashing lights like a win on an old-fashioned pinball machine. This is the stuff of joy and resilience.

"To marvel"

5.12

I was walking with a group of friends in the Lake District in England, where the official pastime is, in fact, walking. There are dedicated walking paths everywhere, even across private property.

The walking guidebooks in the Lake District are a thing to behold in themselves with their descriptive detail. A friend was reading aloud: "Walk along the iron fence to your left for about 35 yards until you come to a wooden shed. Then look to your right and find a small pebble path. Take it and walk around the left edge of a large black rock with a point on top. Walk straight for 50 steps, then stop, look to your left, and marvel at the view."

. . . *47, 48, 49, 50* . . . BAM! Right on cue, an incredible panorama popped into view.

I had never seen the word *marvel* used as a verb in the imperative tone before, but I decided that I loved it. "To marvel." Do it, now. "I command you to marvel."

One summer evening in Rome, I was walking down the street, talking with a colleague. I was so focused on the business that I was not paying attention to the beauty around me.

He stopped me and said, "Patty, turn around."

We were walking away from the Piazza di Spagna (the Spanish Steps), one of the most iconic marble staircases in the world. Normally, the steps are jammed with tourists sitting and taking in the day and the beauty of Rome. I'd seen this before, and I was a little annoyed at the interruption of an important business conversation. But he said again, "Turn around," and gently guided me by the shoulder to do so.

When I turned, what I saw was the enormous expanse of white marble steps glowing in the sunshine. That in itself was extraordinary, because at that moment, the steps were glowing because they were completely empty of people—except for one. A supermodel was standing right in the middle of the gigantic steps, a vision in a red gown with long, flowing silky sleeves and a sort of cape that floated and danced in the breeze. She twirled around while a live orchestra hit a crescendo to initiate a fashion show.

The image of this supermodel in red, who seemed like she was floating over the glowing marble steps of the Piazza di Spagna spinning around to the music, is forever burned into my soul. The amount of sheer beauty in that moment overwhelmed little patty and stopped me dead in my tracks.

For someone always on the search for beauty in the world, this was truly a magnificent moment—one not to be missed. And I would have missed it entirely if my colleague had not demanded that I turn around and marvel.

My friend Bruce Claypool, a nature photographer, always says, "If you are not walking in beauty, it's because you are not paying attention." I do my best to keep his words at the front of my mind, but I know that I can miss a lot.

As a busy, overachieving introvert, it's just too easy for me to get too in my head and too focused on what I am trying to achieve. On some days, finding meaning in life doesn't seem to matter as much as getting to the grocery store. On other days, I languish in an existential crisis and wonder why I do anything. For all these reasons, I can forget to look up at all. I can forget to marvel.

How many times in my life have I not turned around? How many times have I missed the supermodel? How many amazing moments was I too busy or grumpy to notice?

If I want to drive my life forward, if I want to be creative, if I want to stay well, if I want to help others, if I want to succeed professionally, I need to intentionally maintain my life force. And to do that I need to honor little patty's quest for beauty and amazement, which is the main thing that keeps my enthusiasm high and the energy points flowing in.

So, I need to remind myself every day to pay attention . . .

Patty—stop.

Turn around. Look.

Marvel.

Now.

Marvel right now.

Part 6

Humanity at Work

"Be kind whenever possible. It is always possible."

—The Dalai Lama

"Today I shall behave as if this is the day I will be remembered."

—Dr. Seuss

The question

6.1

"**A**s your manager, I am going to worry about what matters to you. So, when I worry about you, what should I worry about?"

That was THE QUESTION.

I had formed this particular question out of Jim's "Talk to everyone and you'll know what to do" advice.

As a leader, I can't even measure the value of this question.

Leaders have to ask all kinds of questions about schedules and budgets and timelines and revenue. But those questions have nothing to do with leadership.

When I would ask *this* question, I would get the most amazing answers—weirdly surprising and specific things people cared deeply about, things I never would have guessed in a million years if I hadn't asked. Grown men would sometimes cry and tell me that in their entire career, no one at work had ever asked them what they cared about before.

No line of conversation was more important to my growth as a leader than this question—because it taught me that *I needed to be a leader for each person individually.*

So, I loved asking THE QUESTION of the people who worked for me because it helped them show me their internal maps. Then I could connect with them in a way that made them feel important and really seen.

I had settled into my big job leading the billion-dollar software business and was feeling good about it. And it was that time of the year when I was asking everyone on my team THE QUESTION.

But there was this one guy who I really didn't want to ask, because I knew he was going to come at me hard. He was a difficult guy. I already knew he wanted a bigger title, more stock options, and more money, as he was recently quite scary when demanding those things from me.

As I waited for him to arrive, I played it out in my mind. *When I tell him I can't give him what wants, he's going to say, "You are clueless about what I do here. You don't appreciate me. You are incompetent. I should have your job."*

I really, really didn't want to open myself up to the attack. THE QUESTION will offer no magic with him. He is one of those men who is loud and aggressive and makes me feel small—like it's weak to be a woman. He will not be open to the discussion. *I'm just going to get my head ripped off. I want to skip this conversation with him.*

He walked into my office in his extra-tall way and unbuttoned his suit jacket, but he didn't take it off, though it felt to me like he was rolling up his sleeves for a fight. He sat down frustrated, letting me know I was already wasting his time.

I thought, *Dammit. I need to be fair. I am asking THE QUESTION of everyone right now, so I need to ask him too.*

So, I said reluctantly, "It's that time of year when I want to find out what is on everyone's mind and what your thoughts are for the coming year."

I took a breath . . .

"As your manager, I worry about what matters to you. So, here's my question for you. When I worry about you, what should I worry about?"

I braced myself and waited . . .

At that moment, his normal aggressive body language shifted. It was softer somehow. He didn't speak.

I was surprised, but I waited . . .

He took a deep breath.

I waited some more . . .

Then he said in a thoughtful tone I had never heard from him before, "What is on my mind right now is that my father is dying. And he is in Boston. And I am in California. And I am working on this critical project, so I can't travel. I'm afraid I am never going to see my father again."

Then he was quiet.

I said to him, "I want you to buy an airplane ticket right now. Go to Boston tonight. I will find someone to cover for you on this project, and if there are any hiccups, I will have your back. There are phones and computers in Boston. Whenever you are ready, check in and we'll figure out what's next. But right now, just go be with your father."

I would like to think that this time with his father in Boston served them both, but I never got any kind of update from him. A few weeks later, paperwork came through for a permanent transfer to Boston for him. I signed off on it and refilled his role in California.

To this day, I think about how close I was to not asking him THE QUESTION because I was worried about my own comfort. But if I had made that choice, a fellow human would never have seen his father again because of me.

Humanity matters.

When I first started my executive career, my instincts were screaming a truth at me that even little patty knew on some level when she was wanting so much for people to like her back: *Why can't we just be nice to each other?*

But kindness was not what I was seeing around me in the executive ranks.

I seemed to be the only one who thought it was important to be kind to the people in my team. Everyone else was just "doing business" without much regard for humanity.

It puzzled me.

As I was trying to figure out what type of executive I was going to be, I tried very hard to keep focused on what felt like an untested theory of leading with humanity, kindness, and respect.

But I would also find that my own humanity would come under pressure, because I was just not prepared for the scale of what was expected of me. The level of the clients I needed to show up for as "the one in charge" staggered me. They were sometimes 30 years older than me and running multibillion-dollar global organizations. The product lines and the budgets and the revenue and the associated business risks under my control got bigger and bigger too.

Then add to that all the press conferences, the big stage presentations, and the media appearances. I was also put in charge of maneuvering the business through complicated corporate partnerships and mergers and deals. All of it suddenly felt gigantic and super high-stakes. And all these big responsibilities were about to fling me across the globe in a much bigger way than I could have ever imagined . . .

The milk around the corner

6.2

One morning during a business trip to Australia, I descended the steps of the Sydney Opera House and walked into a very grand and very luscious and green park across the street, when a dozen giant exotic birds that looked kind of like white parrots suddenly engulfed me. (I have come to learn that they were sulphur-crested cockatoos.) Then they just started sitting on me. I was nose to nose with at least four of them on my left arm. Little patty was flabbergasted, thinking of the small, brown birds in her small, brown world.

As my career advanced, I had the opportunity to encounter countless foreign wonders that delighted the aggressively curious mind of little patty.

Because of my work, I have strolled through amazing architecture in Prague and been stuck in apocalyptic traffic in São Paulo. (Did you know São Paulo is the city with the most helicopters in the world because it also has the worst traffic in the world?)

I can physically recall the giddy, chaotic jolts that ran through my body when I was on a dogsled in Canada as the dogs ran and the sled bounced and teetered along the snowy path. And speaking of winter, I remember how the people in Finland complained that it wasn't a snowy enough winter when I was there. I was thinking, *Man, you people are hardy. Why would you want winter to be worse?* Then they explained that with more snow, it's less dark during the very long nights.

And when I was dressed in a sari in India, ready to be photographed at a press conference for the front page of *The Hindu Business Line*—I remember my absolute terror when I stood up and felt the shocking slice of cold air that hit my bare left side, and I thought, *Oh my God, my clothes are falling off in front of the entire world.*

I so am grateful to my work for actually making me go places. Big, faraway places. Lots of places. Because as much as I longed for my life to be exotic and amazing, travel often traumatized me. Travel is one of those normal things I watch most people do with ease but I struggle with. My fear of getting lost pairs tragically with the fact that I am always actually getting lost, so the big wide world in general is not an easy place for me. I am embarrassed by my fears and my lack of basic navigation abilities. Whether on a nature trail in Kenya or in a crowded train station in Stuttgart, if I am alone on unfamiliar turf, I am a scared bunny rabbit indeed.

When I am trying to find my way in a new place, I am instantly thrown back to kindergarten, where every day, one of us needed to go around the corner inside our tiny schoolhouse, fill the little wheelbarrow with cartons of milk, and bring it back to the class for snack time.

I lived in absolute terror of it being my turn. I'd shudder with alarm each day as one of the kids disappeared around the corner, frightened that they might never come back, dreading the day when it would be my turn to be sent into the abyss. *I've never been around the corner. Will it be dark? Will it be confusing? Will I get lost? Will I be able to find the milk? If I find the milk, will I be able to find my way back? What will happen to me if I can't find my way back? Will I be lost in the inescapable nothingness around the corner forever?*

For me, travel to any unfamiliar place still feels like being afraid to go around the corner to get the milk.

But the thing about pursuing an executive career is that you have to go places. You have to find your way in the world. It is perpetually your turn to get the milk. And you will get lost sometimes.

Exotic world, reluctant traveler

6.3

T he first time I was required go to China, I was to be the important, high-ranking executive in a summit with our biggest clients' important, high-ranking executives to let them know that "we think you are really important."

At this time, China was not on the world stage the way it is today. Very few Americans had ever gone to China or knew anything about it. We did not encounter China in the news—and there was still no internet.

This was one of my first international trips as a new executive. I could not stop thinking, *China seems like a very good place to get lost away from home forever.* I did not want to go to China.

My plane had landed late, and when I got to the airport in Beijing after a flight of approximately infinity hours, customs and immigration took almost two hours more. This was still in the days before mobile phones and flight tracking, so I had no way of contacting anyone to let them know I was late. When I nervously emerged in the exit lobby, I found an American man walking around like, "Hey, what's there to do in China? Where should I go? How do I get a ride someplace? Is there a hotel I can stay at?" Everyone ignored him. No one in the terminal even spoke English.

At that moment, I was so happy to not be him. I even felt a bit smug that I had a plan and he didn't. I had a driver waiting for me, and all I needed to do was find the sign with my name on it. But just watching this man traumatized me. I could not conceive of his situation. *How could he have no plan? How will he possibly survive?*

But when I turned the corner into the exit lobby, my "will I ever find the milk and will I ever see home again?" fears quickly spun up. There were 8 million drivers with 8 million signs. I'd never seen so many people in one place. I panicked. But once I calmed down a bit, I saw that less than 100 signs had the names printed in Western characters. When I finally found the characters that said "Patty Azzarello," I approached the driver, wanting to embrace him for saving my life. But the first thing he said to me was, "You're very late. I was only going to wait five more minutes and then leave."

I was aghast.

To me, just the thought of him leaving amounted to a near-death experience. I had *no other plan* and no way to communicate with anyone. I would have had no choice but to go back to the lobby and join forces with wandering, clueless guy.

I still wonder sometimes what ever happened to him. Gifted travelers always seem to make it work. But with my terrible travel skills, introversion, and social unease, I can only assume that he died, lost away from home forever.

Later that day, I was standing in Tiananmen Square with my local hosts. It was an incredible, almost baffling sight to see something so enormous and so wildly different from anything I had ever seen before. (It would be many years before the internet would give us a preview of where we were going before we got there.)

I was in a crowd of thousands of people, and every time I turned around, someone was tugging on my shoulder. At that time, a Westerner standing in Tiananmen Square was a rare novelty and viewed as a good luck symbol. The conversation with every person basically went the same way.

Them: "You are visiting from Australia, right?"

Me: "No, the US."

Them: "Where is the US?"

Me: "In North America."

Them: "Where is North America?"

I was shocked to realize that these people had never heard of North America. (They didn't have the internet either.)

It was staggering to me that in this country with a population of more than 1 billion people—all of whom seemed to be standing in Tiananmen Square at that moment—for these people, the entire universe that defined my life did not even exist. Finally, that small-town little girl had discovered how truly BIG the world was.

Of course, nowadays, China is a part of our lives, and there is no place hidden in the world, as even the most remote spots are overly selfied online. But in the 1990s, I felt like I had discovered another planet—and specifically, a world full of people who knew nothing of my planet. And I felt so embarrassed that if left to my own devices, without that trip to China, I would have spent the rest of my life never realizing how big the real world is compared to the entirety of the small universe locked within my own brain.

Since then, I have made many trips to Asia, and ultimately, I really enjoyed them. I fulfilled my role adequately as the visiting "highly esteemed executive," and my hosts always took very good care of me, greatly reducing my "what's around the corner?" anxiety. That is, except for the food. Because when you are a highly esteemed guest in Asia, you get served highly esteemed food—which is not noodles and rice.

This time it was hairy crabs.
They weren't kidding.

I was served a split-open duck head (with its brain and tongue), offered things that came to the table still alive, and taught to suck raw crab goo out of giant crab legs like a straw. Every part of travel was life-expanding—and little patty keeps reminding me how important it is to keep learning and to get amazed by new things, and how most of the time it's uncomfortable.

Thankfully, in my executive roles, my international work travel often included business class tickets, in-flight champagne, and, most importantly, a person waiting with a sign with my name on it who would take me exactly where I needed to go. At every step of the trip, I'd be handed off to another member of my team, who would take me to my next hotel, meal, press event, or executive meeting until I was escorted back to the airport for my next curated stop.

Thanks to my guides, I got to see the world, but I never had to rely on myself to strap on a backpack and find my own way in another country. So I didn't die.

Except there was one time it felt like I got pretty close . . .

Lost away from home forever

6.4

It was December 2001, just months after 9/11, a time when traveling as an American felt more uncertain than ever. I had looked up Malaysia, Kuala Lumpur, and saw that it was considered safe for Americans. So, I agreed to be the executive sponsor of a regional partner conference that my team in Asia was hosting there.

After the 12-million-hour flight to get there, I was sitting at the desk in my hotel room casually paging through the book of information and services.

In the book was a map. *OK, let me see more about where I am. There's Malaysia. Here's Kuala Lumpur, with the famous towers . . . but wait. The You Are Here dot is on a different island entirely . . . on Borneo. Borneo? Is this the wrong book?* I started to read the captions. *Wait—I really am on Borneo. How am I on Borneo?*

Reading the map, I learned that Malaysia is a country that is spread across 878 islands, one of which is Borneo. The conference had moved to Kota Kinabalu—on Borneo. And since my travel plans were made for me, and everything was so unfamiliar to me, and I am such a clueless traveler, I hadn't noticed the change ahead of time.

I did a new travel safety check . . . at that time, so soon after 9/11, Borneo was a no-go, high-danger zone for Americans.

Travel is, for me, always both an amazing, expansive experience and an exercise in trying to convince my nervous system that I am not going to die from it.

I set my mai tai down on the map and looked out the window as I considered my situation. A toucan landed on my balcony. A friggin' toucan! Twenty small, brown birds from my hometown could have fit in its multicolor beak. I wanted amazing, and here it was. But I was on Borneo, and I was American, and I was getting nervous.

My staff took me out to a local dinner that first night, and they told me, "Everyone will assume you are Australian. That's important. If you need anything, whisper it in someone's ear. Don't let anyone hear you speaking with an American accent. It will be dangerous for you. But don't worry—you'll be OK as long as you stay with us and no one knows you are an American."

I shouldn't be here kept throbbing in my whole being.

I would have been fine if I had just stayed at the resort, but due to a scheduling hiccup, I had been sent there a full day early. And because I was cranky about having to waste a whole day just sitting in the hotel, my staff had arranged a scuba diving tour for me. Well played.

That morning, I went to the lobby, expecting to meet up with all the other people on the scuba diving tour, thinking I would feel safe enough going outside the resort grounds in a group. But it turned out that I was the only one. I reluctantly got in the hotel van with a driver (and no mobile phone). I had no idea where we were going. And then we drove and drove—for almost two hours.

My fear began to bubble up. *My team would not send me out to be murdered. And I am in the hotel van. But at some point the driver will drop me off and go away, and I will be on my own in Borneo, while being American, which my local team distinctly informed me when we left the hotel last night would be dangerous. Will this be the place I die away from home forever?*

As various scenarios involving my demise played out in my head, we stopped in a deserted, grassy area enclosed with a chain-link fence, and then we walked between two garbage dumpsters and squeezed through a hole in the fence. I could see water in the background and a small shed in the distance. *This is beginning to feel like the part of the movie where it goes bad . . .*

The driver said, "I'll be back later." Then he disappeared between the dumpsters before I could decide whether I should stay there or catch up with him and ask him to take me another two hours back to the hotel without doing the dive tour. I just stood there, frozen. *Will he really come back? Will it matter? Will I even be alive at the end of the day?*

Miraculously, as I walked toward the shed, I found that it was a dive shop. I was hoping I could join a sizable dive group so I could keep a low profile, but it turned out I was the only diver on this tour. My strategy to blend into a group was missing the "group."

We set off—a boat captain, a divemaster, and me—not on a dive boat but in a small motor boat. Very little English was available. As we pulled away from the dock heading out into the open ocean, I thought, *No one is ever going to see me again.*

After a while, the boat stopped. I looked around—wall-to-wall ocean horizon in every direction. No land in sight. The divemaster started putting on his gear, and he pointed to my gear, which I interpreted to mean, "Get ready for the dive." Or the murder.

When we got into the water, all we could see was sand, for about 20 minutes. *Why are we diving here? There is nothing here to see. Is he going to stab me with his knife and leave me here as shark food?*

I knew it . . . no one will ever see me again. My fear continued to simmer.

Eventually, he started swimming away from me with speed and intention. Not willing to be abandoned, I followed. We finally got to a reef where I saw corals and fish and eels and anemones. I felt a sense of relief, daring to hope this was actually a dive excursion and not a death/abandonment scenario.

But then, after this first dive, we got back on the boat and he said, "What are your lunch plans?"

I wasn't sure how to answer this. I responded, "I don't have any lunch plans. I thought lunch would be included in this tour."

He said, "No. We need to eat lunch, and you can't stay on the boat while we do."

Still seeing nothing but ocean in every direction, I thought, *You don't have to feed me, but what do you mean I can't stay on the boat? Do I need to tread water while you eat your lunch?*

They ended up taking me to the tip of a really long dock that disappeared into a cluster of trees on a very tiny island.

"Get out here."

Uh, OK. "When will you be back?" was a rhetorical question I asked, out loud, to myself, as the boat sped away. My fear of being lost away from home forever had never taken such a literal turn. They say that disaster is often a result of several bad decisions that accumulate, and boy, was I racking them up. I walked a slow death march along the bleak, never-ending dock and headed toward the trees.

I entered the trees and, lo and behold, there actually was a place serving lunch on this tiny spit of land in the middle of the ocean. After eating, I raced back to the end of the dock. I was not going to delay and run the risk of them coming back and not finding me . . . then leaving me there forever.

I sat on the end of the dock with my feet dangling.

No one will ever see me again.

About thirty minutes later, the tiny boat appeared in the distance and grew larger. *They are coming back!*

We did another dive. On an even more luscious reef with colorful soft corals, absolutely teeming with every color and size of fish imaginable.

Then, suddenly, in an instant, there were no fish. Nature's subtle signs of danger . . . Why did all the fish disappear? Did the divemaster summon his ninjas to come and kill me? Here it is—the moment I die. I did a 360 turn and laughed, coughing bubbles. I saw that not a murder squad but a lovely, large barracuda was what made all the other fish disappear in a snap.

OK. That was not the moment.

Then we swam a little further up the reef and the divemaster showed me how I could place my hand into an anemone and the clown fish would sit in my hand. If I was going to die before returning to my hotel room, this final dive was a nice consolation prize.

We finished the dive and headed back.

Upon our return to the dive shop, they said, "Wait for your driver over there. It will be more comfortable for you." They were pointing to some bushes. I looked confused, not for the first time this day. So they walked me to the entry of a path I couldn't see before. As I picked my way through the bushes and rounded the corner, the view that unfolded before me took my breath away. I saw a grand and glimmering swimming pool with people sliding down waterfalls and perky waiters bringing guests colorful cocktails. A 5-star resort brimming with delight.

If my driver had walked me this way to the dive shop this morning instead of across the abandoned garbage lot and through the hole in the chain-link fence, I could have spent a relaxed day of fully enjoying this diving instead of being worried that I was going to die, lost away from home forever.

"You're too serious"

6.5

After the conference and another 12-million-hour flight back, I thought about how every return from a big, chaotic, international trip leaves me feeling like I've had a near-death experience—even the ones that didn't offer the fear of actual death like this one did. Every time, I am totally wiped out.

But, as ever, there was no time to recover or process what had happened to me. It was just another Monday, and I was suddenly back at the office, feeling overwhelmed and exhausted. And it was at the end of this very long Monday when my last meeting was a one-on-one with my boss. I was so ready to make my escape and go home to collapse when he abruptly said to me, "You are always so serious."

As we continued talking, he implied that he was concerned that because of my dull demeanor, the other key executives would not find me credible for bigger roles. "They feel like they can relate to your peers (the men) much better, because you seem so serious and closed off. Come to think of it, I don't know anything personal about you."

OMG. How much more do I have to give to earn respect here? I don't want to share my personal life at work. It feels invasive. Will you really take me more seriously if I let you into my family and my soul? What do you want from me?

I was tired, and that conversation had made me grumpy. I walked out of the building into the parking lot, lugging my engine block of briefcase, and wobbling over the uneven pavement in my high heels. I was reminded of an email I'd recently gotten from a guy I worked with in my early 20s that said, "You were always so serious back then."

The "back then" he was referring to was when they told me to wear a short skirt to perform demos, when multiple men from the company and our clients tried to date and/or grope me while I was just trying to do my job, when the engineers and the sales management excluded me from their conversations, and when my boss started kissing me at an offsite meeting.

I don't think being less serious would have helped me "back then."

This is the bizarre course a woman building an executive career needs to navigate. When you are a young woman in the workplace, it's assumed you have been plucked from the "stupid rat" box by default—no one at work takes you seriously. They treat you like a little girl. Your only chance to survive at all is to act overly serious. Then it becomes a habit.

Am I really being told that now, as a female *executive*, if I'm seen as too formal, too prepared, too businesslike, too, well . . . serious, other executives actually *won't* take me seriously?

As I got into my car and nudged my way into the traffic jam between my office and my home, I thought about how many times I had heard this "you're too serious" refrain. I always dismissed it. Because whatever I was doing was clearly working for me. I was the youngest among all of the big shots and all of my peers and all of my teams in every room, and I was good at my job.

The problem of being too serious was hard to get my mind around. I had made good progress being less formal with my teams, but with executives, I was still pretty guarded.

But my boss's comments nagged at me. Was my tidy and efficient work demeanor really coming across as "closed off"? And was that really such a problem?

What is wrong with being competent and efficient?

As I waited four cycles for the light to change in the Silicon Valley rush hour, I began to consider that while "competent and efficient" are generally considered good things, I had been using them defensively—a habit I had built up to be taken seriously. And now I had to admit that defensiveness was not really helping me on my quest to achieve ease and grace.

I am going to need to figure this out.

And I will have an eternity to do so in this traffic.

Big shot

6.6

As Duane Zitzner talked, I listened intently.

Duane was the new chief of a very large part of the company and was speaking at an all-hands meeting. I was standing near the back of the room in the giant crowd.

As I was still getting my footing in my executive role and still committed to respecting humanity as a business leader, I was so inspired by Duane. He was so smart and real. I greatly admired his no-bullshit, plain-speaking straightforwardness.

I thought, *I would love to meet him, but he is so high up in the corporate hierarchy I'm not sure how to make that happen.*

So I kept listening. *Pay attention. Listening creates opportunities.* At one point, amidst the business comments, he said, "I enjoy living in California now—except that I miss good pizza."

There it was. I had my in.

Pizza.

Later that day, I sent him an email: "I really appreciated your talk. And by the way, I had the same disappointing pizza experience when I moved to

California from the East Coast. But I finally found a good pizza. Try Vito's Famous NY Pizza in Sunnyvale."

The next morning, I had an email from Duane. He had gone that very night, and he loved it!

I thought, *Ooh, now I have chance to make an ask.* I replied, "Glad you liked the pizza! Also, you said two things about partner management in your talk that I think could help me solve a big issue in my business. I was wondering, could I get twenty minutes on your calendar? I have three specific questions."

He said yes!

(A mini secret passageway: ***Be super specific when you make an ask. Don't make the person have to figure out how to help you or worry that your vague ask will be an unstructured time sink for them.***)

I walked into my first meeting with Duane in my normal uniform: dark suit, pumps, understated jewelry, 100-pound briefcase. He was sitting at a table wearing a no-frills dress shirt with no tie or suit jacket. I was a bit surprised. Because he was *so* high up in the company, I think I was expecting something more Armani, but there was nothing fancy or formal about him.

As I sat down, I braced myself to be made to feel small, like a pointless woman, like so many big executives before had made me feel. I had my guard up.

As my brain was seizing up trying to figure out how to start, he said, "Man, it's tough out there. I'm struggling. Are you struggling? Margin pressures are crazy. Are you seeing it too? The competition is relentless—sometimes it feels like they're going to steal my pants! Do you have any advice for me?"

I was stunned. *Wait—what's happening here? He is talking to me like a real person. He's such a big executive. And he is telling me that he doesn't have all the answers in his work . . . and he is actually interested in my thoughts.*

I just couldn't believe how open and normal he was being.

Duane was the first really big, out-of-my-league executive I had ever met in my work who talked to *me* like a person—like an equal, even.

But what happened next really caught me off guard.

Before I knew it, my real self just started bubbling over. I let him know what I was struggling with and asked his advice. I told him about mistakes I had made. We talked about pizza. We laughed.

And here's the crazy thing—I had never felt more confident and willing to share my real thoughts in a conversation with any executive. I felt so welcome and normal and relaxed in that conversation. It made me think, *If he can succeed at such a high level and not have to act like a big shot, neither do I—ever.*

It was such a gift that he'd shown me that possibility.

From that moment on, the idea of *not* acting powerful did not seem like a risky choice anymore. Duane's no-nonsense, respectful manner and how comfortable it made me feel was showing me a form of ease and grace that maybe I could achieve one day.

Listen like an introvert

6.7

My boss's comments about my being "too serious" and unrelatable made me think about being an introvert. *I will never be like those smooth, showy extroverts. Can an introvert even be a successful executive?*

I worried about this a lot.

But then I started thinking about how important it is to lean into your natural strengths. Introverts have natural strengths too. Not everyone needs to be smooth.

I thought, *Since I am always going to be an introvert, how can I embrace it instead of worrying about it?*

So what do introverts naturally do really well? We *listen*.

While we introverts shy away from random social interactions and the requisite small talk like vampires from daylight, we are naturally great listeners who love specific, important, rich conversations—we love to go deep. I've heard it said that having a friend who is an introvert is like having a free therapist. We live for a meaty one-on-one session.

I was happy with this idea of deep listening as a strategy because it was built on a long history of successful listening for me.

Deep listening got me into the right conversations as a 17-year-old intern. It got me into various important rooms throughout my career. It was how I got that angry team to stop fighting so we could all move forward. Listening allowed me to meet Duane. I had reaped many rewards with my magic question: "When I worry about you, what should I worry about?"

Listening would be my solution—well, at least part of my solution—to achieving ease and grace. I would listen like a therapist . . . which I call "Listen like an Introvert."

"What do you think?"

6.8

I really leaned into my introvert listening strategy first with my team. I learned from my conversation with Duane that listening with respect makes the people on my team feel like equals. With his straightforward manner and willingness to listen, Duane showed me a type of ease and grace that I felt like I could do too.

So with my team, instead of saying, "Here's what you need to do—make it so," I would say, "Here's what I need you to do. What do you think about this?" And then I would listen.

I was learning that when you ask someone, "What do you think?" and really listen to their answer, you honor their humanity. It increases their confidence and self-worth. It makes them feel motivated to spill their guts, just like I did with Duane. Ordering people around from above just makes them feel small and disrespected.

Listening made the human beings on my team feel safe and ready to personally engage to do the thing we needed to do.

"What do you think?" became my second magic leadership question.

This one was a game changer. I finally had a simple, specific tactic to avert the flash cards problem—where I as the leader am excited about my strategy but no one follows it. The simple question of "What do you think?" became one of my biggest secret passageways:

Ask people what they think about the strategy before you ask them to do it.

I know so many executives who would never dream of having such open and unstructured conversations with their people. "I don't care what they think. It's not going to change my decision. I don't have time for that."

They refuse to step out of their comfy, very busy and important positions in the hierarchy and really listen to the people doing the actual work— the ones who know what's really going on. Sadly, planes have crashed and people have died on operating tables because the person in charge would not listen to the concerns of the people doing the work—the ones who could see the risks.

Here is what I learned by always asking "What do you think?" instead of issuing orders and expecting people to leap into action: Disagreements and concerns and doubts will always exist in your team—whether you know about them or not. So, wouldn't you rather know?

I would rather know. Then I know what I need to do to avoid the risks and obstacles to getting the thing done—*before* the crisis happens.

If I didn't take the time to listen to their ideas, concerns, and opinions first, it would be like shouting my strategy into the darkness, wondering why no one was doing what I told them to do. That's not leadership.

The "What do you think?" secret passageway became such a powerful part of my approach to lead with humanity that it became the subject of my TEDx Talk and my book *MOVE*.

Making real, human connections with people and treating them with respect made me feel like I was getting something right among my much older peer group of men who initially seemed so much more powerful than I was. I was learning that I wanted to share power, not lord it over people. Listening like an introvert was my key to being a successful executive and a big step on my own path to ease and grace.

You can't fake being authentic

6.9

You know that inescapable thrill you get when you are in the very front row of the roller coaster just after it crests the top, and you begin to feel the gravity and the impending speed of the descent? When my team and I found our seats in the very front of a bullet train in Tokyo, that's how it felt. And when I say "the very front," I mean there was only a curved dome of glass separating us from the world outside zooming by at ninety thousand miles per hour. We could have pressed our noses against the glass, but that would have been a distinctly un-Japanese thing to do.

Even my Japanese colleagues who had purchased the tickets had no idea we were getting these seats. But there we all were, amazed, whizzing through the wonders of Tokyo on the tip of the arrow.

Little patty was astonished zooming through this exotic land. This wild, high-speed view of Tokyo was about as far away from being in the woods and playing with dirt as you could get!

As we all settled into the long ride and got out into the countryside, I closed my eyes. I thought about Jim and Al and Duane some more. What was it that made me admire them so much?

I realized it wasn't just their impressive business accomplishments that were inspiring (which they were). It was their no-nonsense, no-bullshit demeanor.

For years, I had been managing myself so carefully to be all business and add value in every moment—and in contrast, they were just unapologetically being their real, informal, straightforward selves. Every time they spoke, I felt like I was in the presence of a truly authentic person. And it was inspiring. It made me want to be in the room with them.

That's the thing about being authentic. Either you are being authentic or you are not. You can't fake being authentic.

And when someone is being authentic, there is absolutely no bullshit. There is no overmanaged formality. There is just a real person saying what they really think.

I started to cast the "you're too serious" feedback in the light of such unapologetic, straightforward authenticity.

I realized that I was coming across as less authentic, not because I was being false, but because there were pieces of my real self that I deemed inappropriate for work that were missing.

Could I also unapologetically be my real, whole self at work like they were?

I liked the idea. But my problem was that I had absolutely no data to suggest that this would work for me based on anything that had ever happened in my life so far.

Let's face it, it did not work for little patty, who would show up unapologetically enthusiastic and full of hope only to be met with, "Ew, you're weird. Go away. We hate you."

I then imagined my younger work self appearing on the scene, smiling, being friendly and open, and my older male colleagues being like, "Well, hey there, honey, you seem fun." My defensive at-work formality, competence, and efficiency had been protecting me for decades. Could I really let that go now?

My internal critic was now in hysterics.

ARE YOU KIDDING ME? YOUR REAL SELF WILL NEVER CUT IT.

OUTSIDE OF WORK, THERE IS NO RISK IN SHOWING YOUR REAL SELF. NOTHING REALLY HAPPENS WHEN PEOPLE DON'T LIKE YOU.

BUT AT WORK . . . AT WORK! PEOPLE WILL THINK YOU'RE WEIRD AND TRIVIAL. THEY WILL LOSE ALL RESPECT FOR YOU. THEY WON'T LET YOU STAY IN THIS BIG ROLE. THIS IS WAY TOO RISKY.

As I considered if and how I might actually bring the real me to work—and if I really should—we neared Tokyo's Narita Airport. There were lights on the walls of tunnel that were specifically spaced and programmed to flash in a way that was synchronized to match the speed of the train, So as you zoomed through the tunnel, what you saw was a fixed work of art on the wall. This bizarre, amazing, train-tunnel art thrilled little patty.

I was still not sure what was possible for me in terms of how (and when) to unapologetically be my real self at work. But I thought, *You know who knows the answer? Mom. I should ask Mom.*

Humanity at work

6.10

When I got back from Tokyo, Mom, Kerry, and I met up in Vail, Colorado, for a girls' weekend trip.

We were sitting on the edge of a big flower bed in the glorious mountain sunshine. I was talking about giving up my formal, all-business persona at work. "But Mom, I'm not sure anyone will respect me if I show more of my real self and my personal life at work. If they know I like to cycle and scuba dive and sing and draw, won't they dismiss me as not serious enough to be a big business leader?"

"That's ridiculous. Male executives don't work all the time. They go out for drinks and play golf, and they call that work. They all have hobbies and families, and they talk about those things all the time. And they have multiple assistants to make their lives easier. Why do you think you are not supposed to show that you have any fun? You need to let people at work know that you, too, experience the world as a normal human."

Mom continued, "People see you as very successful, but if they don't know you have fun or struggle with things, you don't seem human. You might even seem false or intimidating. People relate to people. If you only ever talk to them about work, you give them nothing to relate to—because there is no *you* there."

Something Jim always used to say to me came to mind: "A day that makes you happy makes you wise." That always sounded like it was supposed to be profound, but I was never sure that I really understood it. I wasn't feeling wise or happy. I was never sure what I was supposed to be or feel at work. Was Mom right that I was not showing up as a whole person?

A hummingbird suddenly landed right next to me. He seemed out of sorts, just sitting there panting with his little chest puffing in and out. He looked tired. I was tired too. "I don't know what to do," I said to Mom.

"Tell them about some things in your life. Tell them about being bullied, tell them about your art, tell them about that infernal gingerbread house. You need to give them a person to connect with."

As a kid, Mom was always trying to help me overcome my crippling shyness. And I guess it was still necessary!

I then thought about my dad, who oozed authentic ease and grace and had a lot of influence with people. I never once saw my dad try to impress anyone. He was never formal about anything. He won people over with his smile and humor and big, generous heart. If anyone was unapologetically being themselves, it was Dad.

So, I finally came to see (with some cringeworthy hindsight) an important secret passageway in life:

No one is actually being more impressive when they are trying to be impressive.

People can see you trying, and it's icky. I had to admit that my overly businesslike work self was not as impressive as I had hoped. My 5 points, 3 ideas, and 2 questions might not be the best way to start every conversation.

I realized that in their own ways, Mom and Dad were both teaching me that if I was going to be a successful leader at a high level, I would need to finally let the real human version of Patty out of hiding.

Suffixes and solitude

6.11

Wendy and I were at a restaurant on Anna Maria Island in Florida, sitting at a clunky wooden table right on the beach. We were celebrating our 40th friendship anniversary. As we sipped our margaritas (in marginally acceptable glasses), I curled my toes into the sand.

We laughed. "Do you remember all the stupid games we made up when we lived in the middle of nowhere?"

"Do you remember how many of them involved dirt?"

We were truly masters at entertaining ourselves with nothing.

Wendy became a physical therapist and worked in schools with kids who have learning disabilities. She said, "Having nothing to play with as a kid was good practice for being creative. Now I work in an underfunded school, and if you give me a yardstick and a tennis ball, I can come up with a week's worth of physically and mentally stimulating activities to do in a stairwell!"

We finished our lunch and started walking on the beach, having transferred our second margarita into a plastic cup (which broke my heart a little).

As we approached the water and let the waves splash over our feet, Wendy said, "When we were at school, remember how you made friends with the teachers so you could get out of recess?"

"Yeah, I was so thankful they let me stay inside."

"How did you do that?"

Wendy and me celebrating our decades of friendship

I started thinking, *How did I actually pull that off—getting them to let me stay inside? It's not like I was very socially crafty or influential when I was in second grade.*

Then I remembered. There was a quiz. The teacher's instructions were, "Write down the suffix that goes at the end of the word."

I got to work. There was a list of about 20 words with a blank for you to write the suffix:

I saw the word *forgetful* _____ and I wrote "ness." The word could be *forgetfulness*.

I saw the word *surprising* _____ and I wrote, "ly." *Surprisingly*.

I got a zero on this quiz. I was mortified.

When I asked the teacher what I did wrong, she told me with the word *forgetful*, the answer is "ful." "Ful" is the suffix in *forgetful*. With *surprising*, the answer is "ing."

I was shouting in my silent voice: *Well, that's the stupidest thing I've ever heard. Where is the learning in that? You're giving us the answer—it's right there in front of you. Why is this even a quiz? And more importantly . . . even though I misunderstood the instructions, wasn't it clear to you that I understood what a friggin' suffix was? Do I not get* some *credit for doing something more challenging? I get a zero?*

Anyway, I was required to stay inside at recess to retake that useless quiz. It took me about 10 seconds to get 100 percent.

But suddenly I realized, I was inside—I had infiltrated the empty classroom. Which meant that I was protected from recess on the playground—the main arena of torture.

I was *in*. And man, I needed to *stay in*.

So I asked the teacher, "Is there anything I can help you with while I'm here?" I would have done anything to stay inside that empty classroom.

Task number one was to clean the chalkboards. By the next week, I was staying inside almost every day, and I was grading papers and suggesting lesson plans.

My favorite paper I ever graded was a science test that had the question: If you were at the exact center of a perfect sphere in space, and the sphere was not acted on by the gravity of any other objects around it, what would happen to you? The answer on the paper I was grading: "You would die." I gave partial credit.

That is how my teachers became my friends.

Wendy said, "You were always having interesting conversations with them. It was like watching two adults talking."

It was true, my teachers were so much more interesting to be with than the kids my age, who were shallow and cruel and who poked me to see what fat feels like. I had found my people. I loved having teachers as my friends.

Talking to Wendy on the beach gave me an idea about what I was missing with the executives at work. The teachers controlled what happens. I gave them a reason to want me in the room with them, so they let me in.

Likewise, the executive men at work control what happens. I need to give them a reason to *want me in the room* with them. I was going to need to think about this.

Then Wendy and I sat down in the sand, and I could not help putting down my drink and making a large and texturally detailed sculpture of a sea turtle. I guess I still like to play with dirt.

Will the real Patty please stand up?

6.12

F lying back from Florida, I was dozing off in my seat. I had been traveling a lot recently and was feeling weary from it. As Jim used to say: "Lately, I've been eating most of my meals with an airplane strapped to my ass." Yeah, that.

I thought more about my conversation with Wendy on the beach, and how I'd scored my way inside the room with the teachers. It made me think about my plight with the big executives. *They want to keep consuming my excellent work so they tolerate my presence—but they don't really want me to have a seat at the table with them. They don't really want me in their club.*

Thankfully, I snapped back into consciousness before I missed the beverage cart. I ordered a terrible airplane Chardonnay in a plastic bottle. It was half frozen, so I put it under my knee to thaw. As I considered what would make the big executives *want* me in the room with them, like my teachers ultimately did, I ran right into a roadblock.

The teachers enjoyed my company. The big executives did not. They would need to see me not just as a competent worker but *socially—*as a *peer*. I had mastered so many types of important business conversations that had gotten me really far, but now I had a soul-crushing thought: *None of the conversations I was really good at required any actual socializing:*

- Negotiating/advocating/interviewing—not socializing.
- Asking for help—not socializing.
- The magic question, "When I worry about you, what should I worry about?"—not socializing.
- The other magic question, "What do you think?"—also not socializing.

All of these super high-value conversations always had a point, a practical, desired outcome. So I did great at them. My business persona was perfect—because in those conversations, *it was not necessary for people to like me back*. Little patty could stay safely hidden away.

But now, dammit, I realized that's exactly what was missing: *After a lifetime of practice at avoiding rejection by never even trying to be social with peers, now it seems to be the main objective.*

Little patty bolted forth.

"WAIT. WHAT? Hang on. So what you are basically saying is that you will go up to scary, important people and, in one way or another, say, 'Hi, I'm Patty . . . and I hope we can be *friends*'? Are you fucking kidding me? Come on. That is the one thing, the ONE THING, I have asked you to NEVER MAKE ME DO. Please don't do this."

Despite the fact that little patty was having a nervous breakdown, I was beginning to realize that I was not, in fact, giving the executives a version of Patty that they could figure out why they should like in the first place. I mean, let's face it, *no one wants to have a drink with 5 points, 3 ideas, and 2 questions.*

My thoughts returned to Jim and Al and Duane.

When Jim told me he was worried that his cat was very sick, we made a personal connection. When Al told me about a messy struggle with a dear friend, we made a real heart connection. And to be fair, the whole reason I now had Duane as a mentor was because of the pizza.

What I was coming to see was that they were all being their real, human self at work—someone you *could actually know* (just like Mom said). That's what was inspiring. That's what made me trust them so much. They were not hiding themselves. I was.

The real me was missing in action. I was presenting myself as very competent and efficient, but with a hard, carefully polished shell that protected little patty from further rejection and my career from sexist attacks.

But I was not being social. And I was not showing the real human on the inside at all.

I was still stuck in thinking, *You don't need to know anything about my humanity—just look at my high scores in my work. That's what should matter.*

Jim had told me many times, "The higher up you go, the more *who you are as a human* matters." And Al had kept telling me something Warren Buffett had told him: "I choose people based on character. When it comes to character, intelligence, or work ethic, there is nothing more important than character. *And if someone has poor character, you'd better hope that they are also stupid and lazy.*"

Al and Jim had both been pointing me to the secret passageway for being wanted in the room at a high level, but I had not been ready to accept it: **Be real. Be human. Character and letting people truly know you is what builds trust. That matters more than anything else.**

This was to become a pivotal turning point for me.

The wine had partially thawed. I poured some into the blue plastic cup, which actually seemed an appropriate vessel for this vintage of crappy airplane wine with ice chips in it.

I had to convince myself that showing my own humanity, and the unvarnished reality of my life is the very thing that will inspire people to trust me—and that in fact, those are my best parts. It's connecting with people on human stuff that will make them want to be in the room with me.

So I decided then and there, on that flight, as I was chewing on my frozen slices of Chardonnay, that while I would still do my best to honor little patty's fear of rejection, it was time to push us through.

Little patty, we're going in. I can't promise we'll be OK, but we have to try.

I will say that learning how to be the real me was not going to be an overnight change. It was more of a tentative, multi-decade change.

It felt so unnatural for me to be more social and share the real me at work. But I began to see that it could be an evolution of the "loose hair" persona I was already feeling pretty good about.

I was still afraid that sharing too much would backfire on me. But I put my toe in the water that first day back, committing to never again start with "Here are my 5 points, 3 ideas, and 2 questions" and instead always start with "How is your day going so far?"

It felt so weird.

I wasn't sure I was on the right track. But the final straw came when a work colleague I had actually started socializing with outside of work told another manager we'd been hanging out. The other manager's response? "Why would you ever want to socialize with Patty Azzarello? She is so boring."

I thought, *Dammit, I am delightful. I am interesting and smart and warm and funny—just not at work. And I am weary of putting myself through the personality lobotomy every Monday morning to turn into my boring, work-appropriate self. I actually want people at work to see my real self.*

So, bit by bit, I tried to follow Mom's advice and my mentors' open, straightforward, unpolished, and un-perfect example of humanity. I started to offer a few of my own quirks and struggles in my conversations. "I did a big bike ride this weekend, and after this meeting I probably won't be able to stand up."

Over time, they would hear about my scuba diving and I would hear about their motorcycles. They heard about my PTSD that Crayola didn't introduce proper flesh-toned crayons until 1992. We talked about the best bourbons and laughed about trying to put together flatpack furniture with the little Allen key. I shared my obsession with the perfect glassware and how not only do I dislike blue M&M's, but I can identify them in a blind taste test.

And I became much freer to share things like "I have no idea how to do that. I'll investigate" or "I was really nervous when I did that" without thinking an eject button would open a hatch in the floor that would suck me into oblivion for not knowing something.

It was getting less scary.

Also, I came to realize that I could let people see the real me *without having to share any details about my personal life that I wanted to keep private*. That's never what being "more social" was about.

Also, I took another leap forward when I later read some research that said, "People are more productive after laughing." This I could do—I had a lifetime of training in the laughter department from my family. So I began to start all of my meetings with laughter. I saw that even a fleeting moment of laughter sends a lightning bolt of humanity into any situation. Laughter is deeply real. It builds trust and human connection.

So what happened?

Well, it seemed that people at all levels began to want this more lifelike version of Patty in the room with them.

Real Patty felt so much more relaxed and effective at work than business-formal, carefully managed, gold-star-seeking, defensive Patty ever did. And the reaction was so positive that even little patty thought, *Wow, I'm not scared anymore.* She loved trading in the automatic fear of rejection she had carried for so long for thoughtful, confident, funny, no-bullshit straightforwardness.

I had stopped trying so hard to impress people. People seemed to truly appreciate it when I shared how not perfect I really was. It was kind of like my experience asking for help—doing so seemed to build my credibility, not lower it. I started to care more and more about making a human connection with peers. I was getting invited into more high-level conversations. And I felt like I was finally, truly on my own unique path to ease and grace at work.

So, I decided to take it on a test-drive with a big, scary, important client . . .

The cigar and the feet

6.13

I had been in five different countries in Europe just that week. It was the kind of nonstop planes, trains, and automobiles with built-in sleep deprivation that really wears me down. Now I was in Germany in the back seat of a pristine Mercedes.

I was doing my best to stay classy in my standard suited-up uniform during what felt like a 57-hour drive on the autobahn. At some point, I was probably snoring and drooling. To their credit, the two sales reps up front did not mention this upon our arrival at the big, important client's building.

They'd warned me that this guy could be difficult. They had been trying to break into this account for a while, so they decided to present him with a visiting top executive (*Oh, wait . . . that's me*) as a way of making him feel important and softening up the ground to make a sale.

We entered a very formal office building and took the elevator up. His personal office occupied the entire top floor of the building, which was a glass-and-stainless-steel ghost maze of empty space. It felt kind of like the intro to *Get Smart*: we had to pass through doorway after doorway and empty room after empty room to get to this guy's office. We finally arrived after clearing three checkpoints with three different secretaries.

If surrounding yourself with massive amounts of elegant, empty space was a show of power, this guy was really hamming it up.

We finally walked into his secret lair. He was a round, gray-haired man with glasses. When he saw me, a young woman, the low expectations on his face read, "How quaint," like I had been presented to him straight from the "stupid rat" box. He took out a cigar and put it in his mouth but didn't light it, then leaned back in his chair and put his feet up on his desk, kind of right in my face.

At that moment, I was thinking, *It's my job to turn his disregard for me around and get him interested in our offer. My reputation with the European sales team is on the line here. They are deciding, "Is it useful to bring Patty to our most important customers? Is she going to impress them, or is she going blow it? Will this meeting just be a useless formality?"*

The sales guys had asked me to talk to the client about our stuff and our strategy. But I thought, *Patty, if you want to be impressive, don't try to be impressive. Don't do the talking. And for God's sake, do not start selling. Just listen—listen like an introvert.*

So, I shook off that deflated feeling from his initial low expectations, and I started the conversation. "I have been talking to other companies here in Germany, and they have told me that this [current legal/economic] issue has been causing them challenges. Is that impacting you?"

He took the cigar out of his mouth and, with some surprise in his voice, said, "You know about that? Yes, we are seeing that too."

"Is it causing a big problem for you, or is it just a peripheral issue for your business?"

"No. It's a massive, central problem. We need to solve it."

"Can I ask what you have tried so far to deal with it?"

He told me about an initiative they were working on to mitigate the issue.

I asked, "How's that going? Is your initiative working for you?"

Now his feet came off the desk and the cigar went back in the drawer.

"Actually, it's not. I'm concerned it won't work. Did you learn anything from your other clients?"

Well, how about that? Now he is interested in my opinion. But don't start talking. Don't start selling. Just keep listening.

I continued, "How bad would it be for you if you don't solve this problem?"

He was silent for a minute. But then, for the next two hours, he started spilling his guts.

Wow—being more relaxed and making a personal connection with introvert listening works with big, scary executives too. Score one for a lesson that took 15 years too long to learn.

He talked and talked as the sales reps frantically took notes. He was giving us his internal map—the exact roadmap of what he truly cared about, what was most important to him, what was killing him, how vital it was to his career that he didn't fail, and what, specifically, he most needed help with to succeed.

He was telling us exactly how we could sell our products and services to him—but I never once mentioned what we could offer him. In the last moments of our meeting, all I said was, "We have been able to help other clients solve the central issue you described. May we follow up with you with a proposal for how we can help?"

The client enthusiastically agreed to meet the sales team in two weeks.

After we walked out, the sales reps, practically dancing in the parking lot, said to me, "*Wow!* How did you do that? You must have some kind of magic spell. How did you get all that information out of him? That was amazing!"

The sales reps were able to take all the intel we gathered that day to create a sales plan that they ultimately succeeded with.

If I had tried to impress this customer with impressive talking, I never would have gotten past the cigar and the feet. But genuine curiosity, respect, good questions, and introvert listening did the trick. It made me a hero that day.

Now, *this* was the real thing for me. Listen like an introvert. Ease and grace, baby.

The opposite of *asshole* is not *weak person*

6.14

I 've met several people who have met my resume before meeting me, and they say, "Wow, you're so nice. I expected you to be an asshole."

Little patty is always like, "Are you kidding me? Really? What mean thing have I ever done?"

It was always a hard thing to take: that being in a big corporate role automatically made people assume that I was, by definition, an asshole. Making people feel safe was so important to me, yet my mere existence as an executive made me scary to others.

One time, I was hosting a team lunch with 20 people from my customer support organization in the Netherlands. I sat in the middle of a long table. Each time someone entered the room, they chose the seat as far away from me as possible, filling the table from the outer ends. The latecomers lost this game and had the misfortune to have to sit right next to me.

I'll tell you, it took not a small effort for little patty feel like this happened because my role was seen as powerful and perhaps intimidating, and not just because no one wanted to sit next to me at the lunch table.

A few weeks later, I was in a dark ballroom at a conference where the table topic was leadership style. When I talked about making people feel safe, the other executives were kind of appalled. "Make people feel safe? What are you even talking about? You pay them. Don't waste your time. You can just tell them what to do. You need to make people fear you if you want to get their best efforts. Otherwise they will see you as weak."

This annoyed me. Why did aggressive, scary behaviors seem to be the standard and accepted way to lead? My mind snapped back to "Who are your enemies?"—a question I had discarded years ago.

And why is being kind so automatically equated with being weak?

When I think about kindness and strength, I like to think of ballet dancers. They look so soft and light, right? But here's the thing. You don't get that beautiful lightness and softness without great strength. Compare that to a burly bouncer with a nightstick. I bet he couldn't do even one pirouette.

Throughout my career, as I observed how the aggressive, bullying leaders acted, I saw that many of them were not actually strong at all. They mostly avoided making any of the hard decisions or having the hard conversations. They were just *acting* powerful.

I thought, *Wait a minute—As an executive, I have actually been doing those difficult things, but I do them in a kind and respectful way.*

I am the strong one here.

I want to lead with the ballet dancer kind of strength and grace. I want to respect people's humanity. I want to motivate them to want to engage, not order them around through fear.

The opposite of *asshole* is not *weak person*.

The opposite of *asshole* is *kind person*—and the kindness does not reduce the strength.

I came to realize that those nasty, aggressive managers were not leaders at all. *You are not a leader if people would not follow you by choice.* You might as well just use the nightstick.

All this made me think of my mom. Mom was such a good example of strength and kindness. She had her rigid rules, but she never once made me feel afraid. Mom modeled the perfect combination of accountability and love.

I realized at that moment that I could think of no better name for my personal leadership strategy than Accountability + Love.

And the thing is, my organizations were always high performing. The aggressive leaders' teams were not. And they just could not see the connection between fear and low performance.

Yes, their organizations got stuff done, but it took burning up a lot of suffering people and a lot of extra time.

When I later got to work with people in these abused organizations as a consultant (with the asshole executive not in the room), I was heartbroken to see such brilliant people being so fearful, emotionally broken, and exhausted.

The fundamental truth is this: *People who are self-protecting are not highly productive.*

For me, the good news is that you don't need to be an asshole to succeed. Do assholes succeed? Yes, of course, all the time. But it's not your only option. You can make a different choice. I made a different choice.

There is no question in my mind that if you treat people with respect, communicate well, and make them feel safe, you will get their best work, their best creativity, and their highest motivation.

In reality, I didn't have an actual choice. I just didn't have any slick asshole moves to try to impress people with in the first place. Pretending to be tough would have been ridiculous—I couldn't have pulled that off even if I wanted to. And I owed it to little patty to *never* try.

Superheroes

6.15

I was curled up on my sofa with my laptop and my favorite summer-weight comforter in reach, just beyond my feet, when I got an email from someone I'd worked with a long time ago. It said, "Patty, when I worked for you, I was Superman."

I thought, *Wow! Now, that is a compelling statement. I need to find out what he means by that.* So I replied. And he got right back to me, writing, "I have occasionally reflected on why that was. I'm not sure I know all the answers, but the things I do know are that the environment was real, the energy was high, and the crap was low."

As I read his words, a light went on. And right there, as I grabbed my comforter with my toes and pulled it up so I could gently squish it between my hands—as I pondered his words, I finally landed on how I truly felt about power. My job is to *make the people on my team feel powerful.*

I thought about Mom. Mom made people feel great. While Dad was the fun, showy extrovert, Mom was the one who would go deep. Mom knew the life stories and hopes and dreams of everyone she met. She really cared about each person she was talking to. People *loved* my mom. They felt so seen and understood by her. They always left those conversations lifted up. And Mom was an introvert too. How did she do it? How did she make people feel so good?

I began to consider that it was the way she listened.

When Mom listened to me those afternoons in bed after school, she asked me big questions. I could feel how much she cared about what I was feeling. She helped me understand my situation in a way that gave me new insights and choices. Her listening made me feel powerful because it let her show me ways I could solve my own problems.

Then I thought, perhaps I do this too. My magic questions of "What should I worry about when I worry about you?" and "What do you think?" worked so well because I actually cared, not just about the answers but about the person.

I realized that the secret to being a great listener was to actually listen for what people are *feeling*, not just what they are *saying*. Only then will they start to reveal to you their internal map that shows what they care

about and why. And once you can see their map, only then can you understand what is truly meaningful to them.

People need meaning to feel good and sane and motivated at work.
And people need meaning to feel human. The corporate world does not default to creating meaning for its employees. But it became my goal.

I was finally figuring out the mystery of why super talented, older,
very experienced people liked working for me: It was because I listened like
Mom. I respected them. I actually cared about them as humans. I let them
know I appreciated and admired them, and I wasn't subtle about it.

*Listen because you actually care about the person you are lis-
tening to.* That's the secret passageway.

So, this introvert-listening thing of mine turned out to be pretty powerful
stuff—because it let me help people reach for more of what they wanted in
life with more confidence. I'm glad I somehow got that one right even before
I realized what I was doing.

Getting that email that day from the man who worked for me so long
ago served to solidify an instinct, which then became a concrete goal of
mine, and ultimately a wonderful secret passageway:

*Leadership is an opportunity to create greatness in others.
Don't just stop at making people feel safe and appreciated. Make
them feel like friggin' superheroes.*

The social life of an introvert

6.16

OK. Before we get too carried away with the real Patty coming out and
actually doing well socializing with people, there is still a problem.
People wipe me out.

Many are often surprised to learn I'm an introvert because I am expressive, I laugh a lot, and I talk loud and do the Italian hand-waving thing. And I spend a lot of time out in the world communicating. I do much of my work on stages. And since little patty taught me how to pretend to be OK, I can turn it on whenever I need to. So I don't seem like an introvert.

But that comes at a cost—because interactions with other people cost us introverts energy. Particularly random socializing with small talk. (Kill me now.)

Extroverts, on the other hand, get and restore their energy from other people. Extroverts are a mob of charming, chatty small talkers, out to steal our precious energy points in the game.

As an introvert, I restore my energy only by being alone. Imagine me cowering in a corner with an extrovert looming over me while I'm silently screaming: *Get away from me, you delightfully friendly person!*

Don't get me wrong. I love and need my people. Introverts actually love people. We really do. We just need them to be good ones, and in small doses—and best if one at a time.

When I find someone who makes me feel safe and welcome and appreciated, I am in love—and then I can't shut up. Truly. I am not just putting on a happy face. I am authentically giddy to be with them. A great conversation with a safe person is a true joy in my life.

But no matter how much I enjoyed the experience, afterward, I need to be alone to recover.

Here is my dilemma: I would have little joy or success in life without other people's love and help. But at any given moment, very few social invitations seem more fun to me than staying home by myself.

It is a very high bar to clear indeed that a brunch, a concert, a boat ride, a book club, a sporting event, or an invitation to meet the queen is going to seem more fun than staying home by myself with a comforter, a glass of wine, and a good sofa.

Like many introverts, I am not always good at having fun in the moment. After a big experience out in the world, no matter how much I enjoyed it, I end up with this numb, exhausted feeling, like, *What the hell just happened to me?* I need quiet, alone time to process whatever fantastic thing I have just done. My recovery feels like I am one of those coin-sorting machines in the supermarket—where at first all the memories are disorganized and loud and clanking. Only after all the chaotic details finally navigate their way through my nervous system and settle themselves into stacks of quiet, neatly piled pictures, can I then—in a state of calm—step back and understand which parts of the experience I truly loved. Then, finally, I can think, "*Wow*, that was fun!"

Not-networking

6.17

I was half-heartedly reading an article in the in-flight magazine, strapped into seat 26B on a plane that was not taking off any time soon, when I came across this line: "Instead of making it your networking goal to meet a large number of new people, just set out to make one new friend with some-one you actually like."

I thought, *Wait—that's what I do!*

And with that, my life changed forever. I decided that I would never again think about networking as a goal to meet lots of influential strangers. Instead, I would try to authentically make one new friend at a time. This was the introvert-friendly approach to networking I had been waiting for my whole life—I had just never thought of it as networking before.

Now I had the secret passageway.

What I came to realize through this "make a friend" approach is this: **The active verb—the thing that you are actually doing when you are "networking"—is "being generous" with others.** Networking happens when you put value into your network, not when you try to find new people to get stuff from.

So, in my mind, I have now officially deleted the verb phrase "to net-work" (which always sounded a little icky and self-serving to me anyway) and simply replaced it with "to be generous."

I came to see that my introvert listening approach was its own form of generosity. Because I truly wanted to learn about people's ideas, concerns, gifts, and dreams, and doing so made them feel seen, respected and wel-come. Really listening made me a better leader and a better friend.

And because I created all my new friendships in this authentic way and kept investing in them, they have endured over decades. I am still friends with my fourth-grade teacher.

Today, I do not have a large network, but it is a mighty one.

I love getting people in my network together with each other, then just step-ping back and watching the wonderful possibilities that just start flowing. Together, we (and they without me) have gone on to create amazing new adventures, music, businesses, books, and art. Creating is the true magic of ~~networking~~ being generous with people.

My network is like a team of delightful, undercover ninjas, with diverse talents, ready to spring into action—all of whom make my life richer, more enjoyable, and more successful. These friends are both my expert advisers and my cheerleaders.

First-timers to a party or professional gathering of my people are often blown away by the brilliance, the respect, the warmth, and the laughter.

But it still always feels like a plot twist to me that this awkward introvert has actually created an extraordinary network of friends who have tremendous value and potency in the world at large, and who truly care about me.

Like Warren Buffett says (I'm paraphrasing), "Success in life means that the people you care about love you back."

Much to her amazement, little patty had finally found her people—and they liked her back!

Today, I know that nothing is more important to my success and well-being than choosing the right people to be in my life and avoiding the wrong ones. If only I could have learned that lesson sooner . . .

Part 7

The Right and the Wrong People

"Don't let someone who gave up on their dreams talk you out of going after yours."

—Zig Ziglar

"When people suck the life out of you, wouldn't it be nice if they took some fat too?"

—Someecards

An ugly secret

7.1

I was proud of myself.

I'd gotten into the big room and stayed there. I was doing great at work. My team and my management liked and supported me. The business was thriving.

When I was in this job, my life was great.

Except that it wasn't.

I had an ugly secret.

I was quietly suffering.

Home should have been my sanctuary, the place where I could recover and refuel for the next big day at work, as it had been for my whole life before.

But, each night, when I walked through the doors of my house, I stepped into a different world where my sense of self was disintegrating. On a daily basis, I was made to believe that I was stupid, boring, and unworthy of kindness and respect. I was treated with contempt. I was often forbidden to speak.

The competent, successful, person I was at work, at home, became small and scared. I would hide in my own house, afraid to say what I thought, afraid to breathe, afraid of being in trouble. Afraid of being punished.

Hazard advisory

7.2

E very day he looked into my eyes and smiled, beaming. Someone finally really saw me. He was so funny and smart. The charm was truly swoon-worthy. We got to "I love you" and "soulmates" very quickly. He hugged me and kissed me and told me I was perfect every day. He left love notes all over the house and in my pockets and bags. He gave me gifts and sang songs to me. He showered me with kindness and physical affection. We had long, silly, deeply satisfying conversations. Little patty, who had felt so much rejection in her life, and adult Patty, who had been lonely in her marriage, had finally found true love and belonging. And it was glorious.

Smarter women who are cringing at the red flags here, good for you.

I was not so smart.

The self-help saying goes, "We are not so much victims as volunteers." I raced into this tempest of love bombing without hesitation, feeling so happy, so welcome, and so unguarded for the first time in my life, and I relished every minute of it.

I once read that narcissism is the only psychological disorder that makes the rest of the family need therapy. Victims of narcissism sometimes become drug or alcohol abusers. Many fall into deep depressions or consider suicide. Fun.

Here's how this played out for me. And it was textbook, which I learned only after I got away from it (and read the textbook). While I was in it, I was in way too deep to even look up for years. I was living in an alternate reality and couldn't see what was happening to me.

There Came One Horrifying Moment

After that magical beginning, at the end of one work day, I went to him, beaming. We were always so excited to see each other. I anticipated his broad smile and welcome embrace, just like every time before. But instead, when I got into hugging distance, he turned his back on me. Then he walked off. I was stunned. When I caught up and got in front of him, I could hardly take in what I saw. It was a person I didn't recognize. There was a dark nothingness in his eyes. It scared me.

A switch had flipped.

Suddenly, *everything* felt different. Unrecognizable. From this moment on, my affections were met with repulsion. The loving care I cherished was replaced with loathing, cruelty, and punishment.

And then it got weird.

A New Kind of Low Expectations

What then began was the systematic lowering of my expectations—which I learned only later is in the textbook.

Each day, more types of human connection and kindness were withheld and added to the list of *things I was forbidden to expect* in the relationship anymore. These expectations of mine that were now way too high included things like two-way conversation, basic human respect, having boundaries—or for my presence in the room to be acknowledged at all.

I was also told on a daily basis that I was boring and tedious, and I was often forbidden to speak.

I was made to feel that I was worthless as a human and as a woman.

Yes, that happened to me.

My internal critic:

I NEED TO CHIME IN HERE. I GOTTA TELL YOU, I WAS OUT OF A JOB FOR A WHILE. NOR-MALLY, NO ONE OUT IN THE WORLD SAYS THINGS AS BAD AS I DO TO PATTY. BUT HE HAD ME AT EVERY TURN. IT WAS BRUTAL. AND IT WAS CONSTANT. I USUALLY STICK WITH THE STANDARD INSECURITIES ABOUT NOT BEING GOOD ENOUGH AT HER JOB AND BEING SOCIALLY AWKWARD, AND MAYBE SOME BODY ISSUE STUFF, BUT, MAN, HE WOULD GO DEEP.

IF SHE TRIED TO EVEN SPEAK, HE WOULD RAGE TO SHUT HER DOWN, OR HE WOULD ROLL HIS EYES AND SIGH IN DISGUST OR JUST WALK OUT OF THE ROOM LIKE SHE DIDN'T EXIST AT ALL. IT WAS ROUGH. HE WOULD NOT ONLY ATTACK HER MOST DEEPLY PERSONAL INSECURITIES, BUT HE WOULD ALSO GO AFTER THE THINGS SHE LIKED MOST ABOUT HERSELF. HE WOULD MAKE HER FEEL TERRIBLE FOR BEING CREATIVE, OR FOR SPENDING TIME WITH HER FRIENDS, OR FOR SMILING OR FEELING HAPPY—OR FOR JUST BEING IN THE ROOM. EVEN WORSE, HE WOULD DEMEAN AND PUNISH HER FOR THE EXACT SAME THINGS HE USED TO TELL HER HE LOVED MOST ABOUT HER. IT WAS SURGICAL—AND IT WAS BAFFLING.

HE JUST HATED THAT SHE WAS A JOYFUL PERSON. WHENEVER HE GOT A WHIFF OF HAPPINESS FROM HER, HE WOULD WRECK IT. HE WOULD ERUPT IN ANGER IF SHE SMILED OR OFFERED TO MAKE HIM LUNCH. IT WAS ALL SO TERRIFYING AND CONFUSING. I HAD NOTHING TO CONTRIBUTE THAT CAME EVEN CLOSE. HE WAS SO SCARY SOMETIMES THAT I JUST GOT SHUT DOWN TOO.

It's so surprising that I let this happen to me, because in the workplace I had learned how to identify a narcissist a mile away. At work, when someone would fly into a rage for no rational reason and use anger to bully and be-little people—bingo, you've likely got a narcissist on your hands. It's never about you, it's always about them. They're just a bully on steroids. Get away. Protect yourself.

But in my personal life, I was oblivious. The magical beginning to our relationship had put me into a sort of trance. That's the game. The trance made me miss all the clues. Clues like him flying into a rage for no rational reason and using anger to bully and belittle me.

So was he a narcissist? Maybe. I'm not a medical professional; it's not fair for me to issue an official diagnosis. But, having now studied up on narcissism to the point of a figurative advanced degree on the topic, I can say that *narcissism thoroughly explained all the random, totally confusing, crazy-making torment I endured, and also how I became so injured, weak, and lost.*

So, I use the term *narcissist* perhaps unfairly, but because this term was the missing frame that so completely explained the mind-bending and unexplainable to me. And my understanding narcissism at a deep level is what ultimately let me heal from <u>whatever it was</u>.

The question is, why did I endure that for *years*? Why did I, a person with so much agency, intelligence, strength, and independence, give all of that up to be abused?

That's the magic of narcissism. It alters reality in a few key ways that suck you in and keep you confused and stuck.

One of the signs that you are in a relationship with a narcissist is that you are confused ALL THE TIME. You now live with a stranger and cannot resolve in any way how this could the same person from the beginning. You are kept in a maze of lies and double standards where nothing makes sense, everything is your fault, and they are entitled to all of their bad behaviors with no accountability. My brain would run itself raw trying to resolve all the disconnects.

And the final stage of mind control is that they remain super charming out in the world with everyone else, so you come to believe that you would have no support if you tried to tell anyone about what is happening to you.

Becoming Nothing to Survive

So, to survive, I learned to become a blank. To show no emotion. Any emotion, good or bad, was too dangerous. Breathing felt dangerous. I learned to be as still and invisible as possible.

The result was that I went into a sort of depression where I remained highly functional out in the world, but privately, I had lost myself. I had become numb and blank on the inside to protect myself.

I especially needed to not seem happy around him because it was just too perilous. This act of hiding happiness was the key way *I was ushered to play a role in my own destruction*—I created a world for myself where nothing could be important to me or make me happy.

I stopped doing or feeling anything around him. Eventually, I actually became the boring person he accused me of being all along. My survival strategy was to become too boring to even comment on.

For the first time in my life, home became the scary place in my world.

Another way I was stuck was that I kept telling myself, "All relationships have tough parts." I thought his hurtful behaviors were just part of the nature of our unique "tough parts" and it was my responsibility as a good partner to endure them. My super-student, hard-worker tendencies and my inner patience and fortitude and hope kept me thinking, *I'm strong enough to endure this. I'm smart enough to navigate this. I can see that he is hurting. I can help him, I can fix this, and I am duty bound to do so. And when it gets better, it will be wonderful again.*

So I stayed—for years.

I was living two lives. One on the outside, where I was a high-functioning executive who everyone thought was doing great. And one on the inside, where I was a human woman who was crumbling.

The right and the wrong people

7.3

My lifelong mentor and dear friend Al and I were in the ocean, standing in chest-deep water out beyond the break. It was a glorious summer day. As the rolling swells lifted and lowered us, we were fiercely locked in one of our marathon, super deep, work-life, existential conversations.

I had made a trip to South Carolina to see Al and the rest of the family.

Ross and I had remained good friends after we broke up. Sadly, Ross later died at age 57, but his sister and brother-in-law Al and the whole family adopted me forever after.

On this glorious day, I was thinking, *Why did we not get insulated sports drink bottles and fill them with margaritas?* I had learned, on my scuba diving trips, that the perfect glassware for a cocktail while having life-changing conversations in the ocean is, in fact, a sports drink bottle. (It keeps cold. It floats. It's big.) And if there was ever a perfect moment for a margarita in the ocean, being here with Al on this day was it.

At one point, Al said to me, "Nothing will have a greater impact on your career than the person you wake up with in the morning."

I did not want to believe him. I also did not tell Al what was going on at home, as I was embarrassed by it. And I was still naively hoping I could turn the relationship around.

But if Al was right, I had clearly made a really big mistake with the person I had chosen to be my person.

We all know this—Al was right. It just took me a while to truly believe it.

I've always heard that your personality is largely formed by the five people you spend the most time with. That made some sense to me. People's ideas and tastes and values can rub off on you when you spend a lot of time together.

But recently, I heard a Brenè Brown interview with Dr. David Eagleman, a neuroscientist and author, who was talking about the neuroplasticity of the brain—meaning that your brain is always adapting to every stimulus it encounters and physically rewiring itself to reprogram and optimize for the new information.

He said to Brenè, "You will be a different person after this one-hour conversation with me than you were before we started."

Whoah . . . hang on. Where's the tinfoil? I could feel my introvert brain immediately trying to protect itself from all the intrusive words and ideas and negativity and drama of all the annoying people in the world until I could think this through.

Spending even an hour with you will make me a different person because your inputs will physically re-wire my brain? This interaction will change and shape who I am forever after? Damn—I really do need to choose my people very carefully!

Even if you could change your brain back again after lunch, why waste all that energy to recover from the wrong people, the takers, the ones who bring negativity and judgment or want you to stay small?

Why not spend time with your cheerleaders? The people in your life who instead inspire and push you to become an even better version of yourself? That's the input your brain needs!

I have become very intentional about which people get a seat at my table.

This "brain changing" idea put Al's comment into even sharper focus. You spend a lot of hours with your partner. So they have a frighteningly enormous impact on your brain—on who you are and on what you believe you can be—and therefore what you can actually be.

And I was becoming less and less.

I was still doing great at work, and no one really saw what I was going through, probably because I had become so good at pretending to be OK. But I was starting to see the true harm of being stuck in a situation that was destroying me on the inside.

I pondered Al's comment for months. I couldn't shake the idea that I needed to be more honest with myself about the cost of this emotionally destructive relationship to my health and my brain. I needed to do something different. I needed to protect myself and prioritize my well-being.

My renaissance

7.4

O K, to explain how I got myself out of this situation and got my life back on track, I need to take a brief detour back to the 1600s.

I've always been fascinated with Galileo. Not because of the night sky, which he is most associated with, but because Galileo was such a pioneer of science in general. When I was in school, around age 11, and I first learned about the scientific method—that if you believe something is true, you (and every other scientist in the world) are obligated to try and disprove it before you can claim it as true.

Wow—science says you need to verify something before you can claim it's actually true. OK, I am in love. At 11, I was hooked for life on the scientific method.

Galileo was one of the first scientists to frame this way of thinking. He posed the first questions about what science should answer vs. the church: Does the universe revolve around the earth? The church says, "Yes." The scientific data says, "No, that was disproved." Which do we believe? He went to jail for the data.

Galileo was living and working during the Renaissance, a time when scientists were not only making discoveries about the world but also inventing the idea of science itself.

I also think of the Renaissance artists—contemporaries of Galileo—as scientists. Michelangelo dissected corpses to learn how human muscles and other internal organs worked so he could make his paintings and sculptures more realistic. And he built a marble quarry. I still can't get my head around that one. Leonardo da Vinci invented flying machines and even an early underwater diving suit. The Renaissance artists all pioneered brand-new art techniques—techniques that were like scientific inventions in themselves.

And the epicenter of all of this marvelous knowledge and discovery and art is Florence, Italy. Even though I never wanted to travel anywhere—for these reasons, I always wanted to go to Florence.

One summer, Kerry was renting a house in Lake Como in the north of Italy when I was a busy executive. I had work in Europe, so I was able to join the festivities.

It was one of those trips where I was in London, Amsterdam, Paris, Spain, Germany, and Switzerland in one week. I was thoroughly wiped out. My idea of a good time was to eat Italian food in Italy with my family and stay in one place—without having to set an alarm, touch my suitcase, or get on any type of transport for any number of consecutive days greater than one.

But when I got to Lake Como, Kerry said, "Why don't we go to Florence tomorrow?"

"How would we get there?"

"We'd need to take a train."

"What time would it leave?"

"The train leaves at 6:30am. We'd need to get up at five."

"I don't know." Getting up at 5:00am and traveling somewhere else, like I had been doing every day in the past weeks for work, felt over-whelming.

"What do you want to do instead?"

"Sleep in."

"You've always said you want to see Florence. You're telling me that you have an opportunity to go to the one and only place you've ever actually wanted to go—and you would rather sleep in?"

"Kind of, yeah."

I was down to what felt like about 1 percent energy reserves. But we went to Florence.

As soon as we got there, I had a feeling unlike anything I had ever experienced. I felt like every cell in my body was saying, "We're home." And that was just on the steps outside the train station. It turned out that I absolutely loved it there, not just for all the reasons that everyone loves Florence, but for the unshakable sense of belonging—which is quite notable for me.

Florence is the one place on the planet where I do not feel like an unwelcome, nervous traveler. I am soothed and relaxed. And I am, inexplicably, never lost. I just breathe in the beauty, and despite the crush of tourists, there is a calmness there for me, and it heals me. That "sleep in or go to Florence" trip changed my life forever.

I've since made it a point to go to Florence every year. Even if I could only be there for a night or two on the edge of a business trip, I would visit my emotional home. My visits have evolved to four to six weeks each spring. When I am in Italy, I remain in a constant state of awe. And a near-constant state of eating pizza. I am my father's daughter in this regard.

But let's get back to Galileo and my decision to take back control of my life . . .

Galileo

7.5

Whenever I am in Florence, almost as soon as I arrive, something compels me to walk up the hill to the house Galileo lived in 400 years ago. I've seen it a million times, but still—every single time—I just stand there. I can't tear myself away. It feels like Florence and Galileo and I have some ancient history.

One time, as I lingered outside his home, fixated, wondering, *Why do I do this?* I thought about how the life of Galileo has always inspired me— ever since I did that book report on him at the Italian picnic.

I considered how, when given the choice of being killed for his ideas that the church deemed blasphemous, or accepting imprisonment and agreeing to stop touting his scientific truth so loudly, he chose the stay-alive route. But even then he stayed true to his scientific beliefs. Though he could not voice them publicly, he never totally retracted his findings, and he kept working quietly the whole time.

A painting of Galileo I took a photo of in Florence by the street artist Blub, who paints famous works of art submerged in water. Artist credit: www.blublartesanuotare.com

It made me think about how while I am committed to my beliefs, I would not die for them. I considered the sexism at work that *I didn't directly combat.* Like Galileo's strategy, I chose not to inflame the powers that be enough to kill me—to end my career. My goal was to stay in the room instead of fighting a system I couldn't win against.

And Galileo made some of his most important contributions to science during this period of imprisonment, as he continued making discoveries and quietly writing about them.

Likewise, my own "quiet" approach let me live to fight another day. Which enabled me to continue to succeed in my work, and to get myself into a position where I could help many others later on too.

Better not to get killed for your beliefs. Just keep swimming . . .

One time recently, there was a scientific event hosted in his villa. I actually got to go inside the home where Galileo was imprisoned. I was quite moved to be standing in the very same rooms where he lived and worked.

The villa is on a hilltop with a large outdoor living area and garden, an observation tower, and staggering views of the surrounding Tuscan hills. And there is a servants area downstairs with a rudimentary kitchen and a wine cellar.

Note to self: To maximize productivity, have the pope confine you to a gorgeous villa with a tower and gardens while servants bring you Italian food and wine.

OK, rounding the final bend on the detour to get to how Galileo helped me change my life . . .

I had come to Florence on my own, while I was in stuck in this relationship. And as always, I found myself standing in front of Galileo's house. I remember the exact spot where I was standing, with the red Fiat next to me, the paving stones under my feet, and the radiant blue sky with the one puffy, white cloud.

At this moment, I was not thinking about Galileo, but about a brilliant TEDx Talk by Ash Beckman that I had watched right before I came here. She talked about coming out of the closet. And she emphasized that closets are not just about being gay—that we all have closets. Our closets exist when we are afraid to tell our own truth—when we are hiding.

And she said (I'm paraphrasing): *When you don't speak your truth, it feels like you are locked alone in a closet with a live grenade.* You're afraid to come out and throw the grenade because you know the truth will make a mess and hurt other people. But the alternative is *sitting alone in a closet with a live grenade.*

That's exactly how I felt. I had my own my closet: I was in an abusive relationship. And I was stuck in there, paralyzed with fear over coming out and throwing the grenade—of speaking my truth.

But it was at that very moment there in Florence, outside the home of Galileo, as I rested my hand on the red Fiat and smiled at the puffy cloud, when a sudden surge of clarity and confidence came to me: *If Galileo had to choose between going to jail or getting killed for speaking his truth, I can at least tell mine. I won't die. And I won't even go to jail for it. I've got it easy compared to him. I should do it.*

Thinking about Galileo inspired me to step out of my closet and finally say, "This is not OK. I will not live this way." I was no longer going to stay locked inside all by myself, afraid to breathe or move, like I had been doing for years.

So, what happened?

Well, when I got back home, I threw the grenade. I spoke up. And boy, did it make a mess. But when the dust cleared, I got to live on my own, in my beautiful house on the hilltop in California.

I walked outside one night, looked up at the Milky Way, and thought about how Galileo helped me find the courage to get my peaceful life back. And how he spent his entire life looking up at the night sky. I wondered if he ever tried Leonardo DaVinci's underwater diving suit.

Now my home is the safe and joyful place that it should be, where I share lots of good food and cocktails and deep conversations and laughter with the right people in my life—my family and the dear friends who lift me up.

Save yourself

7.6

Here is a bit of advice here to anyone who needs it:

If you are in a relationship where you went from feeling truly loved to feeling scared and despised, and now they use all the information they gathered about your favorite things to purposefully withhold them, and suddenly *you are being blamed for everything*, and their stories are about how everyone else is wrong or stupid, and they think hurting others is funny, and *they justify hurting you,* and now your definition of a good day is "less volatile," and you are confused all the time, made to feel guilty for wanting basic conversation and respect, and you make yourself smaller and smaller to avoid punishment . . . you might want to pick up a book on narcissism.

Here's what I wish I knew sooner:

1. Know that if someone *justifies hurting you,* and you stay, you will be destroyed.
2. It's so important to recognize that Abuse Strategy 101 is to *keep you confused and injured* so you are too mentally and physically weak to be able to leave
3. Trust that your friends will support you, and get the hell out of there.

Sometimes I didn't want to include this story in this book. But I offer this part of my story as my gift to anyone who is in an abusive relationship to say, IT'S NOT YOU. It's not your fault. Like my mom always said about bullies: It's never about you. It's always about them.

Even if not at the hands of a diagnosable narcissist, many people get stuck in controlling and abusive relationships. Don't think that means you are weak or stupid. Many of us end up there for quite the opposite reason: because we are amazing. Because abusers seek to take from the people who have the most to give, who offer a deep well of talents and kindness and energy they can suck dry for a good, long time. The textbook defines our role as being a "supply."

I got away, but it was not easy. It took years before I made the decision to get out and acted on it. Doctors have described what happens in narcissistic relationships as a form of brainwashing—and you don't just get over that right away.

But once I was out, the more I learned, the more I realized that my situation was not unique. It was just a predictable pattern of behaviors that were always the same. I would read about others' experiences with narcissists and think, *Wait, were you in my kitchen? Were you at that café on our last vacation? Were you there when he ruined Christmas?* When I saw that the behaviors I experienced, which had seemed so incredibly specific and bizarre, were repeated in the stories of others almost word for word, I couldn't believe it. It was like he was using a script.

And as I continued to learn about abuse and understand just how not-unique my situation was, *I finally came to believe that it was not about me. And it was not my fault.*

But for years after I got out, I was still not OK. I was not myself.

Little patty had gone into hiding. I had lost her, and she had taken with her my enthusiasm and bravery and joyful curiosity for life. While I stayed confident in my career, the real me on the inside was lost.

He had convinced me that even though I was successful at work, no one could ever like the real me—and no partner would ever love the annoying, tedious woman that I was. (I also know that I am not the only woman out there who earned all the money to support both people and still was made to feel worthless by their partner.)

It took years of friends and loved ones pulling me out of the dark hole I was hiding in—afraid to express myself or breathe freely. My friends kept saying, "Patty, you keep apologizing. You were never like this before. You don't have to do that. You can want what you want and say what you feel. It's OK."

The healing eventually came from a combination of time and the nurturing people in my life who didn't give up on me (and a therapist who had to define what "nurturing" even meant for me). The people who reminded me that they valued my presence in their lives *just for being Patty*, and who got me laughing again—they saved me.

Al had been right—I have come to learn that nothing is more important than the people I choose to be in my life.

Nothing.

And especially the person I choose to be my person. I have learned to ask myself:

Is your person truly on your team? Do they make you feel more emotionally stable or less? Are they fueling your confidence or making you feel insecure? Do they really see you? Do they honor all of your talents and values? Do they appreciate all of your good and weird parts? Do they want you to shine as yourself or be a reflection of them? Do they want you to be bigger or smaller? Do they light up when you talk about your dreams? Do they celebrate your wins or do they cut you down?

And while you are swimming upstream in your career, do they cheer you on and throw you a rope? Or do they hand you a bag of rocks?

Note to self: *If you want your life to be successful and happy, surround yourself with people who also want your life to be successful and happy. Especially when you choose your person.*

When I finally worked my way out of my depression, little patty, with all her joyful curiosity and enthusiasm for life, came back out and said, "Hooray! It's about time. Now, let's learn to speak Italian."

Sono grata (I am grateful)

7.7

I t started with a nagging feeling. Then it got louder. It grew and grew and then started screaming at me. *Patty, become a better world citizen. Learn to speak another language.*

I had been feeling like an idiot after traveling all over the world where people spoke to me in English no matter where I went, and I did not speak a second language anywhere. It just felt crappy. So I decided to learn Italian.

Learning a language should be relaxed and fun (so I have been told). It should be like music. Getting a feel for the sounds. Trying it out, improvising. Playing with it. But just like I couldn't improvise on the piano at my failed job at the dancing school, I couldn't do it with language either.

It took about six years of daily effort—and when I say "daily effort," I literally mean daily effort—and when I say "literally," I literally mean "literally." Every day. (Super-student mode is unrelenting.) I used every tool and technique and course and app I could find. I studied grammar and vocabulary daily. I also found online tutors and language exchange partners and media content in Italian so I could listen or speak every single day.

Learning a second language as an adult was the hardest thing I have ever done. My effort was epic. My frustration with it was equally epic. During this period, I inspired many others around me to never try to learn a second language.

But now, I can speak Italian.

When people say to me, "Oh, you speak Italian—did you just pick it up during your time there?" I want to kill them.

A happy result is that many of my language partners and teachers became my friends. Now I have people who care about me all over Italy. I've seen corners of the real world in Italy that I never would have found without these friendships. There are young people in my life who I mentor in Italian.

I feel like Italy saved me in so many ways.

For starters, for someone in search of beauty in life, in Italy, you could choke on all the beauty it offers. *Offers* is not the right word. Italy practically assaults you with beauty in every moment, and around every corner. It's truly everywhere: in the architecture, the landscape, the art (not just in museums and churches, but that you trip over on the street) the history, the culture, the language, the people, the fashion, and, of course, the food.

And Italy has also helped me rediscover that I was an artist, and that door has reopened in my life now too. Italy has brought so much beautiful, joyful, and unexpected richness to my life.

So . . . sleep in or go to Florence? I'm so glad my big sister shamed me into the right choice.

The buddy system

7.8

One afternoon, Kerry and I were sitting at her kitchen table. We met every Friday for lunch, and every Friday I picked the avocado off the sandwich, salad, or quesadilla. I asked her yet again, "Why don't you just *not* put avocado on mine?"

"I refuse to have a sister who doesn't like avocado."

Eventually, I came around. She was so right; avocados are now a staple in my life. She also put me though the same type of exposure therapy with gin.

Before we both lived in California, Kerry and I had lived very far apart for many years—like on different coasts, or like me in California and her in Singapore. But we aways stayed connected. We were always interested in each other's lives and loved each other as sisters. But once we were living near each other, we had movie nights with burritos and margaritas, we went shoe shopping, we did hikes on trails with warning signs about aggressive squirrels, we dressed up for cocktails, and we had deep conversations about life, all with lots of laughter. We became best friends.

But one thing we had never done together before was travel.

We decided to try. We went to Bali.

Why start with a weekend in wine country as a test run when instead, you can get on a 30-hour flight and spend two weeks stuck together on the other side of the world to learn if you are good travel companions?

Since this was our first trip together, I was worried because I am a terrible traveler, and Kerry was worried because I am a terrible traveler.

But friends of Kerry's in Bali had invited us to stay in their villa while they were out of town, and we just couldn't pass that up.

Upon arrival, Kerry drove us forever on dirt roads into remote countryside following baffling instructions. (There was still no GPS.) It was a "Drive till you see the field where a green Jeep sometimes parks and turn left when you see three chickens" kind of thing. Getting us there in itself was a mind-blowing feat as far as I was concerned. And my big sister continued to amaze me with her relaxed navigation skills.

I am just not wired for travel exploration on my own. But what I learned from work travel is that I do great when I'm with a guide. With a guide, I can actually find the beauty that I am seeking in the world. I can have the amazing, life-expanding experiences without feeling nervous and hopeless and afraid that I'll get lost away from home forever. And there is no better guide than Kerry. Unlike me, she is an impressive, sturdy, competent traveler and a gifted explorer.

And because of her lifelong passion for getting the hell out of our small town, she has traveled most of the world, and she did it relying solely on her own wits, before the internet, with her own money, a paper map, and a bag of pretzels. She has a knack for finding the most fascinating and beautiful things to see and do wherever she lands.

When we arrived at the villa, we descended a large stone staircase along a massive wall that made me feel like we were in an Indiana Jones movie.

At the bottom of the steps, we came upon a gate that opened up to a stunning lily pond surrounded by orchids and overseen by a giant, beautiful Buddha statue.

We traversed the lily pond on stepping stones. *OK, come on—the entry to the house is a lily pond? And you walk across floating stones to reach the front door?* The door was a marvel of its own—a giant red wooden mass that seemed twice our height and the width of a Toyota, that rotated on an axis to grant us entry. Little patty and Adult Patty were both blown away—and we weren't even inside yet.

This amazing door was a portal to even more new wonders. Inside, we were surrounded by several buildings with soaring thatched roofs, while a swimming pool glistened through freakishly gigantic foliage and an explosion of tropical flowers that might be considered gaudy if they were not flowers.

The kitchen and the living room had no walls. This startled me because they were exquisitely appointed with gorgeous furniture, sculptures, art, colorful fabrics, and cushions. *How does that work in the rain?*

At 7:00pm, one cricket chirped. Then at 7:00pm and one second, as if a conductor had raised his baton, 20 million crickets chirped and were joined by a chorus of frogs. It got so loud it was hard to have a conversation (because the living room had no walls).

Little patty's brain was in a state of shock from the immense beauty and excess of the exoticness of Bali. Once again, my big sister had connected me with genuine amazement, which shook me to my core and said to me, "This is the feeling of being inspired by beauty you have been waiting for your whole life."

And we hadn't yet left the house we were staying in.

Kerry and me on a day tour in Bali

After a couple of days of touring the rice fields and mountains and temples on the ocean, Kerry and I were sitting in a café when I started to feel dizzy and nauseous. I was trying so very hard to be "fine" because I didn't want to be the bad travel companion we both expected me to be by getting sick.

I assumed Kerry was fine because she is such a competent traveler, but a couple of hours later, she said, "I think we should head back to the villa. I am not feeling well."

I thought, *Thank God. Ruining our day is not going to be my fault.* "Oh, I'm sorry you are not feeling well," I said with a straight face. "It's fine with me if we head home."

"They are not expecting us, so we'll need to stop at the supermarket to get something for dinner."

"OK, sure," I said, personally feeling only a total repulsion for the idea of dinner.

At the supermarket, we got out of the car, but as Kerry began to walk toward the store, I said, "I'll wait here"—and once she was out of sight, I proceeded to collapse over the hood. I couldn't move. I was bent over at the waist with my upper body and face pressed against the dirty metal of the hood of the car as people milled about around me.

When she returned, Kerry deduced that I was not feeling well either.

On our drive back, she said, "When we get there, we can go in the pool and cool off. You'll feel better."

When we arrived at the villa, I put on my bathing suit in agony and had just laid down on the ample outdoor bed in the shade by the pool when Kerry announced, "I'm skipping the pool. I don't feel well at all. I want to go to bed."

Thank God. I don't have to pretend to be OK anymore.

So we got into the king bed we were sharing at about 3:00pm and stayed there for the rest of the night, absolutely miserable, with what Kerry called Bali Belly.

Later, in the dark, I was the first to need to throw up, but my fear of throwing up made me resist as long as I could. I finally went outside to the stunning outdoor bathroom (also resplendent with ridiculous tropical flowers), but a big spider was perched on the wall right next to the toilet.

My fear of spiders gripped me even more than my fear of throwing up. I was paralyzed.

I came back in.

Kerry asked, "Did you throw up?

"No."

"Why not?"

"There was a spider. I was scared. What should I do?"

"I'm not getting up to remove the spider for you."

"But I need to throw up."

"Then throw up in a bag."

I got a plastic shopping bag from the closet and carried it over next to her side of the bed.

Kerry said, "What are you doing?"

"How do you throw up in a bag?"

"Just throw up. In the bag. It's not that complicated."

The idea still baffled me a bit, having so little experience as such an unseasoned traveler and so little experience throwing up in general. So, I didn't throw up. An hour later Kerry got up and went outside.

Me: "Did you throw up?"

Kerry: "Yes."

Me: "Do you feel better?"

Kerry: "No."

Me: "Good."

We were in agony for about 18 hours, but it passed the next day.

We realized that we were, in fact, great travel companions. It turns out we are super compatible in terms of what we do and enjoy while traveling, and what the ideal rhythm of a travel day should be, and what and how often you should eat, and how you should always be planning the next meal during the current meal. And enduring this illness together in the ridiculously beautiful villa turned out to be a weirdly sweet bonding experience. We have both laughed about every part of this trip for years.

Whenever we travel anywhere, Kerry is the leader/explorer who handles all the logistics, plans, and navigation, and I am the useless but pleasant companion who tags along and reaps all the benefits of her efforts and skills.

I told Kerry once, one morning when we were out walking on some nature trails near our hotel (before mobile phones), "If you were to have a medical problem and collapse, I would never be able to find my way back to get help. And even if I somehow did, I would never find you again."

I asked her if she was OK with my poor contributions because she works really hard to make everything happen for us. She said, "I like traveling with you. I like being the explorer. Having two explorers on a trip can create friction. And if both people were like you—well, why would you even go anywhere?"

The last laugh

7.9

I am really grateful that I got to have my parents in my life for a long time. Mom and Dad both died in their early 80s. I often think about their big hearts and endless goodwill and how at the end of my legs, I have my father's feet.

Losing my parents was difficult and sad. The world is a very different place without them. But in honor of our family's near constant laugh track, my parents did not fail even in their deaths.

Dad died in the hospital. He was complaining about the food and flirting with the nurses till his last day. When he lost consciousness near the end, I was there accompanied by two dear friends. One was a very spiritual person and the other was an ex-priest. Kerry was on an airplane racing to the scene as fast as possible.

I will just say that attending someone's deathbed is yet another social situation where I had no idea how to be. I don't know how to make small talk with anyone, let alone someone who is unconscious. I told my dad I loved him, but that was all I had. My spiritual friend was talking to him without pause, and the ex-priest was chanting. They made the vibe in the room super lovely. And I just sat there like an idiot.

At one point, all the machines measuring my dad's various functions stopped. Nurses ran in and said there was a technology glitch. They were all poking at the machines and unplugging and rebooting everything. After about five minutes of this, the doctor walked in and said, "Stop fussing with the machines, it's not the machines—he's dead."

Good one, Dad! We all laughed. Instead of a final moment that was only about sadness and loss, Dad gifted us with a comedic exit.

When it was Mom's time, she was at home in her bed. She had lost consciousness for the last few days. Kerry and I were equally ill-equipped to say and do the right things. But I had an idea. I had heard from a friend whose mother had suffered and died from Alzheimer's that even if the person can't understand your words, they can feel your energy. For example—don't have a stressful conversation about their care in front of them.

So Kerry and I decided to lean on our tried-and-true family values of laughter and cocktail hours. If we didn't know how to talk to Mom or recite poetry or chant prayers like our more capable friends, we did know how to laugh. So (hang on and bear with me, it was beautiful, I promise) on those last days, we established "deathbed happy hour."

Kerry and I made Manhattans and sat on opposite sides of Mom's bed. We evaluated the impact of her "you're not allowed to be bored" and "stick with it" rules on our lives, and we pondered whether she *let* us or *made* us be creative when we were kids. We remembered the time the whole family was laughing so hard at the dinner table that we all had to retreat into our bedrooms to be alone so we could stop laughing and actually eat. We told stories about Mom's epic cocktail parties and the silly games she made up to keep everyone laughing. We admired how Mom made Christmas so fun and welcoming with decorations and lasagnas and cookies and drinks and music and laughter that our Jewish friends could not resist coming to our house—and how Mom called it her "Jews for Santa" program. And we toyed with the idea of reviving Marble Cupway.

We laughed and laughed, and it felt like we were supporting Mom in the last moments of her journey in exactly the way she would have wanted —with love and laughter and a cocktail. I did not feel stupid that time. We nailed that one.

Safety check

7.10

Soon after Mom's death, Kerry, who handles the various financial transactions in our family, wanted to get Mom's house sold. Since I was local, I was sent off to meet Mark, the realtor. Mark looked kind of like a rock star, but hiding behind round wire-rimmed glasses and a business-casual, realtor-on-a-Saturday sweater outfit.

He asked me if I was talking to any other realtors. I was still so exhausted from all the emotional and practical things surrounding a death of a parent that I told him I was following Kerry's wishes to do this right away. I said, "I am not going to interview multiple realtors. If you're not an asshole or an idiot, you're getting the listing."

Mark was very concerned that I was OK. He was very sensitive to the context of this transaction and wanted to make sure I didn't find anything about it upsetting. He didn't want me to feel pressured or rushed.

I told him, "I am sad, but I am also OK."

He hugged me.

Then we walked outside to see the back patio. He hugged me again.

Then we waked out the other side to see the garage. We hugged again.

It struck me that this seemed like a lot of hugging for a real estate listing appointment.

Mark was a chatty dude, and for some reason, he told me a story about a man who decades ago was in an arranged marriage. They were each in dangerous situations in their lives, and both accepted that this marriage would be their best path out of harm's way. He asked the man, "Did you love her?"

"No, of course not. I didn't know her. But we were in a scary situation, and we decided to commit to each other that no matter what, we would keep each other safe."

I've got to tell you, that idea shook my world. I had never thought about safety as a basis for a relationship. Making people feel safe was foundational to my leadership strategy at work. It was the most primary of gifts my parents had given me and modeled for my whole life. But in the realm of choosing men, I got that wrong over and over again.

We talked about the idea of safety in a romantic relationship, not just keeping someone physically out of harm's way, but also caring for their emotional safety—keeping your partner protected from the psychological harm of judgment and shame and anger. Mark was really into this making-people-feel-safe thing . . . which explained some of the hugging.

In my own bad relationship choices, it seems I was distracted by the idea that you choose a person based on some sort of fascination and mutual grooviness; the importance of keeping each other safe never came up.

Keep each other safe . . . how did I miss that?

I was determined to be even smarter about the people I let into my personal life in the future. But before you can find the good ones, you have to open yourself up a bit. And that didn't always work out so well . . .

Mario male

7.11

I was at my favorite bridge in Florence enjoying the sunset. I was in my early 50s when a man who looked to be in his mid-30s, in a blue sport coat, classy eyeglass frames, a scarf, bracelets, shoes, no socks, and longish, thick, wavy, good hair—clearly Italian—took a spot nearby. His name was Mario. I will use the name Mario to protect the innocent, because, well, his name was Mario.

After the sun had fully set, when I was no longer glued to my camera, he started talking to me. He was a regional sales manager. Smart, polite, interesting, pleasant. We ended up at a nearby café for a glass of wine.

We made a date for dinner the next day, and he walked me home.

Standing outside my apartment, I said, "See you tomorrow for dinner." But he said he had a long walk home (which was true) and asked to use the bathroom.

So I started the standard female murder-potential checklist in my head. *If I let him in, how likely is it that he will kill me? How likely is it that he will rape me?* I thought, *Not likely.* He seemed actually like a gentle and harmless type: very mild-mannered, thoughtful, and polite. And small. I probably weighed more than him. I remember thinking, as I was calculating the danger level, that I probably would have hired him as a regional sales manager. And I'd like to live in a world where you don't need to deny a regional sales manager who needs to use the bathroom.

Within seconds of being inside my apartment, he grabbed me, pinned me against the wall, and put his hands down the front of my pants.

Then he started grinding his erection into me.

Oh, brother.

How is it that I can be at the "handshake, nice to meet you" phase of an acquaintance, and the man decides his best first move is to stick his hands inside my pants? I literally sighed. *I'm too old for this* . . .

I was really annoyed.

I grabbed his wrists, pulled his hands out of my pants, and said in Italian, just to be super clear, "NO. This is not OK. You need to go away now. *No! Vatene. Adesso!*"

He didn't go.

Then it started . . .

"But why? What is the matter with you?"

"I told you NO. You need to go."

"Why are you being like this?"

"I said NO. This is not OK. You need to leave."

Then, in that whiny tone that horny men use when they want to convince you, he said, "But whyyyy? You are so beautiful. Don't be like this. Do you know how much you are hurting me . . ."

Apparently, *I* was the one behaving badly.

"If you don't want me to touch you, then you just touch me." He grabbed my hand and put it on his erection.

Men and their erections . . .

It's fascinating to me that when a woman says NO, a man thinks that if he shows her his erection, all of sudden she'll be like, "Now *that* changes everything! I can't resist you now that I see *that*. Take me here, right now, on this occasional table."

I pulled my hand away, pushed him aside, and said more forcefully again, "You need to leave now." Whatever I had been thinking about our date the next day, now, clearly, that was never going to happen. He was really awful.

But I could not get him to leave. We went through another several hundred rounds of relentless begging: Why? NO. Why? NO. But why not? Don't you like sex? Are you a prude? Are you a weirdo? Why are you being so unfair? WHY are you being so cruel to me?

I'm thinking, *I'm not exactly afraid of you; if you were going to rape me, you would not be wasting all this time begging.* And I had become very practiced over the years at working my way out of these unwanted-hands-in-the-pants situations before they became dangerous.

I finally got him walking toward the door. He said, "OK, I'll go, but I want you to go out and buy sexy lingerie for tomorrow night. And I don't want to have dinner, I just want to come here and have sex all night on every surface in this apartment."

OMG. You are such a gross idiot. Just get out, please, please, please. Just go.

The way the apartment was laid out, you could see the corner of the guest bed from the top of the steps that led down to the front door.

As he was finally heading for the steps, he saw the bed. He quickly grabbed me, picked me up, threw me down on the bed so I landed on my back, stood over me, unbuckled his belt, and started taking off his pants.

Oh my God . . .

How is this small man so strong?

He had instantly transformed from just annoying to dangerous. I leaped to my feet like a shape-shifting monster from a science fiction movie and drew upon actual rage, and I screamed, this time in English, "GET OUT, NOW."

And he left. Finally.

But he was skipping down the stairs, smiling, laughing, and saying, "See you tomorrow. Don't forget the lingerie."

"See you tomorrow"? Good lord—he actually thinks that was OK. How could anyone think that was OK?

Not all men . . . but enough men

7.12

Once Mario was finally out and the door was locked behind him, I poured a glass of wine and went outside on my terrace overlooking the river and the city lights of Florence.

Mario and his erection were a basic study in:

Woman: "You harassed/assaulted me."

Man: "I didn't do anything wrong. It was fun. You are overreacting. You wanted it. You are lying. Women are crazy."

The reason I included this story is not to be shocking. To most women, this is not shocking at all.

It fascinates me that I have told the Mario experience to four women, and all I said was, "I met this man, it went bad, I couldn't get him to leave"— and they know. They *know*.

They needed no details.

They simply asked, "Are you OK? Were you hurt? Were you scared?" And then when I assured them that I was OK, they just rolled their eyes. One of them imitated octopus arms. They have all been there.

When I Told Good Men . . .

All the men I told were shocked—*shocked*, I tell you, clutching their pearls. They could not imagine any man doing such a thing. They needed to reject the premise that this happens regularly to women. Every single one demanded details and tried to confine the offense to a small population of men that didn't include themselves. "That must just happen in Italy." "That must just happen in America." "That must just happen with older men." "That must just happen with younger men." "That must just happen with Italian regional sales managers named Mario." "No man I know would ever do that."

Why is this so completely understood by virtually *all* women but not at all understood by so many good men—men who enjoy the comfy luxury of thinking this sort of thing doesn't happen to women all the time?

Don't get me wrong. I am absolutely NOT saying that ALL MEN behave this way. In my life, I have had the company of mostly men, and most of them were good to me. Many of them I adore. But ENOUGH men in the world behave this way toward enough women, enough times, that ALL WOMEN experience it.

Sitting on my terrace, I watched as a lightning bolt lit up the Duomo in the skyline in spectacular form.

As I looked out over the city, I thought about how (thankfully) this level of assault never happened to me in the workplace. The unpleasant sexual behaviors of bosses, colleagues, and clients all fell into the "just annoying" category for me.

But I still had the icky feeling of Mario in my nervous system. And it got me thinking about all the men at work who were still *clueless takers*, like Mario—they don't always need to force their hands into your clothes to dehumanize you. There are so many other options.

For example, there were times when a man, making his way through a room, just physically moved me out of his way—no "hello," no "excuse me." It felt like this was his room and I was an inconveniently placed umbrella stand.

Or when a man would steal my ideas in meetings or take credit for my work—not even realizing he did it—as if the gods had implanted my idea directly into his being, and I didn't even exist.

It's so weird that they seem entirely clueless when they do these things. It's like they have no awareness at all that they are taking something from another actual person, with no regard for that person.

(By the way, here's how I've learned to get my idea back when a man steals it in a meeting. To do this, you have to learn to interrupt, and you have to pounce. You can't hesitate at all. If you hesitate, he now owns your idea. So I interrupt before he even finishes restating my idea and say: "Thank you for bringing that up again. As I was saying before . . .")

I was still repulsed by Mario. I needed another glass of wine for this. I brought the whole bottle out.

What was this ugly feeling in my body right now, and why did it feel so similar to those experiences at work?

As the wine kicked in, I saw the connection. It was the *disregard*.

What I was feeling was that grim numbness that comes when I need to dull the part of myself that feels violated when my humanity has been disregarded—whether the disregard is sexual or just when I'm not being considered a full human with a unique identity and the right to an equal existence.

This numbing is a survival skill we women develop. We have to. It's just not practical to get upset about every shitty interaction with a man when we are swimming upstream in a system that dismisses and demeans us so regularly—and so casually. A system that by default labels us a stupid rat, if not a sex object. A system that can absorb debilitating amounts of our talents and work, yet treat us like we are not even there.

How much disregard have I absorbed throughout my life? I thought about how my boundaries of "dangerous or just annoying?" were helpful but not perfect. While that approach kept me safe and kept my career moving forward, it certainly had an energetic cost. *I absorbed a lot of annoying.*

Recently, I had lunch with a former colleague, a man, and he reminisced, "But we had a lot of fun back then, didn't we?" It's the Mario problem in corporate clothing. Not everyone is having fun just because you are.

OK, enough of this. Enough wine.

I was tired.

I went back inside and tidied up the apartment before bed. Mario had already texted me. "I'll see you tomorrow and I want to have lots of sex. Don't forget the lingerie. What time?"

OMG—the disregard. And literally. No. Clue.

I deleted him from my phone, and I wanted to stomp on my phone and set my phone on fire and throw it into the river.

Looking for love in all the wrong places

7.13

In grammar school, even though little patty was an outcast, that did not stop her from being a hopeless romantic. There was a boy she liked so much. He was cute and funny, and he was as smart as she was. In her heart, she knew it was a perfect match. *We are the two smartest people in the class. It's so much fun when we talk, we always win when we are partners on a project, we challenge each other, and we laugh.* She dreamed about being his girlfriend one day.

I recently talked to this boy, and the subject of our being kids together at school decades ago came up. I said to him, not as some big reveal but just as amusing conversation, "You know, I had such a crush on you in grammar school." He replied, "What I remember about you from back then is that you beat me out for valedictorian."

Man, that die was cast early! This basic premise of my problems in the love department started when I was nine and stuck with me like a bad haircut that never grew out.

It cracks me up that it took me decades and many failed relationships (or ones that never started) to realize that the principal thing I chose to make myself "worthy of love" (being a high achiever and collector of gold stars) is the very thing that men hate! *Love me because you're so impressed that I'm as smart and accomplished as you are. Wait, where are you go-ing?*

My career successes seemed to downright repel the men who knew about my career.

I did occasionally meet attractive, single men while traveling who did not already know about me. I learned to take advantage of that and answer questions about myself with something other than "I'm a CEO" or "I'm an author." Instead, I'd say, "I'm here for a conference" (without mentioning that I was the keynote speaker). And then I'd make the conversation all about them. "Wow, that's so interesting, tell me more . . ."

But no matter how much fun or how warm those conversations seemed, or how much of a spark or a connection there seemed to be at the start, I never passed the subsequent Google search or the test of daylight. No one ever called.

So, when I was out and about looking for companionship with men my age and younger—who perceived that they had the same or less status than me—nothing ever started. And with men my age and older—who perceived that they had more status than me—well, they were looking for a younger model.

No one was looking for me.

Seeking single adequate male

7.14

I have a group of single female friends over 50, and we all had the same idea. We'd like some companionship (and sex) but not someone who tells us where we should put the coffee pot. None of us were looking for a long-term commitment.

I made the mistake of thinking men would like this. *Sure, I'll have sex with you, and it doesn't need to be exclusive.*

I was so surprised to find out just how much men seemed to ardently dislike this idea. So, I asked a male friend, "Don't men see this as a good thing?" His answer: "Well, yes, sort of. That's what we men want for ourselves, but we don't want it to be the woman who chooses it for us. We want to have sex with other women, but we don't want you to be OK with that. We want you to only want us, and we definitely don't want you to be with other men."

I asked other male friends in their 20s through 60s and I got the same answer. Huh.

All of my married friends seem to think I have this exciting sex life where there's a steady line of enthusiastic suitors stretching around the corner that I can just choose from at whim. They are so surprised to hear that there is, in fact, no one in that line.

I know single women over 40 or even 50 who have no trouble finding these men. Some have a steady rotation. They use a variety of methods, online and in the real world, that I have determined don't work for people with crippling introversion whose favorite thing to do is stay home alone.

I did have some surprising luck in Italy, though. Just after I turned 50, I had a few fun experiences with men in their 20s. I was certainly not looking for them (both as an introvert and a 50-year-old!). They found me—and they had no life context to be troubled by my career.

One night, on the patio at my favorite pizza place, a young man sat down at the table across from me. We started talking. It was his last night in Florence. He was on a European tour with a group of twenty-somethings, and said he needed a break from them. When I finished my wine, I asked, "Have you seen the city at night?"

"No."

"It's really beautiful, the way they light the old buildings here. I am going to take a stroll through the center. Would you like to join me?"

This was not unusual. I encountered many young people (men and women) traveling on their own, and we would often take walks and share meals together, and then at some point in the evening, they would go off and do their young people things.

But "Lorenzo" (his adopted Italian name for the Italian leg of his tour) was hanging in there with me well into the evening. We had deep conversations and laughed and walked for a couple of hours.

Then he said, "Do you know somewhere to get a drink?"

Ah, this was my cue that he was ready to go. While my brain started jumping through possibilities to recommend to a young, handsome man where he could go meet girls, he started kissing me. And it was very nice. Not at all like Mario.

Lorenzo was an old soul for sure, but in the hard, sculpted, athletic body of a 25-year-old. Did you know that men in their 20s with hard, sculpted, athletic bodies are good-looking? This fact had totally escaped me when I was myself in my 20s.

As we headed back to my apartment, he said, "Can I ask how old you are?"

Damn, I thought I was going to get away with this. Oh well.

I thought carefully about my answer. After some moments, I said, "I don't want to lie, and I think you don't want to know."

"I want to know."

"I'm 51."

He stopped our walk.

Damn. Oh well. That might have been fun.

Then he turned toward me and leaned back, now holding both of my hands, and just looked at me. He smiled and said, "Cool." Then he kissed me again, picked me up, and spun me around under the lights of the Palazzo Vecchio.

We had a lovely night and a lovely morning.

I later asked Kerry, "Where were all these old-soul, mature, interesting, handsome, 20-something men when I was in my 20s?"

"When you were in your 20s, they were all talking to older women."

There were some rare occasions when I connected with a man of a more suitable age. But each time, it felt uncomfortable and unfulfilling. And it gave me that "taking" vibe when they would get weird and closed off and make an unfriendly escape in the morning.

But that unexpected experience with Lorenzo had inspired me that a one-night fling with a man could actually be fun and nourishing with no negative emotional cost.

So I decided from now I would not give up but that I would set the bar very high. Here's what this very high bar looked like:

1. You need to have talked to me enough to like me.
2. You need to be nice to me in the morning.

This cut the field to zero.

One evening, a married, male colleague who seemed oddly fascinated to learn about my sex life was grilling me about this. He wouldn't believe me that there was no one interested.

He said, "I could go out there and find you five men right now who would want to have sex with you tonight."

"Well, OK then! Bring me these five men."

(That didn't happen.)

Pretty universally, no one believed me about how bad I was at this. Let's face it. I am tragically ill-equipped to meet new people in general. So take that and apply it to meeting a man, and I am utterly hopeless. Here's an example.

I was in Zurich, out for a walk in the morning taking photos. I had just walked across a bridge and something compelled me to look back. A person was standing in the middle of the bridge taking a wonderful photo of the river and cityscape that I had missed. I thought, *I want that photo too!* As I approached, I saw that it was a quite handsome man, who was now trying to take a selfie. I said, "Hi. Do you speak English?"

"Yes."

"Would you like me to take a picture of you?"

"Yes, that would be great." He handed me his phone.

I took a picture and handed his phone back to him.

Then I said, "Have a nice day"—and walked away.

Walked. Away.

Not 10 minutes later, along the river, I saw another handsome man trying to take a selfie. I walked up to him and said, "Hi. Would you like me to take a picture of you?"

"That would be great, but my camera is broken and only the selfie camera works, not the distance one." And he had an Italian accent. Swoon.

I said, "OK" . . . and walked away!

Are you sensing a theme here?

This time, two things occurred to me:

1. Patty, if you'd like to meet a man, a handsome one taking a selfie might be a good place to start . . . cause, ya know, "selfie."

2. Go back.

So I turned around and walked back. And, dying a little, I bravely said, "Hey, I just thought, if you would like a nice picture, I could take one with my phone and send it to you."

"That would be great."

So then I switched to Italian. "Sei Italiano, non e' vero?"

It turned out he was an Italian doctor. He was living in Switzerland alone. He did not need to work until the evening.

It was about 10 in the morning. We had a lovely, warm talk for maybe 20 minutes in Italian, and then he asked to take a selfie of us together with my phone, and he sent it to himself. Nice. And then . . .

I WALKED AWAY!

I had no idea how to close that deal. My more competent friend later told me, "Patty, you suggest having lunch together, and then you order wine." *OK. If there is a next time, now I've got my script.*

As time went on, I was also beginning to realize that I was meeting high-quality, single men who were in their seventies. Some of them showed interest in me.

"Maybe that's the secret," I told Kerry. "I'm not ready to be with a 70-year-old now, but maybe my strategy should be to just stay alone for a while and wait until I'm 70, and then I can connect with a high-quality man."

Kerry said, "When you're 70, they'll want someone younger."

Boy, howdy!

7.15

After the sale of my mom's house, Mark, the realtor, and I needed to meet several times to organize various transfers of items, monies, and documents. There were probably more meetings than were strictly necessary. And these meetings migrated to my house and, over time, included drinking Manhattans.

And, like in the old movies when the nerdy secretary takes her glasses off and lets her hair down, when Mark grew his hair out and took his glasses off, now he really did look like a rock star.

At one point, Kerry said, "You know, Mark really went out of his way and did so much extra work for us. We really need to get him something. Buy him a bottle of his favorite bourbon."

Me: "I agree I should do something, but that would be awkward because *he* just gave *me* a bottle of his favorite bourbon."

Kerry: "Then just have sex with him."

Mark and I would sit on the sofa for hours with our Manhattans and have wonderful conversations, which always led to both of us saying in one way or another, "I'm not interested in a serious relationship."

But he kept coming back.

One night, after about seven evenings together, he got very quiet and thoughtful. Then, looking down at his Manhattan, he began: "I need to say something. I am feeling an enormous attraction to you. I know that you don't want a relationship, and neither do I. And I don't want to create any pressure for you if you don't feel the same way, but I just can't not say it anymore."

As it turned out, I was feeling the same way.

So we've been "not having a relationship" together for many years now. And he continues to stress this idea that in any relationship, the most important thing is to keep the other person safe.

In the past, I was always trying to do the emotional work for two by myself. It was frustrating and lonely. Now when I get home after a battle of some sort in the world, Mark will take my hand and bring me to the sofa. He'll say, "Let's just sit here and let our energy settle." We'll tangle our legs together. He'll say, "How did your work make you feel today? Tell me about your dream vacation. Tell me about your favorite scientist. Tell me more about your comforter." He maintains this bubble of safe, connected space for us until I'm relaxed and all talked out. And then he makes me dinner.

It's weird.

He is actively trying to keep our connection strong and keep me physically and emotionally safe all the time. His nurturing kindness is so surprising and unexpected that it's still hard to get my mind around, even after years.

Like, he always opens the car door for me. Always. My brain jolts and stumbles every time. "Wait, what are you doing on this side? I thought you were driving. Why are you standing next to me right now? I thought I was driving. We can't both get in this side." Then I remember, and I see him smiling at me as he reaches for the door handle.

He recently told me that he learned his manners from his mother, who was following an etiquette book from the 1800s. So he also knows how to help me out of a horse-drawn carriage in the rain if that ever comes up.

One Sunday morning, we were having coffee (OK, it was 11:30, and it was champagne). He was telling me a story, and he said, "Boy, howdy, that was something."

"Did you just say 'boy, howdy'?"

"Yeah, why?"

"Boy, howdy? Really? Is that a real thing that people say? Or just you?"

"No. It's a real thing."

Mark has shown me how to expect more and how to give more. He is fully on my team and I am on his. He wants me to reach for

Mark and me at my home in California

my goals. He is excited for me when I am questing and kind to me when I am tired. Al was right. Nothing will have a greater impact on your career and life than who you wake up with in the morning.

And Mark, after having heard one time about my tragic, unfulfilled childhood dream—for my first birthday together, he put glow-in-the-dark stars on my bedroom ceiling.

Boy, howdy!

Part 8

Boy, Are My Arms Tired

"The alarm can ring.
The birds can peep.
My bed is warm.
My pillow's deep.
Today's the day I'm going to sleep."

—Dr. Seuss

Then this happened . . .

8.1

My friend picked this place for its wine selection. We were sitting outside at a bistro table, soaking up a warm, sunny California evening, surrounded by cool shops, and colorful flowers—there was a lively vibe, with groups of happy people wandering by. I began my evaluation of my wineglass. It was too tall and kind of tippy. And the square-ish shape seemed pretentious and not pleasant to drink from.

I greatly admired my friend. She had built her own marketing agency and run it for many years, and I was always wowed by this. The idea of creating and growing a company on my own had always seemed impossible to me—but she had done it. Having brilliant friends like her was one of the things in my life that I loved.

"How are you doing in your work, Patty?" she asked.

I considered how I would answer as I tried to make peace with my wineglass and spun into silent, introvert, hyper-processing mode.

How do I give a short answer? Let's take stock . . . I am in my big dream job, where I successfully implemented a massive transformation. I launched a new strategy globally—and it worked. I deftly avoided the flash cards problem. (Will there ever come a time when I stop thinking about the flash cards?) I have built a high-performing team of truly wonderful people who I love working with. I am well supported by my mentors and management. And, oh yeah . . . just last week I was selected as one of only 10 out of 20,000 people to be part of a special employee retention program. 10 out of 20,000! They put a lot of money on the line to motivate me to stay with the company. They want me there! (Now THAT was a gold star from the teacher that made little patty very proud.)

I snapped out of my introvert brain churn. "I'm doing really well, thanks. The business is on a good growth track and the team is doing great. I'm excited about what I am doing and I feel really good about it."

We picked up our tall, tippy, square glasses to clink. "Cheers to that!"

Now, imagine clouds darkening over our happy scene and the flowers wilting. And cue the suspenseful music . . .

Within a week, my whole world changed.

HP had merged with Compaq. An apocalyptic re-org was unfolding.

Suddenly, everyone above me—all of my management and all of my mentors—were swept away into different organizations or just gone.

Not a single person was left in my world who cared about me.

And I knew that without sponsorship or air cover of some kind, I was at great risk. You simply can't push against the system enough by yourself.

But suddenly, there I was—alone. None of the management in the new regime would even talk to me or return my calls.

And then . . .

I was pushed out of the company.

Let's take a moment to review. I went from being recognized as one of 10 top performers out of 20,000 the company believed they couldn't do without—to being pushed out in a single step.

Weird, right?

The best way I can describe what happened, briefly, was that I was framed for something that I didn't do, then lost my job over it.

OK, the less brief version:

I had been running a software business, which meant "not a hardware business," which meant no physical stuff: no computers, no printers, no storage devices, etc. This also meant that my software business was highly profitable because we didn't need to pay for all that physical stuff.

But here's the plot twist that led to my demise. There came a moment before the re-org when a bunch of expenses in some unrelated hardware businesses needed to be hidden—expenses that were 100 percent focused on physical costs like delivery trucks, storage warehouses, real estate costs, inventory management, and supply chain management. *My software business had none of these costs.*

But a huge amount of these hardware costs were put onto my expense statement, making it look like I was spending way more money than I was actually spending. This maneuver was done to *make a different part of the company look more profitable.* I argued against this to no avail. I was told in no uncertain terms to stop fighting this, it was going to happen, and I needed to be a team player.

So even though my software business was in the real world actually very profitable . . . now on paper, it was showing that it was losing money because of the artificial expenses that had been buried under an obscure line item in my financial statements.

When the new regime came in, well, they couldn't believe that a software business would be losing so much money. They put a new person in charge of the strategy to fix it and told him, "You are forbidden to talk to Patty Azzarello about it because she is an idiot. Clearly she has no idea what she is doing—a software business should be profitable."

The system just disregarded me entirely. No one ever even talked to me about it. I never got to explain what really happened or share my future strategy that I had worked so hard on. As far as they were concerned, I did not exist.

I only learned of this distortion of reality after I was taken out of my job.

Just keep swimming

8.2

D amn.
    I was stunned.

After all those years of swimming against the current, *I had finally arrived upstream.* I was in my dream job and doing really well. I was finally enjoying my work. I was getting paid well. But then, instead of getting to bask in the glorious waterfall, I got swiftly eaten by the bear. I just got bounced out unceremoniously. And no one even noticed.

I had to learn a hard lesson here. It was like the episode of *Star Trek: The Next Generation* where Data, the android, loses a game of *Strategema* to a human. This should not have been possible because his programming did not allow him to make errors in the game. The lesson Data and I both needed to learn was that *you can make no mistakes and still lose.*

After all of that effort over all those years to build my credibility. After doing all those scary things to stand up for myself. After all the relentless challenges to defend my existence to just stay in the room. And after all the great teams and business success that I built. I was just out.

They didn't fire me exactly.

They took me out of my role running the 3,000-person organization and asked me to run a marketing team of two people. It's called "constructive termination." Jim calls this "VP of No Smoking in the Lobby." It's a way to take someone out of a big job but not have to pay them an exit package. The company hopes you are dumb enough to get discouraged and quit for free.

First I called Jim. "Yeah, you are toast. Look for a new job."

And then I called Al. In his inimitable, ninja-teddy-bear manner, he talked me through the whole situation emotionally and strategically. He shared his wisdom about life and success and setbacks. And he said, "Look for a new job."

And then I called Mom. "Patty, remember, this isn't about you. You had no control over this. You've worked so hard and accomplished so much. This sucks. But you'll be OK. Look for a new job."

I guess I need to look for a new job.

But, after a few weeks, I found two silver linings in this dismal turn of events.

First, once I spoke the words "constructive termination," there was no legal battle necessary. The new regime knew they had to cover my contract. And because I was in that elite group of 10 top performers, they had to pay me quite a lot of money to send me away. So that was something.

And second, I realized that in pursuit of my goal of being a CEO of a public company, I would need to leave this dream job at some point anyway. As happy as I was there, I was no longer growing enough or getting the kinds of experiences I would need to meet my ultimate goal.

I decided that I just needed to absorb the new regime's disregard for me and my career and move on. I did my best. But I was angry because this wasn't fair.

But I also knew that it was important to my health and future success to not stay angry.

I thought about the saying that *staying angry is like drinking the poison and waiting for the other person to die.* I'd like to think that someone might have said, "Oh shit, did we make a mistake?" when they realized that I was on that very short "must retain" list, but in reality, no one cared. They were never going to drink the poison. I decided that I was not going to either.

I also came across another gem from Jill Bolte Taylor, a brain scientist, who wrote that anger creates a real, chemical reaction in your body, but the effect only lasts for 90 seconds. So, after 90 seconds, it's entirely up to you to stay angry. I guess that's why staying angry is so exhausting—because you need to keep investing your own effort to do so.

I needed to manage my precious, limited energy points better than that. And it's ineffective to look for a new job while being angry about the last one. People can feel it.

So, even though I felt like my life had been gutted, I felt as duty bound as ever to make practical forward progress. I didn't have room to stay angry. I needed to find a new job—now.

Oops—I hate my job

8.3

Over the next several years, following my "experience paradox" strategy, I thoughtfully chose three different roles that would give me the specific new experiences I would need to ultimately win a public company CEO job. One was the CEO of a Silicon Valley venture-funded company, and two others were top executive roles in larger public companies.

But, distressingly, I found that none of these jobs turned out to be a good match for my strengths. What I was great at was running a large organization. But that is not what any of these jobs were.

In my Silicon Valley CEO job, the first problem was that I was in Silicon Valley again. And as a CEO now, from this higher perch I was even closer to the crazy egos flying around—which I detested. Silicon Valley was never going to be my happy place.

There were only 35 people in my company in the US and another 30 in India. My job was mostly to raise more funding, be a salesperson, and order toilet paper for the bathrooms. I didn't feel like I had a choice, though. It's simply not possible to get placed as a CEO of a large public organization as your first CEO job. If I wanted to be a CEO of a large company, I had to start by being the CEO of a small one.

But as bad as it feels to be in a job you are not good at (like being a bad piano player), I actually find it much more soul-destroying to be in a job that doesn't give a damn about my strengths. I was good at running large organizations, and no one cared.

But there I was, and I was trying to make the best of it.

In the other two executive roles, I was intent on gaining the additional experience I needed, like direct exposure to the board and Wall Street, to later secure my big company CEO job.

But I found that these roles were not really using my strengths either, and the ratio of *money earned* to *life force sacrificed* was not working in my favor. It was quite the opposite. These dues-paying jobs were just pumping the energy points out of me.

Like, one night, I walked through the door to my house after a day that had dragged on forever. It was dark and I was super grumpy. I didn't have the energy to take off my suit before falling onto the sofa.

Man, everybody got so worked up over naming a product that no one is going to buy no matter what we name it—because it's a terrible product. And did we really have to have this mind-numbing debate until 10:00pm? Only to end up deciding to keep the same stupid name we started with? And it's going to land on me to cancel this product when everybody figures out that it's never going to work.

And damn, I have to be back at the office at 6:00am tomorrow for the financial analyst meeting, which means getting up at 4:15am . . . or earlier if I want coffee. Do I want coffee or 15 minutes extra sleep? And oh, right, then tomorrow night is that dinner with the clients from Europe— that's not going to end before 11:00pm. Dammit.

I felt like I was losing the plot to my life. As I finally headed for bed, calculating that I could get 5 hours of sleep max (if I feel asleep while walking there), the reverberating thought in my body was . . . *I hate my job.*

Boy, are my arms tired

8.4

T he next morning, it was still dark when the alarm started stabbing me in the brain. I checked in with all of my limbs and my comforter as a bolt of dread ran through me. I just couldn't believe that the sleep portion of the program was over. It seemed about 37 hours too short. As my upcoming activities for the day clicked through my mind, my most prominent thought was, *I cannot wait to get back into bed tonight.*

That was my waking thought on most days: *I can't wait to get back into bed tonight.* Some days I even thought, *It would be great if I could be hospitalized for a few days for something just major enough that no one could reasonably expect me to show up or respond, but not serious enough to impact my long-term health—and people would bring me pudding.*

And I kept wondering: *Is this what success is supposed to feel like?*

My job, like all executive jobs, had hard parts: high-stakes decisions and negotiations, stressful risks, huge complexity, unreasonable demands from clients, colleagues, employees, and management, difficult conversations, scarce resources, impossible tradeoffs . . . but to be honest, those were not the things that I found tiring or difficult. Those challenges lined up with my skills. I can do those hard things.

If I am being honest, the hardest thing about my job was that it was killing me physically. Even with all of the tools I had developed to manage my time and energy and fitness, they were not enough to combat the energetic demand of a high-level executive job.

Travel made me ill almost 100 percent of the time. And travel was constant.

And there was an always-on, pressure to keep track of everything that was happening with the market, the customers, the partners, the sales force, the competition, the media, the analysts, the products, and the team.

I was exhausted all the time. This was not feeling like success.

As I lay in bed that morning, I thought about being the CEO of a public company in light of how I had been feeling lately in my body, heart, and brain. And I thought about what that role would demand of me in a realistic and practical sense. And then a very clear picture started to form: *That would be a terrible job for me!*

I didn't want to be one of those people who reaches retirement with a lot of money but no health or energy left to enjoy it, or who drop dead five minutes later.

There was deep truth I had been trying to push away, but it was growing . . . and that morning, I began to think the unthinkable. *I think I don't want to be a CEO of a public company anymore.*

I gently squished the squares of my baffle-stitched, high-fill-power comforter to extract some life force from the puffiness.

If I abandon my goal, have I wasted my life? Have I spent all these years working so hard on the wrong goal for nothing? Should I have just disobeyed Mom and become an artist? Did I get my whole life wrong?

At this point, I had abandoned the idea that I could get up early enough to have coffee. I snuggled in a bit deeper to play out this existential crisis.

Yes, it had been hard, but I was proud of what I did. And it was not without its rewards.

First of all, I accomplished what I set out to do. *I did it.* I got to have what they were having. I got to write the narrative of my own life and make my own choices.

I got lots of gold stars along the way. And sometimes the gold stars came in the form of money. I liked the money. I collected enough winnings to get a good start on retirement. I got to buy myself the beautiful home I'd wanted since I was five, with multiple comforters and fluffy carpets—even though Mom would disapprove based on cleanability and allergic risk.

But the best part of surviving my career, and what I carry in my heart, is not the business success; it is the remarkable people I was able to help and cheer on, who have gone on to make their own big differences in the world, and who have become my dear friends.

I would like to believe that the world is a better place because I survived my career.

And I also thought about how after having grown up in such a small, isolated, dull, brown, place on this planet, how thankful I was that work forced me to travel. Without my career, I would have stayed home. And I would have missed so much amazement. My mind flashed through scenes of Sydney Harbour, the Japanese fishing village, the Formula One factory, the original Gutenberg printing press, and being driven inside the Mountain at NORAD. Things I never would have seen if it were not for my career.

I thought, *I'm happy I did it all, even though it made me really tired and now I am thinking about walking away. I did not waste my life.* There were too many good things to discount. And as someone who has always been generally uncomfortable out in the world, I had grown so much stronger and smarter and more comfortable in myself. That would not have happened without all the swimming upstream and the capacity I developed in my career to stay in the room—to not get chased away.

I took one last moment before dragging myself out of bed, and smiled as I recalled walking by a luxury duvet store in Munich with my colleague. Duvets. In Germany. It was like finding the mother ship. I bolted inside. It was a pure delight to wander through all the luxury duvets, with German-castle-level puffiness, and relive that life-changing moment, seeing Julie Andrews with her glorious, billowing comforter in *The Sound of Music.*

So, even though my career stressed and exhausted me, it also fed me some of the most amazing and beautiful experiences of my life. That's how life goes. *There is a cost to seeking amazement—and it's worth it.*

Lying there that morning, I accepted that changing my mind about the future would not negate my past accomplishments.

In the end, I would like to say that my decision to walk away from the goal that had been my North Star for so many years was a result of me smartly outgrowing a dream and confidently making a proactive decision to benefit my life, and not because I was just too tired and gave up, but it was probably a little of both.

Then I got up, suited up, and went to work, without coffee, but with a great sense of relief as I recalled the first secret passageway little patty ever discovered: ***If you don't like how things are going, you get to make your own decision to change your life to make it better.***

I get to write my own story. It was time for a new story.

Walking away

8.5

I was sitting in a California/Thai fusion restaurant in Silicon Valley, waiting for a work dinner to start, desperately wishing I was home instead, and doing the exact math about how few hours of sleep I might get before my early morning meeting the next day.

I was still thinking about changing the course of my career. My mind leaped back to an evening at a restaurant in China.

My team and I were crammed around a low table in the bar when they set out to make Chinese business cards for me. They conferred in a huddle to identify Chinese characters to use to approximate the sound of my name.

They came back with a set of characters that, when spoken, sounded roughly like "Pah-Tee-Ah-Zah-Ray-Low."

"That sounds good, but what do those characters mean?" I asked.

"Something like lovely flowers and morning dew."

I was thinking, *Could you come up with something less tampon-commercial-oriented?* but I said, "Can you make it sound a little stronger and more businesslike?"

"It's tough because we can only use characters that are associated with female names."

"Can you try again?"

After another round of discussion and drinks, they came back from the huddle with an alternative and read it to me. It still sounded enough like "Patty Azzarello" when the characters were pronounced. They seemed pleased with their effort.

"What do these characters mean?"

"Well, we still needed to use characters allowable for female names, so this one translates to something like 'Vengeful Lady God.'"

"Vengeful Lady God? Is there nothing in between?"

"Not really. All the characters for more businesslike words can only be used in male names."

So, my only choices were "Morning Dew" or "Vengeful Lady God."

I had spent my whole career with colleagues, bosses, clients, and employees not quite knowing what to make of me—this ambitious, annoyingly competent woman who just wouldn't go away. And this business card exercise was a good example of how that always felt. *So if I decline to be seen as a fragile beauty, my only other option is omnipotent tyrant?*

Still waiting for my dinner companions to join me, I read the menu a number of times. I kept thinking about the Chinese business cards and the near-constant sense of people wondering, "Why is SHE still here?"

A new, almost blasphemous thought was starting to occur about me and my corporate career: *Why AM I still here? Maybe I actually don't belong here.*

I sat with that bombshell for a while.

Could I really just walk away?

Let's face it, walking away from a corporate executive job means walking away from a powerful role and a fat paycheck. Since my identity had never been tied up in power, the idea of losing that part felt OK. *I'm still just me either way.* But let's face it, my identity has always been hermetically sealed to being a high achiever. Where would little patty get her gold stars if I walk away?

And the paycheck was a real matter to consider. I still needed to earn money for a secure retirement. What else would I do?

I got a text that my dinner companions were running late, so I ordered a drink and thought hard about my job, and what work really meant in my life.

I had put in a monumental effort to build my career and do everything right for such a long time. For decades, my main concern had been, *What do I need to give my work so I can be successful?* I thought about how my company had absorbed as much of my life force as I let them. They didn't really care about me.

But then I started to think, *But what if I turned that upside down? After everything I have accomplished, have I not earned the opportunity by now to instead ask, "What does my work need to give ME?"*

This felt pretty ground shaking. *If I am going to exchange my life force for money, why don't I allow myself to define: What does my work need to give to me to serve my life better?*

I was clear on the kind of things that annoyed me about my work, but were there things that attracted me to my work? There must be parts of my work that I enjoyed or needed in my life outside of the money that helped me to keep going. Even I am not that sturdy!

My guests finally arrived, and we shared the Thai Beef Noodles, which were amazing. Not only was this not the long, boring, agonizing evening I was dreading, but these people turned out to be some of the most fascinating, fun people I had ever met. We talked about business and life and art and fear and anthropology and how quicksand did not turn out to be as big a problem as we feared growing up.

As grumpy as I had been about this dinner, these fabulous people became the turning point for me. I had my answer about what I needed my work to give me:

What I need from my work is to regularly encounter people like these who challenge and stimulate my brain. I need to keep bringing smart, interesting people into my life so I keep thinking and laughing and growing, so I stay enthusiastic and well. And to date, I have only met those people at work.

The next day, I jumped out of bed with plenty of time to have coffee, and with clarity from the night before, I thought, "Well, if I need inspiring, smart people in my life, surely there are other ways to get that than by taking on another big corporate leadership job."

As I was sipping my coffee out of my favorite mug, the one with the gray spots, I started to muse, *What would it look like if I were to do work that put me in the path of brilliant, stimulating people but gave me energy instead of making me wish I could be hospitalized?*

What would the work look like that not only used but demanded my gifts and strengths, and that would let me manage my own schedule?

Well . . . this line of thinking was dreamy!

But before I could even consider the answers to these questions, my internal critic, sensing I was right at the cusp of a breakthrough, leaped into action.

STOP THIS CRAZINESS AT ONCE!

WHAT ARE YOU EVEN THINKING?

THE ONLY WAY TO MAKE YOUR LIFE FEEL THE WAY YOU WANT IT TO FEEL IS TO CREATE YOUR OWN BUSINESS SO YOU CAN DEFINE YOUR OWN WORK AND MAKE YOUR OWN SCHEDULE.

AND YOU'VE ADMITTED ALL ALONG THAT HAVE NO IDEA HOW TO DO THAT. YOU CAN'T DO THAT. THIS IS THE STUPIDEST, RISKIEST THING YOU HAVE EVER THOUGHT ABOUT, AND YOU HAVE THOUGHT OF SOME DOOZIES.

JUST GO GET ANOTHER BIG JOB. THAT'S WHAT YOU DO. THAT'S WHAT YOU ARE SUPPOSED TO DO. THAT'S THE ONLY THING THAT WILL WORK. THIS RIDICULOUS IDEA WILL NOT. JUST STOP.

It really did feel irresponsible to not continue on my chosen path of so many years. It made me feel guilty. It felt subversive. I still needed to earn money. I was the sole financial provider in my life. I was still afraid to order the orange juice.

It took me several weeks and various end-of-workday cocktails in just the right glassware, appropriate for life-changing decisions, to permit myself to even let the thought fully form:

Can I really just walk away?

Better call Al

8.6

When I spend time with Al, it always feels like he finds me struggling to swim upstream and pulls up alongside me in motorboat and says, "Hop in." Then he transports me way further upstream in a flash. Suddenly, I am in a new place I have never conceived of, leaving behind all the things that had me so perplexed, and I think, *WOW, look at all these new possibilities up here! What was I so worried about?*

Having someone who is not just a work mentor but who truly cares about you and helps you in your life is an extraordinary gift. Al was always there for life's biggest questions and decisions. I could always count on him to help me think things through.

photo: Julia Blaukhoph

Al and me at my book launch when MOVE got the store window placement at the Barnes and Noble on Fifth Avenue in New York

Al liked the idea of my starting my own business.

So he invited me to meet him in New York, where we spent three full days brainstorming what my new business and new life could be. We dove deep into my strengths and experience and plumbed the depths of my personal brand. We talked and talked. We rearranged the furniture in his apartment. Our strategy sessions involved lots of walking and many snacks.

After these three days, we had created a basis for my own business. And Al gave me the confidence and motivation to give it a try.

What a crazy coincidence that I had met Al, who had such a big impact on my life and career, by dating Ross decades earlier when I was 19—Ross, whose way of living, by all normal measures, was the precise opposite of an intentional plan or a corporate career. It's funny how life presents its gifts. You can't plan networking. Magic just happens sometimes. My career and life would not be as whole and nourishing if not for Al and my whole extended family that resulted from meeting Ross. I can always feel them all there, rooting for me. I am awed by this and super grateful.

I found my place

8.7

So, with Al's support, I decided to face my fear of the unknown—and my internal critic telling me that I would die if I tried to create my own business—and answer this question: *Can I create a business doing only things that I am good at and enjoy?*

I will admit, this was not some fierce, dedicated commitment to an outcome. At first, it was truly an experiment. If it didn't work out, I'd just go get another big job. That made it way less scary to try.

I had no idea what would happen, but—spoiler alert—to my delight, I created my own business and it worked great. In fact, it took off right away.

As the CEO of the newly formed Azzarello Group, I worked as an advisor to CEOs and their teams to help them avoid the flash cards problem (to reliably execute their important strategies) and also provided leadership and career development programs for humans.

So, in my own business, I get to use my large organization skills to impact many large organizations instead of just one. I help people improve their lives along with their businesses and careers based on the key theme in both my books: respecting humanity at work. And I speak on stages all over the world to share my ideas and experiences—and I haven't fallen off even one of them.

Also, since I could manage my own schedule, I was sleeping more—eight hours, most nights, for the first time in decades. I am not one of those people who equates sleeping to missing out on life. Without enough sleep, I'm just not a good awake person. I need my rest. I need to go home and lie down and process the day, just like I always did with Mom. Those people who say,

"Go big or go home," have no idea how much I really just want to go home.

I would like to say that I never looked back, but from time to time, I wonder if I maybe should have done one more big gig. I could have left my corporate career on a bigger win. But as soon as that thought plays, I know in my bones that the cost to my well-being is just too high. Some things are not worth money.

My goal was never just to accumulate money. My goal was to enjoy my life. Which required some money. But it turned out that by having my own business—one that truly helped others, and without having to sacrifice my health to do it (because it fed me more energy points than it took)—my income actually grew to match that of my corporate tech career.

And now I was working not just in tech, but in all kinds of industries and companies: consumer products, financial services, telecommunications, hospitals, education, manufacturing and design, natural resources, media and entertainment, logistics, and even nature conservation. My world just kept getting bigger and more interesting. I was meeting amazing people all the time who challenged my brain, and the work was feeding little patty a steady flow of learning and amazement and a lot of gold stars.

So, I can say that I finally found my place.

As a competent, ambitious woman, I created a role for myself that landed sensibly somewhere between "flowers and morning dew" and "vengeful lady god."

And here's the headline: Nothing was telling me, "You don't belong here. We don't know what to make of you." That eternal refrain, always playing in the background, making me feel disrespected and unwelcome and panicked about getting bounced out of the room, had finally fallen silent. Patty was no longer weird or unwanted. In fact, it was quite the opposite.

Instead, I was being enthusiastically invited in to help *for the specific reason of being Patty Azzarello*. I was invited into groups all over the world to share the cumulation of my lifetime of experiences with others. I was using my strengths and being highly valued for my knowledge and skills.

I finally came to understand what Jim meant when he said, "A day that makes you happy makes you wise."

The "wise" part comes in because it's not always obvious what makes you happy. You have to figure it out. I was beginning to realize that if you can truly tune into *the simple things in your day* that drop you into your unique, happy, groove (for me, that's great people, beautiful places, learning, and lying down), only then do you get wise enough to design what your life should be.

I defined my life my way. And it all started with finally giving myself the permission to ask, *What does my work need to give ME?*

I felt happier at work than ever.

I had made a good choice.

I was still swimming (because work is still effort) but I wasn't struggling against the current anymore. My efforts in my own business were paying off in money and happiness, and the waters were calm.

Little patty was very comfortable in this world. This was new. This was fun. Work was finally fun.

Me as CEO of Azzarello Group, never too far from a sofa

Part 9

The Rest

"If I had influence with the good fairy who is supposed to preside over the christening of all children, I should ask that her gift to each child in the world be a sense of wonder so indestructible that it would last throughout life, as an unfailing antidote against the boredom and disenchantments of later years."

—Rachel Carson

The hard way

9.1

M om had two full-size sofas in her living room. They were upholstered in a reddish, high-wear, industrial fabric situated in an L configuration. When I went to visit her as an adult, we could both lie down with our feet meeting in the corner of the L. Ever since those afternoons crawling into bed with Mom after school, for me, the best, deepest, loveliest conversations are always to be had when both people are lying down.

Right before her 80th birthday, we were lying on our respective sofas when Mom said,

"You never took the easy path. Never. If you had the choice between an easy path and a hard path, I'd always watch and think, 'Patty is going to invent some third, even harder path.' Why did you always do that?"

Mom replayed some of the hits.

"Why are you taking Physics II before Physics I? Won't that be too hard?"

Me: "Because I want to do a double major, and I'm behind on physics because my adviser screwed up. Don't worry, I'll teach myself Physics I."

Mom: "Why are you taking graduate-level courses for an undergraduate degree? Why don't you just stick with regular undergraduate courses? Wouldn't that be less stressful?"

Me: "But the classes are more advanced in the graduate program. I want to learn more, even if I don't get the advanced degree."

"Remember that friggin' gingerbread house you made?"

"Yes, Mom."

"And you got sick, and I had to clean the whole thing up?"

"Yes, Mom."

Mom reminded me of the gingerbread house for 40 years.

When it came to building my future, I refused the easier path over and over again. I always did extra. I always invented new, difficult challenges for myself.

I always built the gingerbread house.

The harder path was just more attractive to me. Because if you put in a big effort to do the difficult thing, you get a bigger, more wonderful outcome.

And since I wanted big things in my life, I couldn't wait downstream for the good stuff to come to me. I had to do extra stuff, *and* I had to fight the countercurrent of people telling me, in one way or another, "You shouldn't be here."

Try again tomorrow

9.2

I find it so fascinating how on one hand I choose to do difficult, scary things all the time to do extra stuff and get upstream, but for other seemingly normal and less scary things, I deem them too impossible to even try.

Tell me I need to travel to a new city and figure out public transportation by myself, and I'm like, "I am never, ever going to do that. That's just impossible."

But tell me, "Go forge a decades-long career as a woman and an introvert in an environment where you will not be welcome. Then earn enough money to buy your own house, support yourself, and save for your retirement. Do this entirely on your own, without help from a partner," and I'm like, "Sure, that seems fine."

I thought about an article I'd read that said that the percentage of women who had become corporate CEOs relative to all the CEOs in the world was about the same as the percentage of Olympic athletes in the world relative to the general population. I thought, *I wonder if that's true.* It felt true—because there are so few of us, and it certainly required a commitment to decades of steady effort to get there.

It's kind of funny how things worked out for me. I realized that if you don't expect life to be easy and fun and you generally feel like an outcast, it makes more sense to do the uncomfortable stuff that no one else is doing—because everyone thinks you are weird anyway. You do stuff on your own terms, since no one else's terms seem to work for you or welcome you in.

So, the life strategy that solidified for me was this:

The world outside is hard and scary.

Home is safe.

Keep learning.

Be daring.

Stay enthusiastic.

Choose really great people to be in your life.

Be you without apology. Get laughed at and mistreated sometimes for it. (It's never about you. It's always about them.)

Go home. Lie down. Don't skimp on the comforter.

Process. Recover.

Try again tomorrow.

You are not me

9.3

H ey, you. Internal critic.
Come out—I need to talk to you.

WAIT, YOU DON'T GET TO SUMMON ME. I LURK IN THE SHADOWS AND LEAP OUT WHEN I DECIDE IT'S TIME TO MAKE YOU FEEL LIKE CRAP SO YOU'LL STOP REACHING FOR WHAT YOU WANT. YOU CAN'T JUST TELL ME TO COME OUT. THAT'S NOT HOW THIS WORKS.
I'VE GOT NOTHING SPECIFIC TO SAY RIGHT NOW. I'M NOT PREPARED. THIS IS KIND OF EMBARRASSING. BUT . . . UH . . . WHILE I'M HERE . . . YOU LOOK FAT. AND OLD.

I want to tell you that I know your secret.
Yes, I can summon you—because I know that you are not me.
Your voice is not my voice.
You are an asshole whose job it is to sabotage me.
But you are separate from me. I would never be such a jerk to myself.

Dear reader, as we approach the end of this story, I want to muzzle my internal critic for a moment and share one more important secret passageway with you. We all have internal critics. Every one of us. And I have watched so many people let their internal critics define their lives—because they just accept and believe everything it says.

I knew I wanted more than what my internal critic told me I deserved. And it was a constant battle to fight him. (That's right—I've decided my internal critic is a "he" so his voice feels very different from mine.) If it was just my own vague, subtle, quiet inner voice telling me what an undeserving loser I am, I would have believed it—because I tend to believe what my own voice is telling me.

So, to gain an advantage and fortify my resolve, I put that critical voice outside of me and gave it a concrete persona that is separate from me, so my adversary became someone I could better fight against or ignore. I don't want to be my own adversary. I don't want to fight against myself. I do want to fight against *him*.

We wrestled and fought a lot throughout my life. And sometimes he won (and still does). But a lot of times, I won, and I did things despite his constant need to make me stop reaching for the bigger things that I wanted.

So, this is the secret passageway that I want to leave you with: ***You don't always have to do what your internal critic tells you.*** And the more times you don't listen to your internal critic, the bigger and more interesting your life gets.

But don't worry—you don't always have to win against it either. Just remind yourself of this: You don't automatically have to stop trying when your internal critic tells you that you are not ready, or not good enough, or don't belong there. You can still keep going if you want.

Also, know that your internal critic will never go away. So don't waste energy hoping for that.

Accept its annoying presence in your life, and how it shows up every time things start to get good for you. I don't fight with mine so much anymore. It's more like, "Oh, it's you again, right on cue. OK, you can come along for the ride—but you don't get to drive. Sit in the back seat and shut up."

Sofa confessions

9.4

I am again on my sofa, snuggled up, with a comforter.

I am drinking a glass of wine in my favorite wineglass, the one that has the perfect curves and weight and balance, with the Chianti rooster emblem etched onto it. I'm looking out the window watching it get dark outside. But it's not getting dark—because I have moved from California to a high-rise condo in Chicago, and the city skyline starts to sparkle. Little patty likes the sparkles.

Also worth mentioning: In my new home in Chicago, I have refitted an extra bedroom to have the Taj Mahal of a bunk bed/desk combo, with a ridiculously thick, plush rug in it. And this room is also now my art studio. Little patty always gets what she sets her mind to.

When Mom told little patty, "You need to go to college and get a good job and support yourself," little patty didn't really understand what Mom meant exactly, but she thought, "If I do well in school and get a good job, maybe one day that will help me to change all the things that are making me unhappy. Like, I can buy a really pretty house, that has lots of space, and put pretty and fluffy things in it. And when people in the world hurt me, I can just go home and stay in my pretty house by myself, so no one can be mean to me there. I would be happy there."

I smiled deeply, thinking, *We really nailed that one!*

I thought more about little patty, the mini warrior with her lunch tray in the cafeteria, and I wondered, Why is it that she is so present in my life even today? Not just the injured, socially timid and awkward little person, but the little superhero too—the unguarded, daring, enthusiastic version of little patty she was before the world hurt her.

Suddenly, the answer occurred to me. It was because of Mom. (Of course it was because of Mom.) It was because Mom kept reminding me, "You were so sturdy. You struggled with so many things, but you were so brave when you were little. You were always such a happy, enthusiastic little kid. You were always smiling. It was a joy to be your mom."

Mom repeated these things about little patty over and over again throughout my entire life. She replayed little patty's bravery and accomplishments regularly. So it became a natural part of my adult life to remember the strong version of little patty. And that even though she was so little and so bullied and so unwelcome and rejected, she just kept going back in. So, little patty never lets my adult self back away from important, uncomfortable things. It's like having a built-in role model I can call upon to make me less timid and help me battle my internal critic. (She knows he is not right, because she was there before he was).

As I admired the curves and weight and balance of my wineglass, a new picture came into my mind, one of the 29-year-old, pretending-to-be-40 Patty, when I first started walking into the big rooms, in my serious suits and heels. Whenever I would hesitate to enter the room or be nervous about breaking into a tall conversation circle of men, it was little patty who would sternly insist, "Get yourself in there. You need to keep learning."

That's one of the most important secret passageways little patty ever taught me: *Even if you are actually unwelcome—you can still go in.*

I took a sip of wine and thought about Mom and Dad and Kerry, and Wendy and Jack, and Mark, and my lifelong mentors Al and Jim, and all of my dear friends, and all of the kind people all over the world who care about me.

And I thought, *You don't need everyone in the world to like you.* Little patty prepared me to be OK with that too. But boy, does it make a huge difference if you have a few people who do—people who really care about and help you.

At that moment, I was quite moved thinking of the people who have lifted me up and kept me laughing throughout my life. And I thought about how Jack's family and the Ross/Al/Susan extended family have adopted me into theirs.

How odd and wonderful it is that *people* have gone from being the worst part of little patty's life to the best part of mine.

As the city lights began to sparkle even more in the full darkness, I thought about the risk of putting this book out into the world and telling my real personal story. I would be inviting people who like to judge and diagnose and disparage others from the privacy of their screens into my life. Though little patty has been the one to push me into so many scary situations where I was not welcome so I could keep learning, she was not happy about this.

But I reminded her that if some people want to be mean just because I told my story, just like Mom always said, "It's never about you. It's always about them."

My goal in writing this book was to make others feel better after reading it than they did before—because if someone as insecure and nervous as I am on the inside could accomplish such big things, then maybe they can give themselves permission to do their own big things: go for promotions at work, start their own businesses, get on that stage, go back to school, publish their own books, or share their art or music.

I hope this book encourages you to fight off your internal critic and keep trying things, even when you feel insecure or not ready. Since "insecure and not ready" was my starting state for mostly every significant thing I have ever done, please consider my story to offer this: ***Feeling uncomfortable or unwelcome does not disqualify you from your dreams.***

Don't disqualify yourself from your dreams. Don't get chased away.
Listen to little patty.
You can still go in.

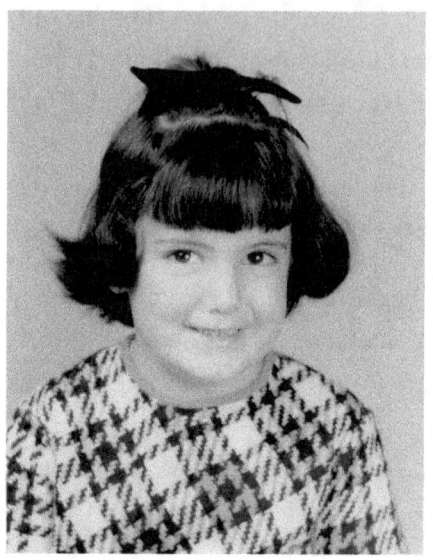

One last thing . . .

9.5

Writing a book about yourself from your heart is like cheap and really effective therapy. It's a journey of self-discovery—you uncover things. Also, other people who read it will ask you questions that reveal new stuff to you about yourself. They will ask things like, "Patty, were you really that uncomfortable, or were you just being dramatic for the book?" Or, more directly, "Do you think you may be autistic?"

That question kind of felt like the end of the movie *The Sixth Sense*. The clues were so obvious as to what the main character really was all along. Why did I not see it sooner?

So, I decided to check out the possibility of autism. Doctor says, "Probably." It turns out that autism in women often does not look like what we tend to imagine autism to look like. It's different for everyone, but one thing it often looks like in women is being very good at hiding discomfort so others can't see it.

The idea of being neurodivergent explained why I can be so uncomfortable with perfectly normal things—things I watch other people do with ease, like not being in a coma after travel, enjoying loud concerts without crying, attending a neighborhood barbecue without being a mortified stone in the corner, or being able to find their way back from the bathroom in a big house.

Neurodivergence also puts my unending quest for and use of scripts, and my mastery of pretending that I am OK when I am dying on the inside, into obvious focus. There are even official names for those things: "modeling" and "masking."

I share this idea here as a sort of epilogue to my story because that is when the idea actually appeared—after I wrote the book.

While I am indeed super sturdy emotionally, my nervous system is prone to frequent meltdowns. Mark describes it like this: I have an impressive amount of extra internal wiring for all the things I am constantly (over)sensing and (over)thinking about. But in order to fit into the available human space, my internal network is made of extra-thin-gauge wire with flimsy insulation. So it's very easy for my nervous system to overheat or short-circuit.

When that happens, I need to be in a quiet place where I can let all that wiring cool down and reset before I can engage with the world again.

In the past when I felt exhausted and in need of this recovery and repair time so often, I would feel guilty and self-conscious about it.

But with this insight, I now understand and accept that I just need time, more time than others do to recover from the people and places and things in the world—even the good ones. And I am no longer embarrassed by this.

I now embrace my brain and its quirks. While my brain does some things marvelously well, it does not do other things *at all*. And that's OK.

I have a unique brain. So do you. So does everyone.

I have several neurodivergent friends. Their brains do amazing things that mine does not. And my brain does things that they find remarkable because theirs do not.

Mark is also neurodivergent. His ADHD brain short-circuits when I make plans for us, as much as my nervous system goes into shock on one of his adventures without plans. But being next to Mark makes the world a magical and much friendlier place, full of possibilities, because of the wild connections his brain is always tuned in to.

While I handle the planning, Mark's unique brain infuses my life with a steady source of amazement—new solutions, opportunities, ideas, laughter, kindness, and beauty in the world—that I would totally miss on my own. We joke that together, we have one really good brain.

If anything, my awareness of being neurodivergent has made my life less stressful and richer and my friendships closer and more interesting. I am more grateful for my gifts. And more importantly, I am no longer embarrassed by my deficiencies.

There is another unexpected outcome of carrying my unique brain around in my head: It has become the basis of my work to help others achieve their own dreams.

Here's what I mean. Since I have always felt outside the mainstream, I needed to relentlessly study successful people to understand what they did and why it worked so I could copy it. And in doing so, I created highly practical systems and scripts so I could replicate the winning approach when my instincts and comfort zone failed me.

As it happened, these tools I created, which enabled me to move ahead in my career despite feeling unwelcome, awkward, and scared, turned out to be super helpful for non-neurodivergent people all over the world—who also feel unwelcome, awkward, and scared.

I share all of the secret passageways I have discovered for building success, confidence, energy, and relationships (all keys to effective leadership) in my books, my business consulting, my leadership programs, and my speaking engagements.

It's a lovely thing to finally recognize that what I have created out of my own "deficiencies" has enabled so many others to move forward more confidently in their own lives.

Everyone, including neurodivergent people (and any of us who find ourselves in an undervalued class), deserves to be successful and happy. We all just need to find the right tools and support to help us navigate through our discomforts in a world that is not always set up for us.

We all need to find our own way forward to let the magic in our unique brains and lives happen, and to enthusiastically share our gifts with others.

So, as it turns out, little patty was never weird. She was just trying her very best to make her own way in a world that kept telling her she was.

I will never be the one to tell you to swim upstream and then laugh at you when you fail. I will always be the one to show you the secret passageway whenever I know it.

Acknowledgments

A ll I can say is thank goodness I am comfortable asking for help, because I needed a lot of it on this book!

I want to first thank those intrepid readers who slogged through the early piles of writing I could hardly call a draft and gave me the insights I needed to find the good parts and shine a brighter light on them: Suzanne Pherigo, Ellen Cohan, Leslie Robertson, Mark Cohan, Allison Cramer, and Sharon Olsen.

Next, I must mention the very talented Neil Gordon. I had worked with Neil earlier to uplevel my stories on the stage, and for this book, he taught me so much about how to find my voice, develop my story, and not be boring.

I probably deleted or rewrote the whole book three times before arriving at what I thought was a solid final draft. I then gave it to another group of readers, who brilliantly pointed out that it was not, in fact, a final draft, as they revealed to me how to fix the still confusing, missing, and annoying parts: Andrew Binstock, Anna Menniti, Ben Kiker, Fran DelBoca, Frank Pope, Jacek Walicki, Kerry Azzarello, Paula Gadsby, and Tess Kessler.

Heartfelt thanks to the featured guest stars in these pages, who are such a big part of my story (in order of appearance): Mom (Jan Sterbenz/Azzarello), Dad (George Azzarello), Kerry Azzarello, my Sicilian and Slovenian grandparents, Wendy (Andrews) Fogler, Adele (Shuttenberg) Manailovich, Dr. Patrick O'Leary, Mike Caprario, Nabi Rafie, Ross Scott, Al Fasola, Susan (Scott) Fasola, Jim Davis, Jacek (Jack) Walicki, Bill Russell, Duane Zitzner, Melissa Lindt, and Mark Cohan.

So many other people contributed examples I used in the story. They offered clever insights on life, work, and happiness; made funny, brilliant comments (and generously allowed me to plagiarize them) and/or provided enthusiastic encouragement to tell my story. You all left an important imprint on this book (and on me): Anna Wenzel, Barbara Nelson, Bonnie (Tiburzi) Srygley, Brian Kilcourse, Bruce Claypool, Danny Gregory, Dave Wright, Elena (Boscherini) Didona, Emmy Sobieski, Jim Grant, Joanna Kulesa, John Fernandez, John Peters, Maura Garau, Meta Mehling, Paul Avenant, Piero Didona, Resa Pearson, Rick Claeys, Saar Shwartz, Scott Eskwitt, Sonia Ognibene, Stefano Tronconi, Stephanie Robinson, Thomas Volk, Trish Schuster, and Vonda Mills.

Also, much appreciation to so many of you I met through my work who played an enormous role in shaping this book and my career.

I want to thank all my local teams and colleagues at SESD, WSY, Verifone, OpenView, Polycom, and Siebel—and all the people in my remote organizations around the world who served as my hosts—who not only supported me and our business but showed me your wonderful cities, architecture, food, and culture. There are too many of you to list here, but please be assured, if you spent time with me in your city, I am grateful to you for sharing your kindness and for acting as my guides so I could experience so much amazing stuff around the world and not get lost away from home forever.

I also want to thank my Azzarello Group consulting and keynote speaking clients, all the corporate women's leadership groups and DEI organizations who have enlisted my services, and the thousands of members of my online *Executive Mentoring Group* over the past 15 years. By so openly sharing your questions and your own experiences of swimming upstream (particularly the women), you have gifted me so many new ideas and insights. If you have ever talked to me about your career, please know that your trust in me has inspired and guided me in the creation of this book.

Thank you to my board of advisors at Azzarello Group, who gave me the courage to change my life and start my own business and guided its development: Barbara Nelson, Robert Kaplan, Brian Kilcourse, Joanna Kulesa, Resa Pearson, Richard Walker, Sandor Kovacs, and Al Fasola (the first three of which are super talented musicians who formed a rock band and let me be the singer).

Finally, for bringing this book into the world, a huge thank-you to the team at Spoonbridge Press: Sarah Kolb-Williams for her brilliant craft in copyediting, which transformed the quality of the finished draft, and Britt Peterson for expertly managing the book design and production. Also, big thanks to Ben Wise for the sound engineering and production of the audiobook, and to the very talented Dave Holmes, who added his voice to my story.

And one final, sweeping thank-you out into the universe just for good measure.

Resources

Why Is SHE Still Here?
My Ungraceful Journey from the Playground to the Boardroom

You can find more from Patty here:
PattyAzzarello.com/resources

Here, you'll find additional useful stuff based on this book and more:

→ **Book group discussion guide**
   ○ Find a free download link

→ **Photo gallery**
   ○ Browse a color photo gallery of the photos in the book and some extras

→ **Summary of secret passageways and key insights**
   ○ Find a free download link

→ **My article series**
   ○ You will find a link to subscribe to my article series "Secret Passageways" on Substack, where I share more of my experiences awkwardly learning things, along with useful tools and scripts. Also, I would love for you to share your own stories there about how you overcame challenges you faced while swimming upstream.

Patty's Other Books

RISE: 3 Practical Steps for Advancing Your Career, Standing Out as a Leader, and Liking Your Life

If you would like to know the specific, practical secret passageways and scripts I used to advance my career, *RISE* is packed with them. Readers have highlighted and Post-it Noted this book to death for its insights. Many keep it close by as their career reference guide. One had her copy of *RISE* taken apart and spiral-bound for faster lookup!

MOVE: How Decisive Leaders Execute Strategy Despite Obstacles, Setbacks, and Stalls

MOVE gives leaders the treasure map to actually implement their strategy instead of just talking about it. It's a practical guide to avoiding all the obstacles that confound groups of humans trying to work together to make big things happen.

More Help For Your Career and Leadership

You will also find links to my *Executive Mentoring Group* and my *Business Leadership Masterclass*. Based on my books *RISE* and *MOVE*, these programs help other leaders to develop their own careers and to lead high-performing teams with more humanity and confidence.

It has been such an honor and so much fun to serve as a mentor for so many people from all over the world through these programs.

About the Author

Patty Azzarello is a business advisor, professional speaker, and the author of two bestsellers, *RISE* and *MOVE*. Her no-BS, humanity-forward approach to leadership propelled her into the highest ranks of management in the male-dominated tech industry. A lifelong learner and enthusiastic sharer (whether you asked or not), she combines her knowledge and insight with humor, heart, and a deep commitment to helping others grow.

She is a high-functioning introvert who loves people—ideally one at a time—and a self-taught artist, writer, and happily mediocre singer. A dual citizen of the U.S. and Italy, Patty currently lives in a groovy high-rise loft in her adopted city of Chicago, where she enjoys time with loved ones and divides her attention between video conferences, lakeside walks, painting, gym workouts, and wondering why adults have to spend so much time cleaning the kitchen. Several weeks each year, you will find her in Italy absorbing the beauty and culture, visiting friends, walking in the hills, sipping prosecco in the sunshine, and mostly eating pizza.

www.ingramcontent.com/pod-product-compliance
Lightning Source LLC
Chambersburg PA
CBHW060406130626
46555CB00005B/1997